D0848852

Widescreen Dreams

LIVING OUT
Gay and Lesbian Autobiographies

Joan Larkin and David Bergman
GENERAL EDITORS

Midlife Queer: Autobiography of a Decade, 1971–1981
Martin Duberman

Widescreen Dreams: Growing Up Gay at the Movies
Patrick E. Horrigan

Eminent Maricones: Arenas, Lorca, Puig, and Me
Jaime Manrique

Taboo
Boyer Rickel

Widescreen Dreams
Growing Up Gay at the Movies

Patrick E. Horrigan

The University of Wisconsin Press

The University of Wisconsin Press
2537 Daniels Street
Madison, Wisconsin 53718

3 Henrietta Street
London WC2E 8LU, England

1   3   5   4   2

Printed in the United States of America

Library of Congress Cataloging-in-Publication Data
Horrigan, Patrick E.
Widescreen dreams: growing up gay at the movies / Patrick E. Horrigan.
250 pp.   cm. — (Living out)
Based on author's dissertation (Columbia University).
Includes bibliographical references and index.
ISBN 0-299-16160-9 (cloth: alk. paper)
1. Horrigan, Patrick E.   2. Gay men — United States — Biography.
3. Gay men — United States — Psychology — Case studies.   4. Motion
pictures — United States — Psychological aspects — Case studies.
I. Title.   II. Series.
HQ75.8.H67A3   1999
305.38′9664 — dc21   98-17528
[B]

in memory of
Gary Lucek

Contents

Acknowledgments

Before anyone else, I am indebted to my parents, Peggy and Jack Horrigan, for enabling me to write this book. They supported me financially and spiritually throughout graduate school, where I conceived of these essays, and from beginning to end they have championed my progress. I am also indebted to my siblings, Mary Jo Dever, Suzanne Johnson, Betsy Rathz, John Horrigan, and Karen Horrigan, for helping to create, in their different ways, an environment within our family where writing this book became possible. In particular, I am grateful to my brother John for reading the manuscript and giving me feedback at a crucial stage in its development. A lot of gay people come from families who didn't love them, who may even have expelled them, and yet they live to tell their stories about it—*Widescreen Dreams* is not that kind of book. What may distinguish it from other memoirs and gay coming-of-age stories is my awareness of the comfort and love, however imperfect, that I received when I was growing up and that I still receive from my family. Among other things, I see this book as an expression of my love for them in return.

Ann Douglas directed my dissertation at Columbia University, out of which these essays grew, and she was the first person to encourage my efforts at bringing together cultural criticism and autobiography. One of the amazing things about Ann is that she can see the value of work that is very different from her own, and she knows how to help her students find and then follow the paths that are most meaningful to them. In this regard, she is the most courageous, unselfish, and imaginative teacher I've ever had. I think that she, more than anyone else, has helped me find my voice as a writer.

Mark Stern shepherded me through every phase of the making of this book, and many of its core ideas have emerged from conversations I've had with him. My life and work would not be the same without him. Wayne Koestenbaum and D. A. Miller encouraged me in the initial stages of this project and mentored me throughout graduate school. They read early drafts of these essays and gave me invaluable feedback; in fact, their comments on my work have so strongly influenced me that I still remember verbatim a number of things they've said. Their own thrilling experiments in bending criticism and autobiography toward each other and their committment to gay male self-expression continue to inspire me, and this book is addressed in part specifically to them and to their work. Margo Jefferson, too, has guided me throughout this project. Her professional advice, her comments on my writing, and her friendship are a gift.

I am indebted to my agent, Malaga Baldi, for her enthusiastic promotion of the book and for her excellent editorial advice. Raphael Kadushin, my editor at the University of Wisconsin Press, has been a joy to work with; he is unfailingly calm, kind, and intelligent.

I've learned a lot about my work and about myself from Maria Russo; she has always supported me in taking the intellectual and emotional risks necessary to write this book. Sara Campbell, Pat Crain, and Michael Perelman have consistently shown an interest in this project and have given me a tremendous amount of feedback. Mario DiGangi and Sarah Chinn read early drafts of some of these essays and, along with other members of the Lesbian and Gay Studies Group at Columbia, gave me useful feedback. Paul Franklin's remarks about several of the chapters have been particularly inspired and inspiring. And I've benefited from conversations with Jeffrey Jullich, Ellen Hurwitz, Vito Russo, and William Bonney during various stages of the project.

Robert K. Martin encouraged me to give an excerpt of chapter 3 at the first Quebec Lesbian and Gay Studies Conference. Joe Falonowitz and the attendees of the Long Island University Faculty Forum gave me a chance to deliver an early draft of chapter 1. And the Trustees of Long Island University and the Research Released Time Committee of LIU's Brooklyn Campus granted me time off from teaching in the spring of 1997 to work on the book. I've also received generous and useful commentary on various chapters from the following people: Rita Achenbach, John Archer, David Bergman, Ron Dotterer, David Doyle, Barb Fedders, Robert Ferguson, Elaine Freedgood, Julia Giordano, Michael Jacobs, Marissa Januzzi, Tom Lunke, Michael Mallick, James Mandrell, Larry Mass, Eric Savoy, James Schamus, John Wagenhauser, Priscilla Wald, Tony Whall, Adrienne Williams, Joe Wolin, and Elizabeth Wood. Special thanks to Steven Estock for consulting with me on the book's title and to my father and Michael Perelman for providing photographs.

Widescreen Dreams is dedicated to the memory of Gary Lucek. Gary was my closest friend and on-again, off-again boyfriend during the late eighties and early nineties. In 1984, as an undergraduate at Columbia, he organized a study group that sought to initiate gay men into current political and theoretical discussions about gay identity, culture, history, and activism. He also conceived of the study group as a much-needed social alternative to gay bars and dance clubs. In the spring of 1987, I joined the study group and became revolutionized by the community of gay men that I met there and by my relationship with Gary. He helped me discover myself as a gay man in mind and body.

At Yale University's third annual Lesbian and Gay Studies Conference in October of 1989, Gary delivered a paper entitled "Out on Vinyl: Readings Between the Grooves in Gay Male Pop Music," a semiautobiographical analysis of the relationship between gay men and 1980s pop music. The paper inspired me to want to write something in the same vein, and so I began to write what has now become the second chapter of this book, "Love Barbra," an essay on my relationship as a gay man and as a proto-gay child to the music and films of Barbra Streisand (I discuss Gary's essay in more detail in that chapter).

In December of 1992, after a severe bout with depression and a series of other misfortunes, Gary killed himself. When Gary died, my world fell apart. Since then I've traveled very far in my grief, but I continue to live out the ripple effects of his death.

At Gary's memorial service, one of our friends recited Elizabeth Bishop's 1976 poem "One Art." The poem is a litany of things the speaker has lost—door keys, spare time, memory, "my mother's watch," beloved houses, cities, rivers, "a continent," and finally, "even . . . you." Somehow, she has learned to live without all of them, "though it may look (*Write* it!) like disaster" (178).

I remember at some point in the late eighties thinking that my life would be unimagineable without Gary in it. This might have occurred to me when I was involved with ACT UP (the AIDS Coalition to Unleash Power) and when, as I recall, Gary had just, mercifully, tested negative for HIV. Or maybe it was around the time of the AIDS-related death of Gary's ex-boyfriend Bill, and I began to ask myself, What if something should happen to Gary? I was afraid that if for any reason Gary were gone, I wouldn't know how to survive.

Now the unimagineable *has* happened: Gary is gone, and I've written his life into mine in ways that I could never have dreamed.

Introduction

The wireless and the telephone have intervened. The letter writer has nothing now to build with except what is most private; and how monotonous after a page or two the intensity of the very private becomes! . . . Instead of letters posterity will have confessions, diaries, notebooks, like M. Gide's—hybrid books in which the writer talks in the dark to himself about himself for a generation yet to be born.
— Virginia Woolf, "The Humane Art"

It seems to me that not only is there loads to be gained from genuinely experimental approaches to critical writing, but that it's intellectually dishonest and deadening to take for granted what critical writing is. . . . I'm . . . interested in how it would be possible to programmatically refuse to exclude the personal, the realm of the autobiographical, or the first person, but at the same time pull those elements into new and unexpected relations to theory and to the writing process.
— Eve Kosofsky Sedgwick, "A Talk with Eve Kosofsky Sedgwick"

Widescreen Dreams: Growing Up Gay at the Movies is a hybrid book. A synthesis of autobiography and cultural criticism, it describes my emergence from childhood into gay male adulthood as a series of encounters with an odd handful of Hollywood movies—*The Sound of Music* (1965), *Hello, Dolly!* (1969), *The Poseidon Adventure* (1972), *Dog Day Afternoon* (1975), and *The Wiz* (1978). These movies were the high points of my growing up years, and they strongly influenced the way I thought about myself and the rest of the world. They also mark stages in time from the rise of gay liberation in the late sixties to its reconfiguration during the AIDS epidemic, which began in the early eighties. My own development as a gay man intersected with this gay American history in unpredictable ways, and my understanding of both myself and my place in history is, and has always been, determined in large measure by the movies.

In their distortive way, Hollywood movies reflected crucial aspects of my world when I was growing up, as they have done for so many people for as long as they existed. The movies were filled with happy families, like my family; unhappy families, also like mine; underdogs and queer heroes, which, in a variety of ways, I understood myself to be; all-embracing mother-figures, like my mother, like my piano teacher; pleasure cruises, like the one my family took in the late sixties while visiting my grandparents in Florida; pretty buildings to look at and live in, like the big old Victorian house in suburban Chicago our friends the

ture during what can loosely be called the Stonewall era, the era of gay liberation just prior to the onslaught of AIDS. Together, the chapters trace an uneven path of gradual—though never complete, never one-way—development from childhood through adolescence and on toward adulthood, from self-ignorance to self-knowledge, and from being "in the closet" to being "out." And this development occurs both on a private, personal level (my story, who I've been, how I've changed) and on a public, cultural level (the story of American popular culture during the sixties and seventies, what that culture looked like, what it tried to say, how it changed during those years).

Chapter 1, "The Happiest Family in All the World!", traces my love of film as well as my self-awareness as a gay person to my childhood obsession with *The Sound of Music* and the hours I spent listening to its original soundtrack while meditating on the accompanying liner notes and film stills. The chapter describes a trinity of female mentors, liberators, and role models—Maria von Trapp, as played and sung by Julie Andrews; my piano teacher, Mrs. Hasbrouck; and my mother—who helped me find my place in the world. And it reveals the interior structure of the large Catholic family, a version of which I glimpsed in *The Sound of Music*, whereby I came to identify myself simultaneously as part of the clan and as deviant from it.

Chapter 2, "Love Barbra," explores my attraction both as a child and as an adult to Barbra Streisand and in particular to one of her most notorious flops, *Hello, Dolly!* It describes the paradox that, on the one hand, certain kinds of gender nonconformity were not tolerated when I was growing up, while, on the other hand, my intense involvement with Barbra Streisand *was* for the most part openly acknowledged and accepted, at least within my family. By charting a series of conversations I've had over the years about Barbra Streisand with family and friends, especially gay male friends, I show how she became an occasion for solidarity and strife among us. I also explain how Barbra Streisand's music and films both validated and helped me cope with feelings of extreme powerlessness.

Chapter 3, "The Wreck of the Family," recalls the ambivalence I experienced growing up gay in a straight milieu; the thrill of imagining, through the medium of the disaster film *The Poseidon Adventure*, home and family torn to shreds; as well as the fear of abandonment and the sense of isolation that come with any revolutionary, catastrophic change. In addition, the chapter examines the possibilities for reading seventies disaster films, especially *The Poseidon Adventure*, as gay texts and, now, as AIDS allegories.

Chapter 4, "Like Home," explores my penchant ever since childhood for creating utopias and alternative spaces, physical and psychological, tracing it to my early interest in architecture, unbuilt houses, and Victorian and modernist mansions. As a kid, my interest in architecture merged with my love of movies and movie architecture, and soon evolved into a devotion to New York City as the ultimate movie set come to life. The chapter culminates in a discussion of my adolescent fascination with *The Wiz,* a movie in which the kingdom of Oz becomes a fantasy vision of New York City and where Dorothy has now grown up to become a young woman in her twenties on the brink of an as-yet-undefined sexual self-transformation.

In Chapter 5, "Coming Out, with Al Pacino," a study of my attraction as a fifteen-year-old to Pacino's character in *Dog Day Afternoon,* I describe the structure of my fantasy life at the pivotal moment—roughly, puberty—when the real possibility of a gay identity and of a loving relationship with another man, glimpsed in the film's portrayal of the hero's relationship with his boyfriend, first entered and altered my mind. I examine the film's attitude toward deviance and urban life, and I show how this influenced my self-image as a teenager. I also use my positive adolescent response to the film as a means to challenge more recent charges of it as being homophobic.

I focus on these particular five films not because they constitute some "canon," popular or otherwise, of Hollywood films during this period (although some of them would, in fact, qualify in one way or another as representative) but rather because they happen to be the movies that meant the most to me as I was growing up and because, in writing about them, I'm trying to understand as fully as possible who I am and why I think and feel as I do. Someone else would cherish his or her own private pantheon of favorite movies (or books or musical compositions or whatever cultural objects mattered the most), and the selection would be, as it is here, partly accidental—accidental, but not meaningless.

One of the recurring themes of *Widescreen Dreams* is that "criticism," whether academic or journalistic, published or spun out in casual conversation over the telephone or on the sidewalk in front of the theater after the movie has ended, is rooted in the particular—and usually concealed—prejudices of the individual critic. These prejudices may best be described not as hard-earned intellectual convictions (though they may be that) or timeless evaluative frameworks (I doubt such things exist) but rather as residuum of the critic's life story. *Widescreen Dreams,* unlike conventional memoir and unlike conventional criticism, brings the life of the critic center stage in order to show how life experience becomes a crucial basis for critical insight, and in turn how critical thinking may illuminate life experience. This does not simply mean that critics' responses to the culture around them are or should be reducible to their life stories (in other words, that "all criticism is always already autobiography"—which, however, I think it is), but that honest, self-aware criticism cannot be done without acknowledging and exploring *within the act of criticism itself* the strange, unpredictable ways that art and life wrap around each other. *Widescreen Dreams* is an extreme example of what all kinds of criticism could in some sense look like.

I've written much of the book as if from a child's perspective—that is, from the perspective of my childhood self—because I want to place "naive" styles of interpretation on a continuum with more critical ways of knowing. Children's misreadings of the world around them, the book implicitly argues, are not some entirely other species of discourse; we should think of them instead as "cartoon" versions of adult analysis and criticism ("cartoon": don't think of Mickey Mouse—think of Leonardo da Vinci's *Cartoon with St. Anne* at the National Gallery in London). The book further conceives of the child's point of view, again implicitly, as a metaphor for a *gay* point of view: children see themselves as the addressees of every cultural statement, the referent of all representation, because they don't fully realize that although they are part of a larger world, they aren't the center of it. Somewhat similarly, we as gay people find ourselves enmeshed in a culture that studiously ignores us or radically misrepresents us; thus, in order to compensate for what the culture withholds from us, we appropriate it (in fantasy, in subculture) and make it say what we need it to say.

But then there's almost no telling when and how some aspect of mainstream culture may be "queered"; the most unsuspecting aspects of the culture may turn out to have queer resonance. This habit of gay interpretation is what Eve Kosofsky Sedgwick, in her *Epistemology of the Closet,* has called "camp-recognition": "[Camp-recognition] says *what if:* What if the right audience for this were exactly *me?* What if, for instance, the resistant, oblique, tangential investments of attention and attraction that I am able to bring to this spectacle are actually uncannily responsive to the resistant, oblique, tangential investments of the person, or of some of the people, who created it? And what if, furthermore, others whom I don't know or recognize can see it from the same "perverse" angle? Unlike kitch-*attribution,* the sensibility of camp-*recognition* always sees that it is dealing in reader relations and in projective fantasy (projective though not infrequently true) about the spaces and practices of cultural production" (156; emphasis in the original).

In Sedgwick's most recent work, this notion of gay interpretive practice becomes the basis for what she defines as a new and much-needed "reparative" approach to cultural criticism:

The desire of a reparative impulse . . . is additive and accretive. Its fear, a realistic one, is that the culture surrounding it is inadequate or inimical to its nurture; it wants to assemble and confer plenitude on an object that will then have resources to offer to an inchoate self. To view camp as, among other things, the communal, historically dense exploration of a variety of reparative practices is to be able to do better justice to many of the defining elements of classic camp performance: the startling, juicy displays of excess erudition, for example; the passionate, often hilarious antiquarianism, the prodigal production of alternate historiographies; the "over"-attachment to fragmentary, marginal, waste, or leftover products; the rich, highly interruptive affective variety; the irrepressible fascination with ventriloquistic experimentation; the disorienting juxtapositions of present with past, and popular with high culture. ("Paranoid" 27–28)

The "presiding image" of such reparative criticism, Sedgwick suggests,

is the interpretive absorption of the child or adolescent whose sense of personal queerness may or may not (yet?) have resolved into a sexual specificity of proscribed object choice, aim, site, or identification. Such a child—if she reads at all—is reading for important news about herself, without knowing what form that news will take; with only the patchiest familiarity with its codes; without, even, more than hungrily hypothesizing to what questions this news may proffer an answer. The model of such reading is hardly the state of complacent adequacy that Jonathan Culler calls "literary competence," but a much more speculative, superstitious, and methodologically adventurous state where recognitions, pleasures, and discoveries seep in only from the most stretched and ragged edges of one's competence. ("Paranoid" 2–3; emphasis in the original)

Not unlike children, then, gay people find themselves in a position to produce particularly talented, imaginative "misreadings" of their cultural surroundings, and it's the structure of misreading as it relates to the problem of identity that *Widescreen Dreams* seeks to explore. (Of course, in no way do I wish to reinforce those old, homophobic stereotypes of gay people as childlike or as mistakes incarnate, though I realize that my argument risks doing so.)

Finally, the book argues that every kind of individual identity, while it may get formed according to widely shared biological and social processes, ends up being "queer" in the broadest sense of that term. "*People are different from each other,*" Sedgwick declares to be the first axiom of gay and lesbian studies ("It's only by being shameless about risking the obvious that we happen into the vicinity of the transformative" [*Epistemology* 22; emphasis in the original]). Any understanding of human identity, gay or otherwise, must take into account the various and winding roads

by which we travel to arrive at the sense of an identity, and so it's important that we tell our stories about how we think we came to be who
we are and that we look critically at those stories. *Widescreen Dreams* tells
how I arrived at my own sense of an identity. You may find elements of
your story in mine.

Widescreen Dreams

home) . . . an eccentric patch of evergreen trees growing on top of a sharp cliff . . . a village peaceful in the shadow of an onion-domed church (*why don't any of our churches in Reading have those pretty domes?*) . . . an aristocrat's palace soaking quietly on the banks of a lake (*I wish we lived in a house like that. I want to go to Disneyland to see Cinderella's castle, which Mom says is modeled on an actual castle in Germany; I want to go to Germany to see the real Cinderella's castle. I want to go to Austria to see where they filmed* The Sound of Music. *I asked Mom, can we go there some time, and she said Honey, I would love to take you there someday when you're a little older; she said she's already been there once but she wouldn't mind going again, it's one of her favorite places in the whole world; she said Honey, someday you'll get to go there if you want to. But I don't understand how I'll get there unless she takes me. I don't want to go there by myself, I wouldn't like it there by myself. I want to go there with my Mom. Will she be gone forever someday? Someone told me that heaven isn't a real place—it's not a place, it's a state of mind, they said—so if heaven isn't a place, what happens to you when you die? I'm scared of infinity: a winding staircase that keeps turning and turning and has no beginning and no end* . . .)

And now something is subtly happening to us as we gaze down at the enchanted world. FAINT SOUNDS are beginning to drift up and penetrate our awareness . . . the tinkle of cowbells . . . the approaching and receding song of a swiftly passing flock of birds . . . the call of a goatheard echoing from one mountain side to another. And with this, we are aware that the ground seems to be rising. The treetops are getting closer. Our speed seems to be increasing. Without knowing it, we have started to approach a mountain.

. . . gliding over a dense forest of trees rushing beneath like water bursting forth from a dam (*Maria's mountain!*) . . . another swath of green trees . . . and beyond, a carpet of green grass on the crest of a shapely, rolling hill . . . flutes twitter their whirling way down a spiral stair in hasty retreat from the onrushing of brass and strings now at their trembling peak!

Faster and faster we skim the treetops. And then suddenly we "explode" into:

To film what is one of the most famous openings in movie history, a helicopter swooped down just as Maria rushed up to her beloved mountain. The timing on that shot had to be perfect. So, to make sure Andrews came up the hill at the moment required, Marc Breaux [co-choreographer, along with Dee Dee Wood] hid in the bushes nearby. As the helicopter ascended, Breaux, using a megaphone, cued Andrews and she rushed up the hill and began singing.

"The funniest memory I have of the movie," said Breaux's wife, Dee Dee Wood, "is of Marc hiding in the bushes yelling '*Go, Julie!*'"

"The helicopter was a jet helicopter," Andrews recalled. "The cameraman was strapped onto the side of the helicopter, hanging out so he could get the shot, and he came at me sideways. I'd start from the end of the field, and I'd hear Marc yelling 'Go!' from a bullhorn. The helicopter would come at me, clanking away, then it would go around me to get back to the beginning to repeat the scene. But when it circled around me, the downdraft from the jets was so strong that it would literally knock me over. I couldn't stay up. They had to do this shot about ten times, and finally I got so angry I yelled, 'That's enough!'" (Hirsch 149–50)

"Our helicopter pilot was the greatest ace, a real daredevil," recalled Pia Arnold [the German production manager on the film]. "But he was too reckless. I heard that he was killed in 1968 working on some film." (Hirsch 83)

I

My mom kept our record player in the little hallway between the kitchen and the downstairs bathroom. I guess she wanted it there so she could listen to music while she worked in the kitchen. There's a photograph of me in front of the record player from around 1967 when I was four years old. I can't say I "remember" the time, the feelings, the experience it refers to. The picture may contain all that's left of my memory; it may even have *created* the memory within me: I lie asleep on the floor in front of the stereo console's speaker panel, flat on my back, my legs spread akimbo like a frog's, my arms flung out on either side of me, my hands gently resting open, my mouth sweetly agape. I'm wearing Charlie Brown pajamas. On the floor to my right, the album jacket of the Broadway cast recording of *Hello, Dolly!;* to my left, the album jacket of the movie soundtrack recording of *The Sound of Music.*

Now I never go to sleep without music playing. And when I awake, the first thing I want is to hear music.

For as long as I can remember, I've known that *The Sound of Music* was my favorite movie. Based on the memoirs of Maria von Trapp, it's the story of a girl who leaves the convent to marry a naval captain, becomes the stepmother to his children, transforms the family into a successful singing group, and leads them in a hair's-breadth escape from Nazi-occupied Austria. The film opened in March of 1965 to mixed, even hostile reviews, such as Pauline Kael's for *McCall's* magazine, which said

Figure 1. Four years old, July 1967.

that *The Sound of Music* is the kind of film "that makes a critic feel that maybe it's all hopeless. Why not just send the director, Robert Wise, a wire: 'You win, I give up'" (qtd. in Hirsch 175).

My parents took me to see the film sometime during its original release, which lasted a record-breaking four-and-a-half years, so I could have been anywhere between eighteen months and six years of age (fig. 1) when I first saw it. When it was rereleased in 1973, I saw it several more times and learned then that lots of people, not just me, were obsessed with this movie. My mother had already seen it five times or so, my Aunt Pauline something like seven times. Seven seemed a crazy number of times to have seen a movie; its being an "odd" number no doubt invited associations with deviance—though wasn't seven also a "lucky" number? Did that then mean, somehow, that to be odd was also to be lucky? And did that in turn mean that if I or anyone else were in any way odd (for example, if I were a sissy, which lots of kids in school thought I was) it might not be such a bad thing after all? *The Sound of Music* seemed to bring about and validate a *counter*-counterculture of nerds, weirdos, sissies, and squares whose obsessions with the film were immediately understood to be as newsworthy as the film itself. The key to the success of the *The Sound of Music*, Joan Barthel argued in a November 1966 *New York Times Magazine* article, was "people"—not just the people behind the scenes who made the film, but also

> the people out front. Not only the extremists like . . . the woman in Wales who sees it every day, or the man in Oregon who saw it so often he sent the studio a copy of the script written from memory, but the average, garden-variety movie-goer who has seen it once, twice, perhaps three times, and has spread the word. Like the people in Moorhead, Minn., where the picture ran for more than a year in the town's only movie house and sparked a protest demonstration by students of the local college who, under the name POOIE (People's Organization of Intelligent Educatees), picketed—"49 Weeks of Schmaltz is Enough"; "Don't Get Caught in the von Trapp"—for a change of bill. Or the people in Manila, who got so unruly in their demand for holiday tickets that police emergency squads had to be dispatched to cope. Or the people in Salt Lake City, where the theater showing it recorded an attendance of 509,516 as of last month, although the city's population was only about 190,000 in the last census. (47)

Between the time of its initial release in 1965 and its rerelease in 1973, my connection to *The Sound of Music* derived mainly from listening to the soundtrack album and from looking tirelessly at the pictures and reading the text in the eight-page, record-album-sized "storybook" that came with the album. Among the pictures in the storybook were twelve black-and-white stills from the movie. Each corresponded more or less to a musical number on the record, and there was a blurb of text adjacent to each film still that explained where the musical number occurred in the story. Paying little attention to the accompanying text, however, I would stare at the pictures and enter into them and animate them as I pleased, the music washing over me all the while.

In one of my favorite stills (fig. 2), the seven von Trapp children sing "So Long, Farewell" at the dinner party given in honor of their father's soon-to-be fiancée, the Baroness Schraeder. The children, whose ages range from five to sixteen, stand on the short flight of stairs that rises up from the parquet floor of the family manse's grand entrance foyer. Below the first step stands Louisa, the second oldest von Trapp girl—who, because she had long blond hair, would have been, to my mind,

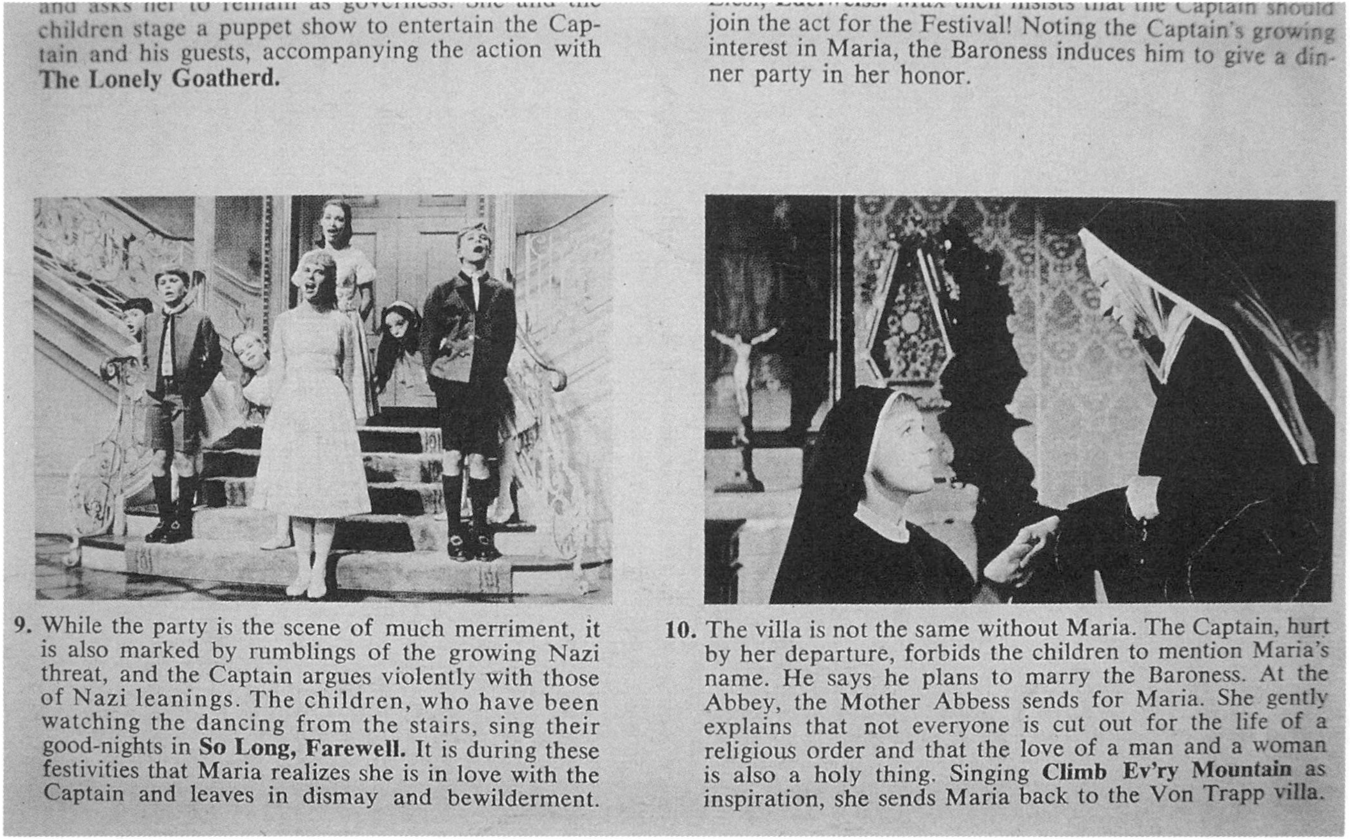

...[illegible]...[illegible]...join the act for the Festival! Noting the Captain's growing interest in Maria, the Baroness induces him to give a dinner party in her honor.

and asks her to remain as governess. She and the children stage a puppet show to entertain the Captain and his guests, accompanying the action with **The Lonely Goatherd.**

9. While the party is the scene of much merriment, it is also marked by rumblings of the growing Nazi threat, and the Captain argues violently with those of Nazi leanings. The children, who have been watching the dancing from the stairs, sing their good-nights in **So Long, Farewell.** It is during these festivities that Maria realizes she is in love with the Captain and leaves in dismay and bewilderment.

10. The villa is not the same without Maria. The Captain, hurt by her departure, forbids the children to mention Maria's name. He says he plans to marry the Baroness. At the Abbey, the Mother Abbess sends for Maria. She gently explains that not everyone is cut out for the life of a religious order and that the love of a man and a woman is also a holy thing. Singing **Climb Ev'ry Mountain** as inspiration, she sends Maria back to the Von Trapp villa.

Figure 2. *The Sound of Music* storybook.

8

Figure 3. John, Patrick, Karen, Betsy, Mary Jo, and Suzanne, Christmas 1967.

my sister Suzanne, who was the second oldest in our family and who also had long blond hair. For at this point I interpreted pretty much everything I heard and saw as having something directly to do with me and my immediate family (fig. 3). On the first step stand the two von Trapp boys, Kurt, the younger one, and Friedrich, the older; to the extent that I could identify the boys with myself and my older brother John, Kurt would have been me, and Friedrich would have been John. Standing on that same step and peeking out from behind Louisa is the youngest, Gretl; though Gretl was the youngest of seven just as I was the youngest of six, she was too inarticulate and fat-faced and infantile for me to have seen myself in her. On the third step peeking out from behind Kurt stands Marta, while behind Friedrich stands Brigitta; neither Marta nor Brigitta fully corresponded with my sisters Karen and Betsy, though like Karen and Betsy they were brunettes and "middle children." On the fourth step stands the oldest, Liesl, by herself; she would have been my oldest sister, Mary Jo, for both Liesl and Mary Jo were beautiful, brunette, interested in boys, and kind to their younger siblings—or at least Mary Jo was attentive to *me* in particular, for I was her biggest fan, I loved to laugh at her jokes, I considered her "my favorite sister," and I would often say so to my other siblings whenever I got into a fight with them.

In the picture, the children's mouths are open wide in song. Not only do they get to enjoy the festivities of the party past their normal bedtime, but now they *themselves* have become the center of attention at the party. As if on stage, they are framed by the ornate, white railings of the stairway, and they are mounted on the steps, so elegant and wide that the carpet need not stretch from side to side. (By contrast, the carpet on our narrower, straight-up-and-down staircase at home was wall-to-wall.) Two slender white pillars rise up from the stairway landing and go somewhere beyond the top of the picture frame, high above the children's heads, suggesting a vast open space—again so unlike our stairs at home, where the low ceiling over the stairs sloped at the same steep angle as the stairs (because another identical staircase led from the second floor to the attic, and everything had to be sandwiched together). I loved the grand, ceremonial, open feeling of the von Trapp family villa: its broad and sweeping arabesque lines, its color scheme of white and gold (only the white and gold baby grand piano in our living room evoked the interior of the von Trapp villa), its theatrical staircases, its high open spaces perfect for seeing and being seen, for watching and putting on shows.

Everything, in fact, that the von Trapp children did, every move they made, had a theatrical quality to it. When Maria first meets them, for example, they march in single file from oldest to youngest, tallest to shortest, down the foyer's elegant stairs (we're supposed to think that they're having a terrible time, marching rigidly like that, but it looked like fun to me); and when it's thundering and lightning, one after another, as if they'd rehearsed it, they race into Maria's bedroom seeking shelter. And then when Uncle Max comes for a visit, he presents them with their very own marionette theater! We got a marionette theater, too, for Christmas one year, only ours was much smaller than the von Trapps', and eventually we had to throw our marionettes away because they got so tangled up we couldn't use them anymore; and anyway we never really figured out how to work them properly, whereas the von Trapps manage to put on a *perfect* show the first time they try it, *and* to the perfect tune of "The Lonely Goatherd." (Why couldn't it have been like that in our house?)

While the picture shows the children singing good night to the party guests, to me it was about the excitement of getting to *stay up late,* of getting to see how adults behaved at night after you had gone to bed—only the difference was, you were still awake to see it! The von Trapp children feel that same excitement when, in an earlier, magical scene (made possible by widescreen cinematography), they stand in one of the tall, widely spaced doorways that open from the brightly lit, gold-encrusted ballroom onto the garden and patio, in the gauzy night air, and watch the elegantly dressed adults inside dancing the Laendler, a traditional Austrian folk dance:

> BRIGITTA: The women look so beautiful.
> KURT: I think they look ugly.
> LOUISA: You just say that because you're scared of them.
> KURT: Silly! Only grown-up men are scared of women.
> GRETL: I think the men look beautiful.
> LOUISA: How would you know?
> [*Gretl gives her a look of mock-disdain.*] 2

Seen through the open doorways, the adults inside look like dainty figurines delicately turning on tiny spindles before the open lid of a music box, or like pirouetting shadows cast on a screen, the darkness of the garden in contrast with the blazing lights of the ballroom evoking the cool, dark, and dreamlike space of a movie theater with its projector rolling.

Although the blurb corresponding to this image in the soundtrack's storybook describes the scene inaccurately—"the children, who have been watching the dancing from the stairs, sing their goodnights" (they were watching the dancing from the patio, not the stairs)—it correctly identifies the basic fantasy enshrined in this scene: whereas "bedtime" means reluctantly having to mount a set of stairs, the rules of bedtime are now happily suspended. This is probably one reason why, some years later, I became enamoured of *Hello, Dolly!* in which, at the climax of that film, Dolly *descends* a staircase: when you're a child, the only time you ever get to come downstairs at night is when, having been banished to your bedroom, all of a sudden, you're invited to come back downstairs again and join the party—Dolly's descent felt like that. Maybe all scenes involving stairways in film musicals—and there are dozens—are meant to evoke this childhood bedtime drama? After all, in *The Sound of Music,* before going off to bed Louisa asks her father, "I'd like to stay and taste my first champagne—yes?" ("No," he replies.)

On New Year's Eve of 1967, my parents took all of us to a party at the house of their friends the Horners. I remember nothing of that occasion except that although I must have fallen asleep long before the stroke of midnight, I was awakened by the tugging rise and fall of being held in my father's arms just as everyone was saying their good nights and he was carrying me, still wearing my party hat and holding a pom pom—I've seen a photograph of this—out into the frigid night, with the snow

falling down and the Horners' outside Christmas lights still blinking and
everyone saying so long, farewell, good night, good night . . .

In another picture, Maria kneels before the Reverend Mother, who in
turn looks down upon Maria benevolently, holding her hand (fig. 2).
It's the scene where Maria, upset because she realizes that she is in love
with Captain von Trapp, has returned to the convent thinking she is now
ready to take her final vows of chastity, obedience, and poverty:

> REVEREND MOTHER: You've been unhappy. I'm sorry.
> MARIA: Reverend Mother.
> REVEREND MOTHER: Why did they send you back to us?
> MARIA: They didn't send me back, Mother, I left.
> REVEREND MOTHER: Sit down, Maria. Tell me what happened.
> MARIA: Well I—I was frightened.
> REVEREND MOTHER: Frightened! Were they unkind to you?
> MARIA: Oh no—no, I—I was confused—I felt—I've never felt that way be-
> fore. I couldn't stay. I knew that here I'd be away from it—I'd be safe.
> REVEREND MOTHER: Maria, our abbey is not to be used as an escape.
> What is it you can't face?
> MARIA: I can't face him again.
> REVEREND MOTHER: [as if what Maria has just said is in some sense unnatural]
> Him? [to Sister Margaretta, who has been listening to the conversation all this
> time] Thank you, Sister Margaretta. [Sister Margaretta leaves] Captain von
> Trapp? Are you in love with him?
> MARIA: I don't know—I don't know—I—the Baroness said I was—she—
> she said that he was in love with me, but I—I didn't want to believe it.
> Oh there were times when we would look at each other. Oh, Mother, I
> could hardly breath.
> REVEREND MOTHER: Did you let him see how you felt?
> MARIA: If I did, I didn't know it. That's what's been torturing me. I was
> there on God's errand. To have asked for his love would have been
> wrong. I couldn't stay, I just couldn't. I'm ready at this moment to take
> my vows. Please help me.
> REVEREND MOTHER: Maria, the love of a man and a woman is holy, too.
> You have a great capacity to love. What you must find out is how God
> wants you to spend your love.
> MARIA: But I've pledged my life to God. I—I've pledged my life to His
> service.
> REVEREND MOTHER: My daughter, if you love this man it doesn't mean
> you love God less. No. You must find out. You must go back.
> MARIA: Oh Mother, you can't ask me to do this. Please let me stay, I beg
> of you.
> REVEREND MOTHER: Maria, these walls were not built to keep out prob-

lems. You have to face them. You have to live the life you were born to live.

If only my mother or father had said (or *sung!*) that to me—about how our house wasn't built to keep out problems, how we have to face our problems—when boys at school used to call me "faggot," and then when I began to feel overwhelmed by my physical attraction to those same boys. If only I'd felt, like Maria, that I could seek safety from my sexuality in the places most familiar to me, the places where God dwelled—home, the church, Catholic school. If only my parents hadn't been afraid to discuss those things openly with me, even if they like the Reverend Mother had insisted that I could never solve my problems by hiding from them at home. If only: *The Sound of Music* has always appealed to the part of me that wishes dreams could come true. For one of the amazing things about this scene was the way the Reverend Mother lovingly confronts Maria's anxieties about her sexual identity. She acknowledges, to begin with, Maria's unhappiness, whether or not she thinks Maria ought to be feeling that way and without even knowing why she's unhappy: "you've been unhappy. I'm sorry."

During my sophomore year in college, I started falling in love with my best friend Martin. The fears that I'd had ever since high school that I might be gay were coming true. One night my parents called me, as they regularly did, to say hello and see how I was doing. "How are you? What's new?" my mom asked. I wasn't sure how much she really wanted an answer to her questions.

"Oh, I'm not too good," I began to say.

"Why *not,* honey?" she asked with a worried intensity.

"Oh, I don't know . . ."

But before I got very far in trying to explain (though I wasn't ready at that point to come out to her), she showered me with protestations of "Oh, honey, we all feel sad once in a while, but we just have to look on the bright side of things. Sure, there are days I don't feel like getting out of bed" (*were* there, I suddenly wanted to know? Why don't you tell me about *that?*), "but I do it anyway, and as the day goes on, I feel better, and I forget about my troubles—we all have to, you know. You can't just sit and do nothing and feel sorry for yourself, honey. Talk to God when you're feeling blue, that's what I do, and it helps, it really does help. Okay? You know your father and I are always here for you and we love you—all of you kids—very much . . ." I remained silent.

The Reverend Mother asks tactful but pointed questions to find out what's bothering Maria: "Why did they send you back to us?" "Tell me what happened." "Were they unkind to you?" "What is it you can't face?" "Are you in love with him?" And not only does she help Maria to admit that she *is* in love with a man, but she reassures Maria that loving a man is something good: "Maria, the love of a man and a woman is holy, too. You have a great capacity to love. . . . if you love this man it doesn't mean you love God less." Although this scene examines the tension between a woman's love of God and her love for a man, not the tension between heterosexual and homosexual love, Maria's love for the captain is so unexpected, so forbidden, and so seductive within the terms of the story that this might as well have been a gay coming out scene. It was always possible for me to hear in the Reverend Mother's speech the simple promise that loving a man is good . . . if you are in love with a man it doesn't mean that you are less the person you already are.

Although my parents and I never directly addressed the possibility of my being gay in the way that the Reverend Mother urges Maria to embrace the possibility that her calling might be a heterosexual rather than a celibate one, still when I was ready, finally, to come out, my parents were the first people I came out to. It was August of 1985, the summer after I graduated from Catholic University and one month before I was set to move to New York City to begin working as an editorial assistant in a publishing firm. I had just spent the weekend down at Catholic U., in Washington D.C., visiting my friend Patrick, who had also been my boyfriend for a few months during my senior year until he dumped me, having decided, he told me, that he wasn't really gay after all. A full ten months after our breakup I still wasn't over Patrick, and so I came home feeling dejected and lonely. I arrived, however, only to discover that my dad was planning to leave town that very night for a business trip and my mom was going with him, leaving me by myself for the next three days (by this time, none of my siblings lived at home anymore). I couldn't bear the thought of being alone with myself and my feelings of unrequited love for Patrick for three whole days, so I began to cry.

"What's wrong, honey?" my mom asked me.

"Oh, nothing," I said, still crying.

"Yes there is something, tell me what it is."

"Nothing," I said, afraid to tell the truth but unable to conceal it any longer.

"If it were nothing, you wouldn't be crying like this. Now, please, honey, tell us. What is it? You can tell us."

I decided to fib.

"It's my friend Robert. I'm feeling sad about him." Robert was an acquaintance from college who at that time was dying of leukemia and whom I'd also seen the previous weekend in Washington. My mom had met him at my graduation and so she knew about his illness, but she also knew that although I was fond of him, his illness—even his death—would not have affected me in quite this way.

Turning to my dad, she said, "Jack, you go without me, I can't leave him here like this."

"I'm not leaving either," my dad said.

"I'm going to make a pot of coffee and we're gonna go sit down in the living room and talk about this.

"No, I don't want you to stay home because of me," I protested.

"No, honey, we don't mind at all. This is more important. We want to stay here with you. Now let's go into the living room."

What followed was the beginning of a long, uneven, sometimes unpleasant process of becoming reacquainted with one another, a process that continues to this day. Many—perhaps most—gay men come out to their parents having first developed some kind of support system of gay friends and lovers, but I came out to my parents in the same moment that I came out to myself and before knowing intimately anyone who was openly gay. I think I did it this way because, despite my parents' limitations, in some sense I *did* experience home, family, and even the Church, as welcoming and loving. And this scene from *The Sound of Music*, where in the end the Reverend Mother sends Maria back into the arms of the man she fears but knows deep down she loves, would have confirmed in me that feeling from the very first time I saw it.

When I was a child, the first thing I decided I wanted to be when I grew up was a priest. Ideas about eternity, uphill struggles, self-sacrifice, and strong leadership had already been planted within me by the time I first saw *The Sound of Music*. My family made friends with certain of our parish priests, in particular Father Mike, who was handsome and extremely sweet-tempered, and who everybody said looked like me, or at least as though he could be my older brother, because we both had the same auburn hair and the same pattern of freckles on our faces. Mike was in his mid-twenties when he came to our parish and must have needed the security and the sense of belonging my family provided him. He seemed to be around a lot, joining us for summers at the beach in Ocean City, New Jersey, where his mother lived year round.

I haven't seen Father Mike since he was transferred to another parish in 1970. The only concrete thing that I have left of him is a picture someone took of the two of us at his going away party in the cafeteria of our parish grade school, a picture I keep on the wall in my bedroom. Whoever took the picture—probably my dad—was adding to the myth that Mike and I were related in some fundamental way, a myth that I now cherish as I search for usable pieces of my past with which

Figure 4. Father Mike and me, June 1970.

to surround myself. In this five-by-seven-inch color photograph (fig. 4), Mike, seen in profile, stands at the back of the auditorium, intently observing something that is happening at the front of the room—it might have been someone paying tribute to him and his invaluable service to Sacred Heart Parish, his inspiring sermons, his appeal to young parishioners, and so on. He is holding what looks like a folded piece of paper, maybe his notes for the farewell speech he is about to give. There is a serious, almost frightened look in his eyes; he might have been thinking, "I don't ever want to leave this place. Where am I going? Will I make new friends? How many times in my life will this happen to me, getting settled only to have to tear up my roots and start all over again?" He is dressed entirely in black—black pants, a black short-sleeved shirt and Roman collar, and a black leather belt. He has (easy for me to see this now) beautiful forearms covered in light-auburn hair and fleshy biceps just visible beneath his short-sleeves. The photographer has caught his shiny auburn hair and sideburns perfectly in the light. (Did I think then, in any way, that he was "sexy"? What does a six-year-old know about sex? I don't remember what I felt for Mike, except that I'm pretty sure "I liked him," whatever that might have meant.) To his left and in the background of the picture, there are several long, cafeteria-style tables, covered in white paper tablecloths and decorated with green, red, and blue crepe paper flowers. I am sitting by myself on one of these tables, facing in the same direction as Mike, with the same serious, attentive look, holding a Coke cup. I'm wearing a short-sleeved dark blue shirt and dark blue pants with blueprint-style drawings of sailing ships all over them, my tiny pair of black shoes dangling a few feet off the floor, my auburn hair echoing Mike's—right down to the faux sideburns cut around my ears. "Bookends," my parents liked to say about us when they looked at this picture, thinking how much of a matched pair we made.

My parents loved Father Mike's sermons, and they even invited him to say mass at our house a few times, in the dining room. As years went by, they would often quote things they remembered him saying. In a letter I got from my mom a few years ago, she wrote, "a thought came to mind Tuesday evening of a time way back in the 60's when you kids were little. We went to adult Education classes run by Fr. [Mike] and I remembered a point he made to the young adults who were there. He said, 'you don't have to find out if you are compatible with someone "below the waistline"—that's already been proven, that 99 times out of 100 that works out. It's whether you can get along "above the shoulders" that really counts.' I never forgot that." Mom's letter came in the wake of an argument we'd had the week before. I had gone back to my home-town of Reading to visit my parents for a few days, and while I was there my mother had inadvertently come across my diary and started read-ing it. She was shocked when she read about the sex I'd recently been having with my boyfriend, and she was upset that I'd acknowledged her anger at me for not having visited Reading in several months (to admit her anger about this would have meant admitting how drastically things have changed between us over the past several years, how much less we now trust each other). My mother's letter to me, in which she quotes Father Mike as a way of expressing her disapproval of my sex life, re-minds me that I know very little about Mike. What would *he* think of me if he knew me today, no longer the sweet little redheaded boy who everyone said looked so much like him?

My mother's letter reminds me, too, that the figures I've used in constructing a mythology for myself about who I am and where I came from (Mom and Dad, my siblings, Father Mike, the scene in *The Sound of Music* where Maria confesses her love of Captain von Trapp to the Reverend Mother, and many others) exceed my grasp, don't do everything I want and need them to do for me, have a life of their own quite apart from the use to which I've put them, can in fact be used against me. And yet, without them, how else would I conceive of myself? What I've made of them is partly a fiction, but I can't live without *some* kind of fiction about who I am. For one thing, I would never be able to communicate my sense of who I am to anyone else without some amount of cutting, pasting, editing, quoting, sampling, shaping, framing—that is, without some kind of fiction-making.

More than anything else, I was absorbed by the picture that served as the promotional image for *The Sound of Music*—the one that appeared on the cover of the soundtrack album as well as on the front page of its storybook (fig. 5). I don't think I fully understood (a) that I was looking at a painting, not a photograph, and (b) that what appeared in the painting didn't necessarily happen exactly that way in the film. In the picture we see Maria, the largest and central figure, her suitcase in one hand, her guitar in the other, bounding over the crest of a grassy hill. The seven children race up the hill behind her, all of them laughing joyously (the film's promotional slogan was "The Happiest Sound in All the World"). Captain von Trapp stands off to the right, observing them with a disapproving look; a dog or a cat, it was hard to tell which, is huddled at his feet (in fact, my sense of perspective was faulty: it was neither a dog nor a cat, but a horse, farther off in the distance). On the left-hand side of the picture, a man rides a bicycle downhill, away from Maria and the children (a reference to the character of Rolf, Liesl's somewhat androgynous, blond boyfriend, who delivers telegrams on his bike and later ends up in cahoots with the Nazis). We see a fountain on the left spurting a thin stream of white water; a statue on the right; from one end of the picture to the other, the top few stories and rooftops of buildings, denoting the city of Salzburg, massed in the valley out of which Maria and the children have sprung; and behind Salzburg, the purple, triangular Alps.

The picture held a perverse fascination for me because it looked like Maria and all seven children were covered with mud (the shadows on the characters' faces and clothes were painted with colors that made them look "muddier" than actual shadows would appear). I couldn't

Figure 5. Poster for *The Sound of Music.*

quite understand why everybody was smiling when they were caked with mud from head to toe; I knew I would have hated to get mud on my face and hands and clothes. There was, of course, a scene in the movie where Maria and the children fall, *kerplunk!*, into a lake when their row-boat tips over, and although they get soaking wet, they laugh about it, so I could understand if they were shown in the picture all smiling and laughing and singing and soaking wet, all covered with mud *from the lake*. But if that, in fact, was what the picture was supposed to be showing, where was the lake? Where was the capsized row boat? And why wasn't anyone's hair wet?

That was another weird thing about this picture—the children's hair. All the girls in the movie had long hair, but in the picture Brigitta, Marta, and Gretl seemed to have short, "boy" haircuts. True, they were pictured face forward, so perhaps they were wearing their long hair in ponytails and we just couldn't see them; but that didn't really explain the artist's rendering, since Leisl and Louisa were *also* pictured face for-ward, and yet we could see *their* ponytails bouncing behind their heads. One result of this confusion for me was to wonder if these particular children—some of whom, like Leisl, even looked too old to be chil-dren—were somehow not the same children as the ones in the movie.

Perhaps the weirdest and most fascinating thing in the picture were Maria's legs. Her dress was shown fluttering up above her knees because she was obviously doing some kind of a hop or a jump; one foot was raised higher than the other, and both were well off the ground (a flying nun? I knew all about that. I also knew that Julie Andrews had played Mary Poppins not long before she appeared in *The Sound of Music,* and I may have assumed that because she could fly in *Mary Poppins* she could also fly, by virtue of her outstretched guitar and carpetbag, in *The Sound of Music,* or maybe even that she could therefore fly in *all* of her movies, no matter who or what she played). But it was hard for me to tell which of Maria's legs was *in front of* the other. It looked like her left leg was in front of her right, because we see her left knee clearly but not much of her right knee. Also, her left leg seemed less muddy, or less in shadow, than her right, which again would have suggested—even to someone like me not completely aware of how artists create the illusion of perspective—that her left leg was supposed to be in front of her right. But her left foot looked exactly the same size as her right, both shoes were the same muddy red color, and though her right foot was all brown while her left was brown and yellow (which might have suggested that the left foot was out in front of the other), still there was something about the way her left foot was drawn to match perfectly the curve of what would have been her right *calf* that made me think that the left foot could have been either behind, next to, or in front of the right leg—it was difficult to decide.

And the sky was an unnatural pea green.

Finally, at the upper-right-hand corner of the album sat the little RCA dog (Nipper) looking into that thing that at the time I didn't know was an old-fashioned record player but which I nevertheless understood to be something that hypnotized the dog in the way that music always hypnotized me. It never occurred to me *not* to imagine that the dog was supposed to be me, even though I knew that animals and humans were not the same species. I recognized something about myself in his dumb, rapt attention, in the way he went around and around and around in dizzy circles on the round, black record label.

II

My mother and I both love *The Sound of Music,* but for different reasons. My favorite scene is probably the opening sequence of the film, leading up to Julie Andrews's rendition of the title song. I remember my mother telling me once when I was a kid that her favorite scene is the one near the end of the movie where the von Trapp family perform together in the Salzburg music festival singing competition while secretly planning to flee Austria, now occupied by the Nazis. I couldn't understand why this was her favorite scene; for one thing, as musical numbers go, it was pretty staid—we see them just standing there, singing on stage. But the particular thing my mother loved about this scene, she always said, was when Captain von Trapp sings "Edelweiss" and loses his voice. He stands alone before the audience, his guitar in hand: "My fellow Austrians," he announces, "I shall not be seeing you again, perhaps, for a very long time. I would like to sing for you now a love song. I know you share this love. I pray that you will never let it die." He begins to sing the heartbreaking waltz "Edelweiss" (the last song Rodgers and Hammerstein wrote together), and not far into the song his voice begins to falter: "Edelweiss, Edel . . . ," he quietly gasps. Maria, standing off to the side with the children, out of the spotlight, sees that he is losing his voice and goes to him, center stage, to pick up where he left off. She then motions to the children to enter the spotlight and join her and the captain. Finally, the captain gestures to the entire audience to join him and his family in finishing the song.

I still wonder why my mother cares so much about this scene. In what ways, for example, has she ever felt, over the forty-three years that she and my dad have been married, that she had to support him in the way that Maria here supports her husband? That is, assuming that my mother was identifying at this point with Maria as a woman, wife, and mother. In what ways have my parents needed each other in the way that Maria and the captain need each other in this scene, and why, though I know how much my parents love each other and always have—so they have always said—why don't I know much more than simply that about their love? Why do I know so little about the close, everyday texture of their love—the ups and downs, frustrations, ambivalences, hurts, and angers? (Why are there so many things we never talk about?) Could remembering, perhaps, how she once saved him, as Maria here saves the Captain, or how she continues to save him year after year, day after day (but save him from what?), make tears come into her eyes as they do when she even so much as describes this scene from *The Sound of Music*? (Even as a child I knew that men, apparently, sometimes thought of women as their saviors: in one scene, the captain assures the baroness, "I'd hardly call you a mere distraction, darling." "Well what would you call me, Georg?" she flirts. He answers, "Lovely, charming, witty, graceful, the perfect hostess, and—you're gonna hate me for this—in a way, my savior. . . . I would be an ungrateful wretch if I didn't tell you at least once that it was you who bought some meaning back into my life." And a little later, he gratefully tells Maria, "you brought music back into the house—I'd forgotten.")

But then, maybe my mother identifies not with the vocal competence of Maria, the effectively supportive wife and mother, but with the vocal *crisis* of Captain von Trapp, the crumbling, needy patriarch. But then who supported my mother through *her* trials and dark nights and public humiliations—through *her* vocal crisis?[3] And what did that consist of? Who lent her a voice when she lost hers? When in her life has she ever felt voiceless?

Several years ago, my mother was diagnosed with throat cancer. She received radiation treatment on her throat, which rid her of the cancer but also severely damaged her voice box so that she couldn't speak for over a month, and to this day, though it is restored for the most part, her voice lacks the power it had before the treatment. It was extremely painful for me to see my mother unable to speak, reduced to the crudest of physical gestures to communicate her most basic needs, having to write things down on a pad of paper and, more often than not, settling for just leaving things unspoken because it would be too difficult to communicate through body language or it would take too long to write things out, and then her hand would grow tired from all the writing she had to do. It seemed to me that here was someone whose whole life was dedicated to taking care of other people—her husband, her six children, more recently her ten grandchildren—and who asked relatively little for herself, and now she couldn't even do that. So much of her vocation in life has involved speaking kind and reassuring words to other people: singing lullabies into our baby ears as we drifted blissfully off to sleep (softly she would sing to me when I was a child, "Little lamb you're tired, / I know why you're blue, / Someone took your kiddy car away. / Better go to sleep now little man, / You've had a busy day. / You've been playing soldiers, / The battle has been won, / The enemy is out of sight. / Put away your soldiers, / And put away your guns, / The enemy is gone for tonight"); making promises that everything would be all right when someone had hurt our feelings; promising to pray for the sick; fasting in solidarity for someone if they were taking a test, or hoping for a mortgage to come through, or undergoing some difficulty, such as an operation. She fasted for me on the day of my Ph.D. qualifying oral examination and on the day of my dissertation defense, and she prayed for three months with special intentions for me after my boyfriend Gary died; she gave up eating Baby Ruth chocolate bars, her favorite, for nearly fifteen years for a friend of hers whose husband died in an automobile accident early on in their marriage and who had never, it seemed, fully recovered from the loss. Even when my mother's reassuring words and good intentions weren't enough to help the person in need or to solve the problem, as I often felt they weren't when I needed her support, the constancy with which she made her offerings was impressive, making you feel that if nothing else could save you, her unbending faith would.

I used to think we were the happiest family in the world. From a thousand little things I heard my parents say when I was a child, I came to believe that we were definitely "lucky." They would often distinguish our family from people who lived in California—for example, our distant California relatives who apparently had endless problems with their kids. My parents were under the general impression that life in California was more permissive, more wild, less conducive than the east coast to raising children and instilling in them the proper values. But only in certain places on the east coast: for example, New York was out of the question—a place to visit, maybe, but never to live in. We lived in the suburbs, and that was best. My parents would often say how none of us kids ever gave them any trouble. We were, all of us, healthy, thank God; all exceptionally good students. We were hard workers and good sports. All of my siblings were accomplished athletes: Mary Jo played field hockey; Sue played basketball and field hockey; Betsy played basketball and field hockey; John played football, baseball, and basketball; Karen played softball and field hockey; plus all of the girls were swimmers and

large family. I was also feeling a little homesick, despite the fact that Mrs. Freymoyer did probably as much as anyone could have to make me feel secure, welcome, and at home.

"I feel really lucky to have such a big family," I said. "With the exception of me and my sister Karen, who is two years older than me, all of my other siblings are one year apart. So we're really close."

"Your poor mother!" Mrs. Freymoyer exclaimed. "Having babies for six years in a row! How did she survive being pregnant all those years?" Everyone always asked that question.

"I don't know. She had some back trouble during some of her pregnancies, but she says that she and my dad would have had more children after me if they had been able to. They seem to love children more than anything else in the world."

"Is that right! Well, what's it like to have all those older brothers and sisters?"

What's it like? No one had ever asked me such a question. It's not like anything, was my initial thought, it's just the way it is. But how *is* it? What makes being part of this family different from being part of some other family or from not having a family at all? Rather than think too deeply about it, I fell back on the kind of thing I usually told people.

"I love it. I never have to worry about having someone to play with."

"Do you get along with your brother and sisters?"

"Uh huh."

"That's amazing. I used to fight like crazy with my sister and my parents. I couldn't wait until I was old enough to go to college and get out on my own. I mean, I can appreciate my sister now, and of course my parents are both dead, but I just wanted to be on my own so badly and do things my way. I guess I've never been a team player, and so I wonder how you manage with your big family. What makes your family so cohesive? The truth is I envy you, Patrick."

I usually liked it when people envied me for my big, happy family. But Mrs. Freymoyer wasn't just complimenting me on my family to be polite, and she wasn't speaking superficially. I could see that she was trying to understand something for herself, and she was giving me permission to do the same—to make conversation not as a way of filling the air with received wisdom or rehearsing conventional pieties (like most of the conversation around my house) but as a means toward deeper, critical insight into whatever it was that I felt I needed to explore. But what did I need to explore? Did I dare tell her that my family wasn't always as happy as we liked to say we were? We never said anything bad about the family to people outside the family. Whenever anyone asked, "How's Betsy?" or "How's Suzanne?" or "How's [some other member of the family]," we would always say, "Oh, she's fine," or "Oh, he's just great," and we would proceed to rattle off a list of his or her most recent accomplishments. But things weren't always fine and we weren't always just great. As far as I could tell, there were goings-on in my family that no one wanted to talk about. For example, one of my sisters seemed to have an eating disorder. Another of my sisters was so unhappy with her weight, her appearance in general, that she used to pluck out her eyelashes. And from about the time I was eight, I developed the habit of pulling out locks of hair from my scalp, causing a bald spot to develop on top of my head that was increasingly visible to everyone.[4] I was always amazed at how kids at school felt entitled to just walk up to me and brazenly say, with an insincere gasp, "*[gasp!] You have a bald spot on top of your head!*" But apparently the humiliation of having my bald spot pointed out to me and the damage I was doing to my appearance wasn't strong enough to deter me from ripping out my hair (and always with that tiny pin-prick of pleasure every time a knot of hair was torn away from the scalp!). I found out that my third grade teacher said something about it to my parents because she found little knots of red hair all over the floor around and underneath my desk, and our cleaning lady, too (she came twice a week), found knots of my hair around the house, hidden under chairs or behind the sofa, and would from time to time alert my mom to this. But I don't remember the conversations, if any, that I had about it with my parents, except that my mom told me periodically not to pull out my hair because I had such a beautiful head of hair and it was a shame to do that to it.

For as long as I can remember I didn't like myself, and I must have learned to feel that way in part from cues I was getting at home. I could tell that my parents vaguely disapproved of something about me—the way I walked, was that it? The sound of my voice—was that it? My mother was always telling me to stick out my chest and throw back my shoulders when I sat at the table or when she would happen to see me just standing around somewhere. And she would say it in a low tone of voice that presaged doom: "*Patrick Horrigan, sit up straight.*"

When I would answer the telephone, the voice on the other end would invariably say without hesitation, "Peggy—." They thought I was my mother because my voice sounded feminine.

"Just a minute, I'll get her."

When my mother would take the phone from my hand, and the other person, assuming I was mortified, would apologize for having called me "Peggy" (it was universally understood to be a crime to mistake a boy for his mother), she would pretend that it was she, not I, whose gender identity had been called into question: "I know," she would joke, as much directing her comment to me as to her friend, "I have a deep voice. I sound like a man. . . . [*with a brisk laugh*] Oh, it's no problem at all! But now, how are ya? I haven't talked to you in ages!" (By contrast, the sound of a girl's voice issuing from a boy's mouth was greeted with warmth and affection in *The Sound of Music:* at one point during the von Trapp children's performance of "So Long, Farewell," Kurt lip-synchs the second syllable of "good-bye" while one of his sisters supplies the impossibly high note, at which point Captain von Trapp smiles and gives Kurt a friendly wave of the hand.)

But I couldn't explain any of this to Mrs. Freymoyer. It was enough that she was interested in learning about my family and in what I had to say about them. The only language I had for speaking about my family was the one I inherited from my parents: "We are happy and good and everything is fine. Period."

"My favorite thing in the whole world is Christmas Eve, when all of us kids exchange gifts with each other after going to midnight mass," I told Mrs. Freymoyer. (She was nonreligious, and I sometimes liked to make people who weren't practicing Catholics feel like they were missing out on something.) "The other thing I love is going to the shore with my family every summer."

"I don't suppose you have your own room."

What was she getting at? Each of her kids had their own room, which seemed like a strange luxury to me.

"No. I share a room with my brother."

"Do you get along with your brother?" That question again.

"Yeah. Pretty much. I mean, I can't do all the things he can, like he's a really good athlete, and I can't do stuff like that. He plays baseball and basketball and football and tennis and a million other things. He's a junior in high school. He's on the student council."

"What kinds of things do you and your brother do together?"

"Well, we don't really do that much together." (But I mustn't betray him or my family. John is my brother! I love John! John loves me!) "When I was born he was so excited that one day he picked me up out of my crib and carried me downstairs to show me to the milkman. My parents were afraid that he would drop me because he was only three years old."

"Oh, how sweet! He must have been so happy to finally get a brother after having all those sisters."

"Yeah." I thought for a moment. "But we don't really have much in common."

"Does he play an instrument?"

"No." (But I mustn't betray him or my family.) "My sisters do, though. Mary Jo and Sue play the piano, and Betsy and Karen play the guitar!"

"Wow! That's wonderful. I guess you can have concerts right in your own home!"

"Yeah."

"Have you ever done that—played a duet with you on the piano and one of your sisters on the guitar?"

"No."

"Oh, you should try it sometime! I used to play the piano with my friend Lucy, and she played the flute, and we had such wonderful times! And we would sing too! My god, we weren't very good singers, but we had fun. We would try to sing Beatles songs! We were madly in love with Paul McCartney, even though he was a little too young for us at that point!"

"Oh, we've never done that."

"So what do you do when you want to be by yourself? Where do you go in that big house full of brothers and sisters?" Another question no one had ever asked me. I never thought of the hours I spent by myself (painting, building model houses and airplanes, listening to records, playing the piano, playing with Lego, bouncing a ball on the driveway, playing by myself in the woods near our house, talking to myself whenever I found a place where no one could hear me) as having any kind of integrity or reason for being. I never imagined that a person might actually *need* to separate themselves from their family from time to time, maybe even for a long time, maybe even for a lifetime.

"Well, I guess sometimes I play by myself, but—"

"What do you do when you're by yourself?"

I ran my fingers through my hair and felt the bald spot underneath my fingers.

"Some of the things I like to do you can't really do when you're with another person . . ."

"Like what?"

I didn't know where to begin.

If someone had asked me when I was twelve or thirteen what I loved about *The Sound of Music*, I might have said something about the way Maria teaches the children to sing "Do Re Mi" and dance with complete abandon around the city of Salzburg and the local countryside. But now I think that *The Sound of Music* must have meant more to me even than that, though I still think that is pretty momentous. For although on the surface my family resembled the von Trapp family in its size, its relative number of girls and boys, and its more or less sunny public disposition, especially once Maria had arrived and taught the children to sing, there were also grimmer, more serious undercurrents running through the von Trapp children's life at home that must have echoed the uglier realities of life in my household as well. I suspect one of the things about Maria that was so compelling to me as an adolescent was not just her winning personality and the guarantee that life in her presence could become a song and dance at any moment, but—just as important—in one crucial scene she told the Captain the truth about the unhappiness each of his children felt deep down:

CAPTAIN: Do you mean to tell me that my children have been roaming about Salzburg dressed up in nothing but some old drapes?
MARIA: Mm hm. And having a marvelous time.
CAPTAIN: They have uniforms—
MARIA: Straitjackets, if you'll forgive me.
CAPTAIN: I will not forgive you for that.
MARIA: The children cannot do all the things they're supposed to if they have to worry about spoiling their precious clothes.
CAPTAIN: I haven't heard them complain yet.
MARIA: Well they wouldn't dare! They love you too much—they fear you too much.
CAPTAIN: I do not wish you to discuss my children in this manner.
MARIA: Well you've got to hear from someone. You're never home long enough to know them.
CAPTAIN: I said I don't want to hear any more from you about my children!
MARIA: I know you don't, but you've got to! Now take Liesl—
CAPTAIN: You'll not say one word about Liesl, Fraulein.
MARIA: She's not a child anymore. One of these days you're going to wake up and find she's a woman. You won't even know her. And Friedrich— he's a boy, but he wants to be a man like you and there's no one to show him how.
CAPTAIN: Don't you dare tell me about my son!
MARIA: Brigitta could tell you about him if you'd let her get close to you, she notices everything. And Kurt . . .
CAPTAIN: [*interrupting her*] Fraulein—
MARIA: . . . pretends he's tough not to show how hurt he is when you brush him aside . . .
CAPTAIN: [*interrupting again*] That will do!
MARIA: . . . the way you do all of them.
CAPTAIN: I said, that will do!
MARIA: Louisa I don't know about yet, but someone has to find out about her, and the little ones just want to be loved. Oh please Captain, love them. Love them all!
CAPTAIN: I don't care to hear anything further from you about my children!
MARIA: I am not finished yet, Captain!
CAPTAIN: Oh yes you are, Captain!
[*Maria suppresses a smile at his faux pas.*]

On one level, I could best see my own particular situation in that of the von Trapp boys, Friedrich and Kurt, while on another, there was at least something Maria said about each of the children, boys and girls alike, that I felt was true for me too. It was true, there were times when I felt my father brush me aside, like the captain brushes Kurt aside, and it would hurt me just like it did Kurt (even though we never exactly witness in the film any of the particular infractions on the captain's part that Maria accuses him of here, indicating—though I couldn't have known this when I was young—how routine we take this kind of neglect to be within families and how we don't even need to see evidence of it to believe that it exists. It's as if we feel, *of course* fathers brush their sons aside and don't teach them who they ought to be, *of course* fathers are never home long enough to get to know their children, *of course* children suffer in silence, and so on, even if it's not 100 percent true).

For example, once when I was practicing the piano and getting particularly ardent about the Brahms rhapsody that I was learning (op. 79, no. 2; "*Molto passionato, ma non troppo allegro*"—to be played "very passionately, but not with too much liveliness"), my dad was sitting in the living room listening to me and reading a magazine—my memory now tells me it was *Forbes,* but I could be just making that up. As I filled the room with as much of the romantic drama as I could squeeze out of my Brahms rhapsody (I wasn't "banging," as my siblings liked to complain—and then they would *bang* the door shut between the living room and the den, where they sat watching TV—I was *soaring!,* in the same way that the camera and Julie Andrews's voice soar at the beginning of *The Sound of Music*[5]), my dad rustled his magazine and said, "Does it have to be so loud? Can't you tone it down a little?"

"No!" I cried, suddenly out of all patience with him, "I'm playing it exactly how it's written," which wasn't true; "it's *supposed* to be played like this!" And I got up brusquely and stomped out of the room and ran upstairs and slammed my bedroom door behind me so hard I scared myself and accidentally knocked one of my brother's trophies off its shelf.

And Maria told the Captain that Friedrich had "no one to show him" how to be a man. That was illuminating to me, not because I consciously thought I needed to learn from some other man how to become like him, but because it spoke the truth about gender as I was living it out day after day: you're not just born a man or a woman, a boy or a girl; you have to be taught how to be one, and your parents are supposed to teach you how, and often they don't. Like Friedrich, I wasn't, it seemed, learning how to be a man. For example, on the night that *The Sound of Music* premiered on television in February of 1976, my parents and I were caught in traffic coming home from a Philadelphia Phillies game and I was losing my mind at the thought of missing even one minute of the film.

My dad always got us exclusive seats in the Bank of Pennsylvania Superbox because his company did business with the bank. In the Superbox you could watch the baseball game on a big color TV in the private, air-conditioned lounge if it was too hot to sit outside in the seats; there was an open bar with a meat, vegetable, fruit, and cheese buffet that was replenished by the waitress every fifteen minutes or so, and then everything from chocolate cake to banana splits for desert; plus a private bathroom so you didn't have to wait in line in one of those big, smelly public men's rooms along with everybody else. This was great for me because I was—and still am for the most part—irreparably pee shy, and no matter how bad I had to go, if there was even just one person standing behind me waiting his turn at the urinal, I'd never in a million years be able to do it; so that was another reason why I liked the Superbox. I had no real taste for baseball, but I felt if I had to watch a baseball game, it might as well be from the Superbox.

On the night of *The Sound of Music* TV premiere, however, it was all I could do to conceal my impatience with baseball. I complained persistently about the traffic the whole way home. It seemed cosmically unfair that on *this* night of all nights (a) I had to be dragged off to a baseball game in Philadelphia, which my parents had promised me would be over in plenty of time for us to get home to watch *The Sound of Music* but then looked like it wouldn't be, and (b) I had to get stuck in traffic on the way home, and then I got really annoyed with my mom when she insisted that it didn't matter if I missed the first half hour or so of the movie since I'd already seen it at least three times in the movie theater, and how many times did I have to see *The Sound of Music* anyway? I practically knew the whole thing by heart as it is! How could I be so ungrateful, when your father gets you *superbox* tickets to a Philadelphia Phillies game at Veterans Stadium? Do you know how many boys would love to have such good seats? And all you can think about is rushing home in time to watch some movie on TV! ("*Some movie on TV??*" I thought to myself, floored by the understatement.) "I like *The Sound of Music* too," my mom would concede, "but my life doesn't revolve around it! I mean, let's put things into perspective!"

All of this meant, somehow, that I wasn't learning to act the way a boy ought to act (preferring Hollywood musicals to baseball games and making a big fuss over it), and that, like Friedrich in *The Sound of Music,* I needed and lacked someone to teach me how I should be acting. But lacking an effective masculine role model also implied that whatever was supposedly wrong with me wasn't all my fault—which, if that were true, would have dealt a major blow to the fantasy that we were the happiest, most perfect family in the world. I had already become accustomed to holding together in my mind the contradictory ideas that, on the one hand, my family was perfect and that, on the other, I deviated from the family norm—in a sense, I believed that I was not an integral part of this perfect family, that I was only supplemental to it. But Maria's argument that Captain von Trapp was implicated in his children's suffering encouraged me to see myself as perhaps still damaged, but *belonging* nonetheless. For she argued, in effect, that the problems in the von Trapp family were systemic, not isolated to this or that particular, deviant child. And so if I was both deviant *and* a fully entitled member of my family, then the same was true of my father and every other member of the family! That thought came to me as somewhat of a relief.

Captain von Trapp, Maria said, would "wake up one day and find [Liesl] a woman" and not know who she is anymore. It was amazing to think of one's parents as fallible, as being too blind to notice something. But, of course, at times, my parents did *nothing but* not notice things about me—about all of us, about the whole world around us—or rather, their love for us made them notice things about us and about our environment only selectively.

Then there was Louisa. Maria felt an obligation toward even the child she knew least: "Louisa I don't know about yet, but someone has to find out about her." Maria's duty as a "parent," it seemed, was precisely to get to know each child as an individual. It was stunning to think that different children in the same family could actually have different personalities and therefore different needs that parents might understand only partially—that children, according to Maria, were in some significant way *different from* their parents and from each other and that this was something to be acknowledged and respected, not minimized or denied.

And it was thrilling, how Maria said that Brigitta—one of the middle children, and a *girl*—was the one who "notices everything." But her father wouldn't "let her get close" to him. I wasn't exactly sure what "being close" to a father entailed, but dimly it occurred to me that I might not be as close to my father as I might deserve, or wish, to be.

(Things have changed somewhat between my father and me over the last several years. An accumulation of events, major and minor, some of them disastrous—my mother's bout with cancer, my boyfriend Gary's suicide, and, in a less obvious but, I think, still profound way, the constant challenge over the past fifteen or so years of getting to know me now not just as his grown son but as his grown *gay* son—all these things have made my dad more physically and emotionally present to me than ever before. When my dad called to tell me about my mother's cancer, he wept audibly and unashamedly and didn't rush to hang up the phone to conceal his grief; when Gary died, my dad drove me to the funeral in New Jersey, stayed by my side the whole time, and kissed and hugged my friends, even though he had only once, briefly, met Gary and, until Gary's death, knew almost nothing about our relationship.)

III

I started taking piano lessons when I was five, around the same time that I first saw *The Sound of Music*. I don't remember thinking that my piano teacher, Mrs. Hasbrouck, was anything like Maria in *The Sound of Music*—Mrs. Hasbrouck and Maria didn't look or act like each other at all—but the story of a woman who transforms the inner lives of seven sad, angry children through the agency of music must have resonated in my mind with the relationship that was developing between Mrs. Hasbrouck and me. Although Maria eventually becomes the von Trapp children's mother, she never really behaves like a mother, at least not in the way I thought mothers were supposed to behave. Maria was more like a fun baby-sitter—like Janie Distelhorse, the daughter of friends of my parents, who used to baby-sit us occasionally during the late sixties and early seventies. Almost everything that came out of Janie's mouth made me laugh. She was particularly good at playing zany language games and making up goofy names for us—she named me "Patrikimus," which my brother, for years afterward, shortened to "The Mus" and eventually just "Mus" (rhymes with "puss"). Mrs. Hasbrouck, on the other hand, was even older than my mother—she was practically old enough to be my grandmother. While Maria was girlish in her shiny, auburn page boy haircut, Mrs. Hasbrouck had soft, curly white hair and wore glasses. Maria was agile and bursting with energy: on her way to meet the von Trapps, she sings "I Have Confidence." As she sings, with her carpetbag in one hand and her guitar in the other, she trips, skips, kicks up her heels, runs down the street and gets all out of breath and then pulls herself together and is ready for more. Mrs. Hasbrouck, on the other hand, was deliberate and slow. For most of our time together, we sat. And as the years went by, Mrs. Hasbrouck's step grew more and more hesitant. Sometimes I would walk her home after my lesson—her apartment was across the street from the mall where she taught. She would hold onto my arm the way frail old people do. Although I was happy to walk with her, once I had delivered her safely to her door I would run full speed back to the parking lot where I'd left my car, just because I needed to let loose. (My mom frequently tells a story about her friend Annette who was walking across a lawn one day with her five- or six-year-old daughter Katie. They came to a hedge, and instead of walking all the way around the hedge, as Annette would usually have done, Annette just jumped over the hedge. Katie rejoiced: "Now *that's* the kind of mother I want!"

Whenever my mom wants to joke with me about how she struggles to stay "with it," or how there are some things she just can't bring herself to do no matter how much I might want her to do them, she tells that story.)

When Maria tries to teach the von Trapp children to sing, they're puzzled at first. They don't understand the meaning of notes and scales (do re mi fa so la ti) until Maria makes up a song that explains it all: "Doe—a deer, a female deer . . ." and so on. Thereafter, the children sing, dance, and harmonize unbidden. They even jump up and down, forward and backward, on a flight of stairs, in perfect synchronicity with the music they are singing, just like notes arranged on a staff—they don't just learn music, they become music incarnate (in so many ways, like Maria).

It was more complicated with me and Mrs. Hasbrouck. My parents noticed my interest in the piano when I was three or four. Mary Jo and Suzanne were already taking lessons with Mrs. Hasbrouck, and I would try to imitate them at the piano. Somehow I started playing renditions of songs they *weren't* practicing, like "Sons of God," a folk-style church hymn that was popular in Vatican II–era Catholic churches in the late sixties. Immediately my parents took me to see Mrs. Hasbrouck, and although her policy had always been that a child isn't ready to start playing until he turns eight, she agreed to take me on, impressed by my eagerness to play and my ability to play by ear. I was a deceptively fast learner. Mrs. Hasbrouck would play a piece for me, and I would pretty much play it back to her. Soon she realized that I wasn't reading the notes— I was imitating what I'd heard her play. She decided that if I was ever going to learn to read music, I would have to work out the notes for myself without the benefit of first hearing how the piece was supposed to sound. It took me over six years to learn to read music, and even then I was a slow reader (I still am).

While playing the piano never came as easily to me as singing did to the von Trapp children, in other ways it was just as magical a carpet ride to another world. For music was an alternative language; if I couldn't change the way things worked within the tight structure of my family, at least I could learn about other ways of structuring the universe and inhabit those structures whenever I practiced the piano. And the bond that grew between me and Mrs. Hasbrouck was, ultimately, as revolutionary as the bond between Maria and her adoptive children. Quite apart from the business of my lesson, Mrs. Hasbrouck and I enjoyed talking to each other, and we talked about all kinds of things. She was one of the first people in my life who fulfilled my need for intelligent, mutually rewarding conversation (Mrs. Freymoyer was another), the kind of conversation I felt there wasn't enough of at home. She once told me a story about how, several years earlier, sometime in the early 1970s, she had been sitting on a bench one afternoon in Philadelphia's Fairmount Park when along came a very distinguished-looking old gentleman who sat down next to her on the bench. It was Richard Rodgers.

"Did you say anything to him?" I gasped with excitement.

"Oh no, people like that usually don't want to be recognized in public by total strangers. Besides I'm not the biggest fan of musicals in the world, as you know, Mr. Horrigan."

I giggled. I knew she wasn't.

"But he seemed like a sweet man. It was nice just to see him there."

"Was Hammerstein with him?"

"Oh dear no, he's been dead since . . . I think he died in 1960. No, he was with a nurse or a companion or maybe it was his daughter. I don't know."

"Wow."

Nor was Mrs. Hasbrouck all that fond of *The Sound of Music:* "I think it trivializes the history of Germany's takeover of Austria and the spread of Nazism throughout Europe. Not once does that film mention the Jews, and when the von Trapps escape to Switzerland, it's as if we're supposed to forget about all the people who *didn't* escape the Nazis. Plus, I find the idea of a singing nun a little bit ludicrous. And I especially don't like the captain in that movie. I'm very fond of Christopher Plummer as an actor. He's a great Shakespearean actor." (I had no idea.) "But the Captain von Trapp is just a cardboard figure of a man. I don't find him to be much of a character at all."

I was puzzled by Mrs. Hasbrouck's criticism of the captain. The idea of an emotionally crippled, often physically absent father, if that's what she meant by "cardboard," apparently made such perfect sense to me that I hardly noticed the captain's deficiencies at all, or if I did, I never imagined that he might have been any different. To me, his presence—his *absent* presence—was simply a given, one of the basic conditions of a story about children finding themselves through the love and music of a surrogate mother figure. If Christopher Plummer's performance was "cardboard," wasn't he just performing the role as it should be? Weren't all fathers—all men—more or less cardboard figures in the lives of women and children? It was strange but interesting to imagine Mrs. Hasbrouck wanting the captain to be *more* of a man, as if there were anything more in being a man than the little that Christopher Plummer demonstrated, and as if that could in any way be considered a good thing. Apparently Mrs. Hasbrouck didn't think all men were alike or that they were all as bad as Captain von Trapp. Hmm!

The majority of the music Mrs. Hasbrouck taught me was "classical"

(Bach, Mozart, Beethoven, Chopin, Schubert, Schumann, Brahms, Debussy, Ravel, Rachmaninoff, Prokofief), but she also let me branch out occasionally into Broadway show music. After I saw *Sweeney Todd,* with music and lyrics by Stephen Sondheim, on Broadway in 1979, I became an instant and obsessive admirer of Sondheim's music. I bought a collection of songs from his shows, which Mrs. Hasbrouck and I worked through. I don't think even Sondheim's music interested her very much, though she did seem to recognize his importance in the history of the Broadway musical (how, with musicals like *Company* [1970], *Follies* [1971], and *Pacific Overtures* [1976], he and his collaborators succeeded in integrating book, music, lyrics, choreography, and production design into a single overarching concept; at the time I was reading all about it in a big, glossy, coffee-table book on the subject, *Broadway Musicals* [1979] by Martin Gottfried, that I'd gotten for Christmas that year). As we rehearsed selections from the Sondheim songbook, Mrs. Hasbrouck remarked, "his music is more complex than most Broadway show music. Some of it is very pretty. I can see why his musicals are not always popular or successful. You don't exactly go around humming these songs, do you?"

"No," I answered, and proceeded to lecture her on the importance of Sondheim's innovations in *Sweeney Todd*—how, for example, the score was really more like opera and how the chorus at times commented on the action as would the chorus of an ancient Greek drama (I'd just written a paper about it in my eleventh grade English class). Mrs. Hasbrouck seemed to see *Sweeney Todd* my way. "Yes," she said, "it is like opera and very clever. And I must say I prefer this music to Gilbert and Sullivan, whom I really can't stand. All that oom pah pah, oom pah pah, and those silly Victorian love stories."

"And Stephen Sondheim uses songs dramatically in ways that don't seem to fit the way the songs sound or what the words are about, like in *Sweeney Todd,* when Sweeney sings 'Pretty Women,' about how beautiful and graceful and touching women are, and he sings it as a duet with Judge Turpin who is sitting in the barber chair getting a shave from Sweeney, and it's this gorgeous melody, but really Sweeney is preparing, as he sings, to slit the judge's throat, and he's using the song to lull the judge to sleep so he can murder him!"

"I see. Very interesting," Mrs. Hasbrouck would say. Then, looking at the Stephen Sondheim songbook, with the photograph of Sondheim on the cover, one last time before we turned back to our main business for the week—it might have been Ravel's "Pavane (Pour une infante defunte)," the dirge for a dead princess—she said, "he is quite a handsome man."

Was he? I wondered. I'd never thought of adult men as attractive, though there was a picture of Sondheim in my copy of the *Sweeney Todd* souvenir program—from when he was in his early thirties, with long-ish hair, his brooding, unsmiling face hidden mostly in shadow—that I thought looked thrillingly demonic, as I felt the face of the composer of *Sweeney Todd* should look. I became momentarily aware of how standards of physical beauty varied from person to person, and how women who were attracted to men looked at them.

I was pleasantly surprised to discover that although she thought little of Broadway musicals in general and only slightly more of the works of Stephen Sondheim, Mrs. Hasbrouck did have the Broadway cast album of *Pacific Overtures,* possibly Sondheim's most obscure and eccentric, and certainly his least successful, show to date. Mrs. Hasbrouck and her husband were interested in all things Japanese (*Pacific Overtures* is a kabuki-style musical about Commodore Perry's infamous trip to Japan in 1854, which succeeded in forever exposing Japanese culture to what the show styles as the pernicious influence of Western values), and their cast album of *Pacific Overtures* had been a gift from their son Allan. Mrs. Hasbrouck was, in fact, one of the lucky people to have seen the show in 1976 before it closed after just a few performances. She lent the album to me, and I liked it so much that for Christmas the following year she bought me my own copy. I showed it to some of my friends from high school one night, knowing they would think it strange and partly *wanting* them to think it strange (for at least in that way I would get their attention). Predictably, they laughed at the actors' funny names like Mako, Yuki Shimoda, and Sab Shimono, so obviously not "big names" (I laughed along with them because from their point of view, I could see, it *was* comical). Broadway musicals were already a laughingstock among most kids my age, and Japanese-style Broadway musicals all the more so. But my best friend Beth, at least, took it as still more evidence that I was smarter and subtler than the rest of our friends. (At least twice a year during high school, Beth and I took day trips to New York City to see shows and soak up as much "big city life" as we could before getting back on the bus to Reading.)

The cast album of *Pacific Overtures* was one of several things Mrs. Hasbrouck gave me during the thirteen years I studied full-time with her— queer little tokens of her affection.

Frequently during my lesson, Mrs. Hasbrouck would suck on smooth, highly aromatic white candies the size and shape of small bird eggs, which she called "violets" because they had the strange, almost nauseating taste of purple—not grape, but sheer *purple.* They came in an elegant cardboard box covered in satiny white paper attractively decorated with flowers. She bought them somewhere in one of the ladies' departments at Wanamakers, which was the main department store in our local mall. She would always offer me one of these candies, and I would take one—and one was always enough. I'm not sure if I liked or disliked the taste, but they were unusual, and I definitely liked that. Once Mrs. Hasbrouck either bought me a whole box for myself or, more likely, gave me her box, which my mother could smell when she came to pick me up after my lesson as soon as I got into the car, even though I had held them pressed against my shirt with my music books (I held books in my arms the way only girls were supposed to hold books—pressed against the chest; boys were supposed to be able to grasp them with one hand and support them against their hip, or, even more masculine, carry them in a duffel bag slung over the shoulder).

"Did Mrs. Hasbrouck give you those lavender candies again?! Blyech!!" my mom would say, and comically stick out her tongue. "You two characters!"

Knowing she'd refuse but wanting to keep up the situation comedy, I would answer my mom back, "Do you want one?"

"Oh, honey, you know I can't stand those things! I tried one once and had to throw it out," and she would put her hand over her mouth, and I'd laugh. "They're so perfumey. I don't know what they put in those things. I think she buys them at a perfume counter in Wanamakers." And we would keep on laughing.

"I like them," I'd insist.

"Well they're all yours, then!"

One time I drove everybody in the house crazy with a pair of castanets that Mrs. Hasbrouck lent me. I couldn't get the hang of them, and no one in my family could believe that I was actually trying to use them or, for that matter, that a pair of castanets had actually found its way into our house. Castanets represented a culture that was so foreign to us as to seem unreal—the kind of ridiculous thing you only saw on *The Lawrence Welk Show* or in a Bugs Bunny cartoon, with Bugs dressed in drag like Carmen Miranda, pretending to be a sexy Spanish dancing girl, luring Elmer Fudd into some kind of humiliating trap (Fudd, perhaps, would try to kiss "her" and end up with a black eye or a rubber plunger stuck to his mouth instead of Bugs' thick, lipstick-red lips). Castanets could only have connoted slapstick and degradation in my family. I think my mother insisted that I immediately return them to Mrs. Hasbrouck the next week, "and be sure to tell her thank you, but we've had our experiment, and enough's enough!" Sometimes, my mother must have thought, Mrs. Hasbrouck could go too far—in the same way that, in *The Sound of Music,* Captain von Trapp was appalled to discover, on his return from Vienna, that while he was gone Maria made play clothes for the children out of the curtains that used to hang in her bedroom, and she led them singing and dancing, in broad daylight for all the world to see, through the streets of Salzburg.

But though they didn't share the same appetite for cultural exotica, my mom and Mrs. Hasbrouck did have one big thing in common: they were smoking buddies. One of the things they loved to joke about was how there seemed to be fewer and fewer "real smokers" left in the world. They never asked people, "Do you mind if I smoke?" if they went out to dinner or visited somebody's house, for fear that the person might say "Yes, I do mind, thank you for asking." They would double over with laughter when telling stories about some smug nonsmoker who spoiled their fun for an evening by asking them not to smoke. Now and then they would talk about how they know they ought to cut down or quit, and they would commiserate about how joyless life became when they tried. One of the funniest things my mom thought Mrs. Hasbrouck ever said to her was when they were comparing notes about trying out the various newfangled low-tar cigarettes, and Mrs. Hasbrouck said, "they taste like they just went out!" My mom loved Mrs. Hasbrouck for that: "Ann, I know I can always count on you! When we're both in our nineties and still puffing away and everyone else is dead and gone, I'm coming over to your house!" Mom would shout with laughter, and they would hug and kiss each other so long: "I'll see you next week, sweetie."

"OK, Peggy." Then to me, "Now Patrick, you watch out for her. Don't let her get into trouble!"

Little by little, Mrs. Hasbrouck gave away a good deal of her piano music to me over the years, including her precious, deteriorating copy of Bach's "Jesu, joy of man's desiring" for two pianos (which both Suzanne and Mary Jo, as well as I, had the honor of performing at piano recitals with Mrs. Hasbrouck); the two-piano Mozart Piano Concerto no. 21, which, incredibly, Mrs. Hasbrouck thought I might just feel like picking up one day and having some fun with; and a book of Chopin études, "sure to keep you up nights for the rest of your life," Mrs. Hasbrouck assured me. She began to develop arthritis in her hands not long after I started taking lessons from her in 1968; by the late seventies she could no longer stretch a full octave, and her hands would be in pain after playing for even just a few minutes. So the music she passed on to me was material that she herself could no longer handle physically, much as she adored it. She was entrusting it to me for safekeeping.

Then, she claimed, as the seventies wore on and she started teaching the children of some of her former pupils and even her own rambunctious grandchildren, young people were becoming increasingly unfit to learn the piano. They were too impatient, too overstimulated by other things like TV and minor league this and that. To be frank, children weren't nice anymore; they were rude, demanding, didn't say "thank you" or "please" for anything. Mrs. Hasbrouck thought the younger parents of today were to blame—they only wanted their children to learn to play the piano because it would impress the neighbors or because it would help them get into posh boarding schools. Parents enjoyed buying big, expensive pianos as furniture, but they couldn't tell a good piano from a bad one. In short, they sent their children to piano lessons for all the wrong reasons.

"Not like your parents. They are such lovely people," she would say. "And they're so proud of you. They must love to hear you play." This was a touchy subject. I didn't believe it. I wasn't convinced my parents thought I played well—or rather, their praise often meant little to me because it didn't seem to have any solid basis in anything other than the fact that I was their son and they loved me. (What did they know about music or about playing the piano? My mother played when she was a girl, but her teacher used to bang her fingers against the keyboard, so she gave it up as soon as she could. Whenever she would describe her piano lessons to me, the feeling of pain she experienced would come back on her face, as if just thinking about it had the power to make her fingers ache all over again.) I'd make my way through the pieces I was practicing, then I'd go out into the kitchen to see my mother. I'd go to her, hoping for praise or applause, knowing that I didn't deserve it, and invariably she would say something like, "that was beautiful, Patrick. You play so wonderfully! What was that piece?"

Immediately I would feel frustrated. "Well, which one do you mean? I was playing several different ones."

"Oh, they're all beautiful. What was that last one you played?"

At this point, I wondered, did she even hear *anything* I was playing?

At the annual recital one year, I played Chopin's Nocturne op. 9, no. 2—the first piece of "difficult" piano music I ever learned. Afterward, Mrs. Hasbrouck was talking to me and my parents. She was saying how one of her other students, an older boy named Stuart, whom we all thought was destined to become a professional musician, had criticized my rendition of the Chopin nocturne. "Stuart came up to me afterward and said, 'Patrick played that nocturne too slowly. It's supposed to be a nighttime piece, but there has to be more momentum.' Well, I told him,

'Stuart, that may be how *you* would play it, and that may even be how the piece was written, but you have no right to tell Patrick how to play it. He has his own interpretation, which is different from yours.' "

"Oh, I'm sure Stuart didn't mean to be critical," my mom said immediately, unaccountably rushing to defend a boy she didn't know instead of her son, and making me think that there was a difference between what my parents told me in private and what they said about me in public (the weird thing was that whereas I could imagine most other parents bragging about their kids in public and then ignoring them or putting them down in private, here it seemed to be just the reverse).

But this was a powerful statement coming from Mrs. Hasbrouck. I didn't realize that what I was doing was "interpreting" the piece. I was playing it the way I thought it was supposed to be played, or at least the way I liked hearing it given the limits of what I could do at the piano. First, I was shocked to hear that Mrs. Hasbrouck agreed with Stuart that I hadn't played it correctly; but then I was *thrilled* to learn that she thought so much of me and my "incorrect interpretation" that, as far as she was concerned, I could play Chopin as I pleased. (Years later in graduate school, I felt similarly when the administrator of the English department told me that one of my professors "really admires your work—she doesn't agree with you, but she loves what you're doing." *Doesn't agree with me?*, I thought, how come I don't know anything about this?! On the other hand, what a thrill to hear it confirmed from someone else that she likes my work!)

But then the shadow of a doubt: What was the standard against which Mrs. Hasbrouck judged my work, if it wasn't what, of all people, *Chopin* intended? What did Mrs. Hasbrouck's approval of my work say about Mrs. Hasbrouck herself? Did she know what she was talking about? To some extent I always disbelieved Mrs. Hasbrouck's praise of me. I'd heard with my own ears other of her students playing (*especially* Stuart), and I figured there were things they could play that I would never be able to play. I felt her love for me blinded her to my inadequacies.

It was around this time, I think, that Mrs. Hasbrouck started crying when I played the piano at recitals. One year I played several Broadway show tunes, including "A Lovely Night" and "Ten Minutes Ago" from Rodgers and Hammerstein's *Cinderella,* and as a finale, Richard Rodgers's "The Sweetest Sounds" from *No Strings.* Mrs. Hasbrouck told me after the recital that by the time I finished playing, she had tears in her eyes. (And I hadn't forgotten, when she told me this, that she really wasn't fond of show tunes to begin with.)

So, though I loved getting Mrs. Hasbrouck's praise, somehow it seemed off the mark, and the delight that my parents were, according to Mrs. Hasbrouck, supposedly taking in my music seemed slightly less than self-evident. I would never lie outright to Mrs. Hasbrouck by agreeing with her that, yes, I too thought my parents loved the way I played. But I could never bring myself to really talk with her about it either. Instead, I would say something ambiguous like, "oh, yeah, I'm sure they do," and then change the subject pretty quickly. I didn't know how to broach this subject with Mrs. Hasbrouck—just as, years later, I never quite knew how to come out to her (she must have known anyway). I think I've always wanted to keep my relationship with Mrs. Hasbrouck as a refuge from the intractible realities of the rest of the world; I wanted the time and space we shared to stay pure, abstract, and musical. But was our relationship ever so ideal?

The first half of *The Sound of Music* ends as Maria leaves the von Trapp family villa while the party in honor of Baroness Schraeder merrily goes on in the ballroom. Maria realizes she is in love with the captain, and she feels his desire for her in return; so to avoid the possibility of their mutual attraction developing any further, she decides to leave. To the sound of a rousing rendition of "Edelweis" played by the ballroom orchestra (making her departure all the more heartbreaking—the happy, up-tempo music knows nothing of the painful action it underscores), Maria rushes down the grand staircase, leaves a white envelope on a side table beneath a large, gilt mirror, makes her way to the front door, and, before turning to exit, takes one last, regretful look at the grand entrance foyer—the place where she first met the children, where she first laid eyes on the captain, and where the captain thanked her for bringing music back into the house—music he'd forgotten. When, during the second half of the film, she returns, hoping, as the Reverend Mother has encouraged her, to face her problems, to "find out how God wants you to spend your love," and "to live the life you were born to live," the Captain greets her with a flirtatious air of wounded relief that she has come back:

CAPTAIN: You left without saying good-bye. Even to the children.
MARIA: Well it was wrong of me. Forgive me.
CAPTAIN: Why did you?
MARIA: Please don't ask me.

When Mrs. Hasbrouck died in the winter of 1994, I didn't go to her funeral. Although I continued to visit her regularly for years after I moved away from home, by the early nineties I'd virtually stopped playing the piano and my visits with Mrs. Hasbrouck had come down to one a year at most. Our lives had changed: Mrs. Hasbrouck's husband died in 1990, she retired from teaching in 1992, and, increasingly incapacitated by Parkinson's disease, she entered a nursing home near Philadelphia not long after that. I came out as a gay man in the mid-eighties, entered graduate school, struggled to redefine my relationship to nearly everyone I had ever known up until that time, and became more and more alienated from my immediate family. Around the time of her retirement, Mrs. Hasbrouck wrote me this letter not long after we'd spoken briefly on the telephone:

Dear Patrick,
    It was so wonderful to hear from you. I miss seeing you very much but I realize that you must have very little time for writing letters or visiting. I had a very pleasant talk with your mother several weeks ago. She had called me because Suzie wanted to buy a piano and needed some advice. It gave me a chance to hear about what is happening in your life.
    Poor Patrick! You must be having a terrible time reading my handwriting. It's getting worse all the time. In the first place the Parkinson's disease is getting worse with age and then my eyesight is nearly gone which was the reason made [sic] music almost impossible.
[. . .]
    On the way up [to Vermont the previous week with her son Allan] we stopped at West Point to visit my brother's grave. He died a few weeks ago and I'm finding it difficult to accept. I have only one brother left.
[. . .]
    Patrick dear, I apologize for this writing but I do miss you and want to send you my
Love,
Ann H.

When Maria comes back, the children are the first to see her. They're trying to cheer themselves up by singing one of the songs Maria taught them, "My Favorite Things," but their song is forlorn and funereal until Brigitta (the one, as Maria had reminded the captain, who "notices everything") hears Maria's voice, faint, in the distance, picking up the tune: "snowflakes that stay on my nose and eyelashes." They see her coming through the trees across the lawn, her carpetbag and guitar in hand. Maria! Maria! they cry. They race toward her with open arms, and she receives them all in her embrace. Gretl holds up a bandaged index finger for Maria's inspection:

MARIA: Gretl, what happened to your finger?
GRETL: It got caught.

MARIA: Caught in what?
GRETL: Freidrich's teeth.

Poor Gretl! Poor von Trapp children! The love Maria felt for them was pure and uncomplicated, and once she had taught them to sing, she had forever unblocked their ability to love her in return. And when Maria left them, they felt nothing but the purest sadness.

But when I read "Poor Patrick!" in Mrs. Hasbrouck's letter to me, I thought, she must be kidding! *I'm* not the one who's suffering, *she* is. When I read how Mrs. Hasbrouck missed *me* and was struggling to get *my* attention ("I miss seeing you very much. . . . I do miss you"), I thought, How could she love me so much? She hardly even knows me anymore. What have I done to deserve her love?

A few weeks before Mrs. Hasbrouck's death, my Grandmother Horrigan died. She and I had enjoyed a special friendship during her last years, and, like Mrs. Hasbrouck, my grandmother seemed to understand something about me that no one else in my family understood, or if they did, they couldn't acknowledge it in the same way that she could. In the eulogy I delivered at my grandmother's funeral, I tried to talk about the kind of relationship we had:

> Last year Nana seemed to be going through a phase where it felt necessary to her to start giving things away to people—certain special objects she set aside for specific people.
>
> Her gift to me was a piece of crystal in the shape of a small tree bending gracefully but irrevocably sideways, as if in a strong wind, or in a hurricane, its glass branches curling, fluttering like ribbons made out of silk. Instantly I remembered a conversation I had with Nana when I was around ten. We were by ourselves, and she said to me, "you know, Pat, you're a loner. I think you like to be alone."
>
> Now I don't remember the context in which she said this, but she was right—I did spend a lot of my time alone, and I felt guilty about it. I wanted instead what I thought everyone else in my family had, which seemed to be lots of friends and lots of activity and no sadness or hurt feelings and no burdensome interior life of any consequence—so I thought.
>
> "No, I'm not a loner," I said defensively, feeling criticized and not wanting to share with her what I dimly felt was something important about myself, even though, just possibly, she might understand and accept it no matter what anyone else thought.

Then when Mrs. Hasbrouck died a few weeks later, I didn't want to share my feelings about her death with anyone else, though I couldn't say why. I wanted to keep her death, and the memories of my life with her, to myself. The weekend of Mrs. Hasbrouck's funeral I was scheduled to give a talk in Kentucky at a conference on twentieth-century literature. I canceled my talk, but not so that I could attend Mrs. Hasbrouck's funeral. Instead, I stayed at home in New York, alone.

Recently, I wanted to play the piano for my boyfriend, Rob, even though I hadn't played in at least seven years. He came over to my apartment one day and brought along his friend Vivian, a piano teacher, who was visiting from Los Angeles. After I struggled but made it through the Brahms Intermezzo op. 118, no. 2—a piece I used to know by heart and was particularly fond of playing for Mrs. Hasbrouck (partly, I think, because for years I thought it was simply the most beautiful melody I'd ever heard, and it was a piece I could play well)—Vivian talked about how painful it is, even for her, to play the piano; how it can sometimes seem like a contest between you and the instrument; how important it is not to give up in the middle of a piece but to keep going and get to the end; how hard it is not to let mistakes, imperfections, even lack of talent deter you from staying with the music. A few days later, Rob told me how, soon after Vivian had returned to L.A., she played, imperfectly, one of Bach's Two-Part Inventions for him over the phone and then spent the rest of the day in wrenching pain because she hadn't managed to play for him as well as she had wanted. "It's Okay," he told her, "I loved what you played. I couldn't hear the mistakes. Now I want to get a recording of Bach's piano music because what you played really inspired me to want to learn more." But she was hard to console. Rob did buy a CD of Bach's piano music, and lately he's been listening to it as he paints—it's completely changed his mental state while he makes art, he says, and he's grateful to me and to Vivian, despite all our complaints about our musical faults, for opening up this new world to him.

Near the end of *The Sound of Music,* Maria, the captain, and the children take refuge from the Nazis in the abbey where Maria had been a postulant. The Reverend Mother ushers the family into the churchyard and behind a row of tombstones where they won't be seen. Before leaving them there, she says good-bye to Maria, whom she realizes she may never see again:

> REVEREND MOTHER: You will not be alone. Remember, "I will lift mine eyes into the hills from whence cometh my help."
> MARIA: Yes, Mother.
> [*They give each other one long, last embrace.*]

In the final scene of the film, the von Trapp family cross a wind-swept mountain to a new and uncertain life.

The Sound of Music means more to me now than it did when I was a child: now it whispers through hollowed hands of the urge for leaving and the difficulty of saying good-bye. But it also looks forward, one day, every day, to the possibility of return.

OUTTAKES I

Cinderella (1964)

I've never seen the original 1957 television production of this Rodgers and Hammerstein musical that starred—it must have been sublime!—Julie Andrews in the title role, but there are two things I remember most about the 1964 TV remake, starring Leslie Ann Warren. First, I strongly identified as a child with Cinderella's theme song, "In My Own Little Corner," in which she describes her elaborate fantasy life (she imagines herself a Norwegian princess, an opera singer, an eccentric heiress, "a girl men go mad for," an East Indian slave, a Peruvian queen, a mermaid, and an African huntress) despite—or is it *because of?*—her confinement in a corner of her stepmother's house. And second, I was impressed by the ballroom at the palace of the prince, which seemed unnaturally polished and so huge that it engulfed the dancing ladies and gentlemen (the camera's fish-eye lens and the deliberately minimal set design contribute to this artificial, dreamlike effect). But that wasn't all: midway through their dance together (they have the entire floor to themselves because everyone has stood aside for them, so perfect and striking a couple do they make), the prince and Cinderella spin out through a large, open doorway and into another vast, polished, empty space—the patio adjacent to the ballroom. I didn't even know that the patio existed—that more space existed than the space I had already seen and become familiar with—until Cinderella and the prince found themselves engulfed by it! I remember feeling that we were now in the middle of a limitless expanse of space, as if we had fallen through the television screen itself and found ourselves drifting weightless through colorless, shapeless, endless, timeless space.

The Flying Nun (1967–1970)

"There was always one thing you could expect from Sister Bertrille—whatever you didn't expect."[1] The Convent San Tanco's Mother Superior speaks these words in a voiceover at the beginning of one episode in which Sister Bertrille, played by Sally Field, crashes the convent station wagon at an intersection in downtown San Juan into another car being driven, it turns out, by the members of one of her favorite rock groups, Paper Balloon. At first she's distraught over what just happened until she realizes that she crashed into Paper Balloon, whereupon she screams with delight, "I have all your records!"

Like Maria in *The Sound of Music*, Sister Bertrille was a fun-loving, troublemaking young woman who in so many ways was not meant for

48

religious life, and yet she remained in the Church, wreaking havoc, working her own kind of magic, and, of course, *flying* (although clearly it was her perky personality and her sense of humor as much as—perhaps more than—her never-explained ability to fly that made her special and a true child of God).

I remember more than anything else about this series the closing credit sequence, where we see Sister Bertrille trying to hit a baseball in an alley with some local Spanish kids; walking past what looks like a war monument with a canon on top and peeking into the canon's mouth as she passes by; and walking between buildings, away from the camera, up a pedestrian street, and, once or twice, looking back over her shoulder at the camera, as if to say, good-bye, see you again soon, are you still there watching me? I got the feeling from these images that Sister Bertrille, like me, spent a lot of her time alone, that although she was part of a larger family (the Convent San Tanco and the city of San Juan, Puerto Rico, in which the convent played such an important part), she was also, ultimately, a loner. It seemed that when she turned back to look at the camera one last time before the closing credit sequence ended, she was acknowledging her loneliness—as if she liked knowing that we in the audience were there all the time, watching her, following her, by her side, even as she went about her daily, melancholy routine. And it made sense that, in these closing images, she didn't fly but, rather, walked liked the rest of us. The point seemed to be that her ability to fly is just a metaphor for something inside of her, something psychological or emotional, a metaphor for her imagination. And normally, when a person is somewhere else inside her head, to the rest of the world it looks like she's just walking down the street, or playing baseball, or doing chores or homework, or saying prayers. But really, she's flying over the Alps or sailing across New York Harbor on a tug boat or shedding her habit, her normal, everyday suit of clothing, for a different outfit—leaving the convent, leaving the safety of home, of her "own little corner," as Cinderella called it, walking out into the clear and brilliant sunshine, on her way to a new job, a new family, a new home, an unknown future that could be so exciting if only it weren't so frightening.

The Flying Nun is memorable to me now for one other reason—Carlos Ramirez (played by Alejandro Rey), one of the other main characters on the show, the handsome owner of Carlos's Casino and, though it was never made explicit, Sister Bertrille's boyfriend (he, like everyone else, found her exasperating: "If Mr. Trouble comes knocking on my door, it's usually Sister Bertrille who gave him the address," he fumes in the Paper Balloon episode). I don't know whether or not I thought Carlos was good looking when I was a kid (I do now), but I did think his apartment was strange. His front door, made of thick, scrolling iron trellis work, seemed more like a castle gate than a normal front door (was that how all bachelors' front doors looked in the Caribbean?). And there seemed to be nothing but closets along one of the walls in his living room, with floor-to-ceiling, shutter-style doors, which I don't remember Carlos ever opening; I wondered what, if anything, was behind them. His living room seemed to double as a bedroom, which only intensified the association between bachelorhood and sex as well as the idea that Carlos's friendship with Sister Bertrille, at least on his part, was more than just straight friendship.

The Partridge Family (1970–1974)

"In August of 1969, Bernard Slade, creator of *The Flying Nun, Love on a Rooftop,* and *Mr. Deeds Goes to Town,* was under contract to Screen Gems, the television subsidiary of Columbia Pictures, to develop three pilots a year. Inspired by *The Sound of Music,* he decided that 'it would be interesting to do a show about a family that sings together.' His idea for a new situation comedy, originally titled *Family Business,* centered around the trials and tribulations of a widow with five children who is forced to become a permanent member of her children's rock band when their girl singer gets the mumps" (Green 5).

The first episode of *The Partridge Family* begins with the following words, a voice-over spoken by Shirley Partridge (Shirley Jones), as the family take their bows at the end of their first concert: "If I look a little stunned it's because until recently the only bow I'd ever taken was for an occasional well-cooked roast. You see, we're not your average show-biz family. So how come we're on national television?"[2]

I used to pretend that my brother and sisters and I were a famous singing group known as "The Horrigan Family," or sometimes just "The Horrigans." We were accidentally discovered one day fiddling around with instruments in a music store, and the next thing we knew we were an overnight hit, not unlike the Partridges (over the show's opening credits, David Cassidy as Keith Partridge sings about his family's quick rise to stardom, and how "it really came together when Mom sang along!").

Little by little, our image as a singing group hardened (that may be when we changed our name from "The Horrigan Family," which sounded a little too nice and safe, too obedient, to "The Horrigans," which sounded somehow a little more threatening, as if maybe the Horrigans were a mob or a gang). On one album cover, which I thought was a sign of our new, meaner attitude, we were photographed standing in no apparent order (another sign that we had gone bad—in a family photo we had had taken secretly in the fall of 1972 as a Christmas present for my parents, the photographer arranged us, by contrast, in an almost perfect triangular shape [fig. 15, in chapter 3]); everyone was standing around, sort of aloof, as if not talking to one another, as if we'd all just had some kind of big fight, on the bleachers by the side of an outdoor athletic field (the sports setting, too, seemed "bad" to me because I was always so miserable whenever I had to go to a football game or to see my sisters play field hockey or my brother play basketball. I was always bored and couldn't wait to get home again, but we of course had to be the last ones to leave the field or the gymnasium because we had to wait for the athletes to come out of the locker room or to collect their dirty, sweaty, ugly things; and then we had to hear all about the game from the athlete's point of view the whole way home in the car, as if having watched the entire game from the bleachers or from the side lines wasn't torture enough). Mary Jo, Suzanne, and Betsy were standing more in the foreground than the rest of us because they were the lead singers (I assumed they would be the lead singers because they were the oldest. In *The Sound of Music,* Gretl asks her uncle Max "why am I always last?" when Max reads the children's names in the order in which they appear—from oldest to youngest—on a concert program; he answers, "because *you* are the most important." "Oh!" Gretl cries.). One or more of the girls was wearing a bandanna or a turban with a long piece of cloth hanging down the side like the hippies wore, which was another way of showing how bad we had become. And one of the imaginary songs on the album was called "Hooker," which was not about a prostitute but about a guy named Hooker whom all the girls were supposed to be in love with, putting themselves in danger because he was such a creep, but instead he was sexy and irresistible, sort of like the "Dud" on the board game Mystery Date—cute, perhaps, but a slob, dressed in khakis and a tee shirt instead of a suit and tie.

Contrary to my family's rock band image, the Partridges' image never hardened as their career progressed. They continued to celebrate the possibilities of being happy and coming out into the bright sunshiny day and coming down off your shelf, stop being such a wallflower, take a good look at yourself and see how beautiful you are: "The leaves of life are fallin' down around you girl." This was the Partridge Family's breakthrough song ("Let the Good Times In," written by Carole Bayer Sager and Neil Sedaka), the song that, in the premiere episode, wins them an agent and an instant booking at Caesar's Palace in Las Vegas. It was the sound of someone starting to smile and even laugh through their tears because everything really *was* going to be all right after all.

I don't remember thinking that David Cassidy as Keith Partridge was especially cute (and in fact I was annoyed by how increasingly shape-less and lumpy his hair got from season to season), but now, looking at photographs of David Cassidy from the early seventies and at epi-sodes of *The Partridge Family*, I see how fabulously attractive he was—how randy, lithe and sweet in a dirty kind of way. Yet it was *Laurie* Partridge, played by Susan Dey, who was always my favorite character. She was tall, thin, cool and sharp-witted, but also "feminine," with her pretty, bouncy long brown hair and her pouty mouth, as if, like me, she had buck teeth (she reminded me of Karen Carpenter). Laurie was the most introspec-tive, the most psychologically complex of all the Partridge children; in one episode, after careful research and reflection, she endorses the plat-form of a high school feminist group called Power of Women (POW), even though she doesn't like the fact that Keith committed the family to performing at a POW rally without first bringing it to a family vote (which is how Laurie prefers that decisions get made in the family) be-cause he was dating one of POW's leading members, another pretty, long-brown-haired, pouty-mouthed girl named Tina. And there always seemed to be some kind of flirtation going on between Laurie and Keith (not unlike what seemed to be going on between Karen and Richard Carpenter). I wanted to be Laurie Partridge, first, because I liked her. But being Laurie also meant, somehow, having Keith. I didn't want to *be* Keith—he was older and bigger and badder than me and the possi-bility of being him didn't appeal to me or even, I think, occur to me. *Having* him probably didn't occur to me either, except through my iden-tification with Laurie. And I don't think having Laurie was on my mind either, although my siblings would often tease me, saying that Laurie was my "girlfriend," implying that something more than just friendship and the meeting of minds was going on between us.

I joined the Partridge Family Fan Club (I got the address off the back of their 1972 *Up to Date* album), and I thought it was strange that, in an article they sent me, Susan Dey said one of her favorite hobbies was read-ing. I'd never really read a book on my own just for pleasure, and I'm not sure I knew anyone who did either (though I do recall, a few years later, my mother staying up late one night and reading from start to finish a new novel called *Jaws*, which at first I didn't know was about a shark, I thought "jaws" referred to someone's mouth, maybe a killer's mouth, maybe an ugly mouth with lots of silver fillings in it or maybe chipped, rotten teeth). Another hobby, Laurie/Susan said, was meeting people, which I thought was even more strange than reading, partly because meeting people didn't seem like something anyone would ever do for a hobby. I didn't like meeting people. In general, new people scared me—especially people my age—especially *boys* my age. I was always afraid they wouldn't like me, and often I didn't like them, sometimes at first sight. Plus, meeting people was, in my experience, something that was inflicted upon you, not something that you freely chose to do. So I wondered if maybe Laurie wasn't as cool as I always thought she was, and I worried that maybe we didn't have all that much in common after all. But I was also kind of impressed by the fact that she liked to read and to meet people, because it made her seem serious and brave and more of a nonconformist and, therefore, someone I might like being friends with after all, even if I didn't like to do all the things she did. It's not like she said her hobbies were bowling or hiking or raising farm animals or something like that, which would have seemed so far removed from my everyday experience as to be plainly ridiculous.

2

Love Barbra

I was outdoors, walking behind the bleachers of a sports stadium, and the top- and back-most row was level to the ground I stood on. The bleachers were filled, and as I walked along I met Barbra Streisand. She was sitting in the back row—she seemed to be directing a film there—and we came face to face. I spoke to her: "You have been very important to me," I said. She answered by talking rapidly about something, I don't remember what. Then she put her head down and fell asleep. A young woman came along and kissed her on the forehead. Barbra awoke, and they began to speak, excluding me from their conversation . . .

Then I awoke.

I

It wasn't until I turned nineteen and had gone five thousand miles away from home, to spend my junior year of college at the University of London, that someone directly asked me the question that I had never dared ask myself before, so self-evident, or so elusive, seemed the answer:

"What is it exactly about Barbra Streisand that you love so much?" my friend Jenny asked me, as if the question were something we could profitably discuss in the way that we might, say, discuss Virginia Woolf, or Anton Chekhov's *The Cherry Orchard* (fig. 6).

Because she had theories about everything, I imagine that Jenny had one about why I loved Barbra Streisand—perhaps that "many men like Barbra Streisand because they are attracted to strong women." She may even have said that men liked her (Jenny) for the same reasons, even though she also spent a lot of time feeling underappreciated and overlooked by men and by people in general (by all accounts, like Barbra herself).

I could see why. Jenny wasn't easy to like. She talked incessantly, to

54

Figure 6. Leicester Square, London, spring 1984.

the point where if you wanted to respond to the things she said, you had to interrupt her. She had strong opinions on the most trivial of subjects (like whether it was better to visit Hampton Court on a cloudy or a sunny day), and she made sweeping generalizations about people and things, implying a knowledge of the world and a power of insight into human nature that, if they were founded on experience, would have been amazing in someone so relatively young. So I vacillated between thinking she was brilliant and thinking she was just crazy.

She seemed to have an almost tragic confidence in herself. She wore lots of makeup, she died her hair orange, and she overdressed for class, as if in costume, making her creativity and intelligence seem parodic instead of the real thing. Most of our classmates found her unbearable, as I did some of the time. (Likewise, the audience "didn't know whether to laugh or groan" at the sight of Barbara Streisand when she appeared in a talent contest at the Lion, a New York City West Village gay bar, in May of 1960: "On top of her head she had bobby-pinned a Dynel hairpiece that looked, in the words of a friend, 'like a cheese Danish.' From under it her real hair fell stringily to her shoulders. She wore a short purple sheath and a jacket festooned with purple ostrich feathers, which the thrift shop clerk told her had once belonged to a countess. With feathers wisping around her shoulders and the audience ready to pounce, Barbara stood stock still under the spotlight, closed her eyes, and dramatically drew back her head as Patty [the bar's pianist] tinkled out her introduction. Someone in the audience muttered 'Oh, boy'" [Spada, *Streisand* 66]. And a few nights later, the gay comedian Michael Greer recalled, "she looked like she had dressed herself from a garage sale. As I remember she wore a tiny high-heeled shoe in her hair because she liked the rhinestones in it" [qtd. in Spada, *Streisand* 67].)

But Jenny entertained me and made me feel special, like I was a particularly important friend. One day she invited me over to her room for tea for no other reason than that she just wanted to spend time with me. She played a Mozart piano concerto on her stereo, a cheap rickety thing that she'd had ever since she was five, she told me—she had inherited it from some relative or friend and she was always threatening to replace it but it kept on working, and so why get rid of it, she didn't need the latest in stereo equipment in order to appreciate music; after all, she said, if the music's really good, does it matter what kind of stereo equipment it's playing on? I'd never thought of it that way—but before I could respond, she launched into a tirade about her classics professor, how she disliked him even though he was a genius, and I should read Juvenal and Heinrich von Kleist because, Jenny thought, I would like them, and she was writing a term paper about Juvenal. And then there was the whole complicated story of her friendship with Sally Ann, and how they fought all the time even though everyone thought they were best friends, and how hurt she was by Sally Ann, how angry Sally Ann made her, and how I should be careful of Sally Ann because she would pretend to be my friend but it would really only be because she was trying to use me to get back at Jenny. (Likewise, the columnist Liz Smith recalls how Barbra Streisand's insecurities were revealed by *her* rambling, self-referential discourse: "At night we would sometimes go to her house for dinner. And later she would show us still pictures of herself from *Funny Girl*, which wasn't released yet. She would ask me what I thought of each one. I knew she needed a more astute opinion than mine, and she would get exasperated when I'd say, 'That one is okay, that's nice,' and on and on. It was too bizarre. It was all *her*. The idea that you are so fascinating that people would be happy to stay up until three in the morning looking at pictures of yourself, seemed so *strange* to me; sort of like Norma Desmond' " [qtd. in Considine 139]. However, *Hello, Dolly!* producer and screenwriter Ernest Lehman [who also wrote the screenplay for *The Sound of Music*] thought differently of Barbra's behavior during this period: " 'Barbra wasn't full of herself; she didn't have an ego. I think just the opposite. If she were full of herself she wouldn't have been so concerned about everything being just right. She's never been a person who feels her own perfection. She was a very insecure person, doubting her own worth, especially interpersonally.' . . . Doubtless this affection led Lehman to welcome—and to miss, on the rare occasions when they didn't come—the dozens of late-night telephone calls from Barbra during the filming. . . . 'When she *didn't* call I'd think, Call and harass me, *please!*' " [Spada, *Streisand* 218–19])

The last I remember, Jenny was applying for jobs in banking (she majored in German literature), and I wondered why she wanted to work in business when she obviously had so many other, more artistic talents. Maybe she didn't have a family like I did and, so, needed to start supporting herself. Gradually I stopped spending time with her, partly, I think, because she reminded me of some former version of myself that I was trying to escape. Like Jenny, I had a knack for drawing a lot of negative attention to myself at home and at school when I was a kid. Everybody noticed me—because I had red hair; because I had a bald spot; because I had buck teeth; because my voice sounded sissy; because I was the only one in the class who got an A; because I was the only one in the class who couldn't hit the baseball; because I was the only boy in the class who had female friends. I wanted to be noticed, but I also wanted to be *liked*.

I don't remember anything of my conversation with Jenny about Barbra Streisand. All I know is that she asked the question.

II

Although I cannot precisely recall the first time I saw, heard, or started loving Barbra Streisand, I remember seeing the comedienne Marilyn Michaels impersonate her on *The Kopycats,* a comedy show that aired on TV briefly in 1972. Now I forget how the sketch ran, but it must have involved someone making a list of all the things that come a dime a dozen—generic things; things that come in great quantities; everyday, ordinary things (something like, "there's more than 1 city named Athens, 3 persons in the Holy Trinity, 57 varieties of Heinz ketchup, 88 keys on the piano, 101 reasons why the chicken crossed the road"; I might have added, "5 bossy older siblings, and 60 boring first cousins")—because it ended, by contrast, with Marilyn Michaels done up as Barbra

Streisand, sitting at a dressing room mirror, wearing a big floppy hat
with feathers, turning to the camera and saying, ". . . but there's only *one*
Barbra Streisand!"

This wouldn't have been the first time I'd heard her name or seen
her face. My parents owned a couple of her early records from the mid-
sixties, including *The Second Barbra Streisand Album* (the cover photo of
Barbra made me uncomfortable because she had bare shoulders, suggesting that she'd been photographed topless, and she gave you a knowing look that said, "I know what *you're* thinking . . .") and *My Name is
Barbra, Two.* And I have a dim memory (which may actually be a composite of two separate incidents) of being in an arcade with my siblings
in Ocean City, New Jersey some time during the early seventies, and
while they played ping pong or pinball, I turned over the Broadway cast
album of *Funny Girl* (the photograph of Barbra on the back, singing,
made her look incredibly odd with her large, misshapen mouth and her
Chinese eyes) and strained to hear the music coming faintly out of the
speakers. (But what arcade had a stereo for anyone to use, and record
albums that anyone could pick up and handle?)

I remember being drawn to Barbra Streisand's voice and acting talents
when *Funny Girl* (1968) was shown on TV in the early seventies. Actually,
I was drifting in and out of the room during the movie, but several other
people in my family were watching it intently (it might have been my
mother and a couple of my older sisters, probably Mary Jo and Suzanne,
and maybe some other adult who was not a member of my immediate
family—my mom's sister Rita?—perhaps, because Aunt Rita has always
been a big Barbra Streisand fan). Partly I was compelled by the fact that
here was a group of women doing something together and I wanted to
be a part of the group (if it had been a group of men watching TV—you
can imagine that scene—my reaction would have been just the opposite:
get me out of here!), but then at a certain point something in the movie
itself captured my attention and I forgot about the people watching it
with me and I became transfixed by what was going on in the movie. I
remember someone saying that this was a movie about the life of Fanny
Brice, and from the look of it (dirty old city buildings, funny old clothes)
and because I didn't know who Fanny Brice was ("she sang in the Ziegfeld Follies," someone said, "she was a commedienne"), I wasn't all that
interested at first. But then there was this young woman (Fanny/Barbra)
and she was wearing a brown dress with what looked like little brown
Christmas tree balls all around the chest and shoulders, and she had her
brown hair wrapped up in a pretty, shiny bouffant with a braid running
around the middle (which made me want to touch it), and she had allur-
ing Egyptian eyes, and everyone who was watching the movie kept de-

bating whether or not she was pretty and they said one moment she was and the next she wasn't (someone called her "homely," a word I'd never heard before, but I immediately understood that it meant not pretty) but they all agreed that she had incredible talent. And she was talking to a dark-eyed man dressed in a tuxedo (Nick Arnstein/Omar Sharif) on a city sidewalk in front of a short flight of stairs—it must have been a poor part of town because I had seen front stoops like that when we would drive through downtown Reading. And it was nighttime and they had just come from a party, and it was clear that this was one of the most exciting moments of her entire life because here she was, walking and talking with this dark, handsome man. But it was also sad because for some reason he was going away and she might never see him again, and so no sooner had her dream come true than it was being snatched away. And then she began to sing a song—a beautiful, sad song about how people need each other and how lucky you are if you need someone, and it was so sad because she needed him and he was leaving and she was singing about how lucky she was and I wondered, how could you be lucky when your heart is breaking? Wouldn't it be better to love someone and to have them love you in return? Didn't needing someone mean that you didn't have the thing you wanted? And so how could you be lucky not to have what you wanted? But as the song continued and the camera circled around her as she stood alone on the stairs, leaning against the railing, her head thrown back, her eyes closed, accentuating her exotic, heavy eye makeup, her hands twitching in front of her, lost in the tender song she was singing, I felt as taken by her as he did when he finally said: "Fanny, you're an enchanting girl. I wish I could get to know you better."

"So give me six good reasons why not," she says.

"Just one," he says—he has to catch a train for Kentucky in the morning, and then maybe on to Europe or the coast after that—"I never have definite plans. They make me feel too tied down," he tells her as her heart is breaking.[1] She's heard it all before—men letting her down for one reason or another. He kisses her good-bye and leaves.

Now in a high-angle long shot from across the street, we see her drift along the empty sidewalk like a lonely kid with too much time on her hands. Her arms outstretched as if she were balancing a tight rope, she tiptoes along the edge of the sidewalk, begins to hum the melody of the song she had been singing a few moments ago ("People"), and restlessly drops her arms down at her sides. Next, she wanders over toward the front stoop, listlessly running her hands over the railing, singing in the shadows, her head turned away from the camera (which, all the while, has been slowly approaching her, descending from above). She walks toward a lamppost, singing, still half in shadow. Coming into the light, she grips the lamppost and sings, her song rising to its dramatic peak, the camera pulling in for a closeup, "*But first, be a person who needs people!*" and she tilts her head forward on the word "needs," then throws it back with abandon on the word "people." One moment she sings with full-chested gusto, then suddenly she speaks the words of the song with a quiet laugh, and then again she sings in her purest head tones. Once she has stopped singing, she looks pensive for a few seconds, still enveloped in the emotion of the song, but then catches herself, realizes with a touch of embarassment where she is and what she has been doing (singing her heart out on a deserted city sidewalk), and rushes back to the party around the corner at her mother's saloon.

By this time I knew that no matter how miserable her life was, it was better to be her—better to look like that and talk like that and walk like that and *sing* like that—better to be her than anyone else in the world. For even though a part of her went with him when he left, something remained that no one could take away from her: she had an *inner life.* And it was only after he'd gone that her inner life came fully out into the open. It was *only* after he went away that the movie turned its full attention to her, and in that moment she became sensational! At that moment, it didn't matter what she looked like on the outside, didn't matter whether she was pretty or not, didn't matter what people said about her. All that mattered was, all of this was going on inside of her. In that moment, she made it supremely okay to be cast out. Because of her, being rejected acquired beauty and dignity. She became someone to turn to, someone to emulate.

But for some reason I didn't stay to watch the rest of the movie. I kept wandering in and out of the room until I was, again, drawn to the television set as she ran down a corridor with a big bouquet of yellow roses in her arms and a suitcase in each hand. She was singing about how she was determined to have him after all and no one was going to stand in her way—the music was catchy and pulsating—and then there was a train belching smoke as it wound around the side of a mountain and the camera descended from high above, all the way down to a window of the train, and there she was, inside the train, singing about how "nobody is gonna rain on my parade," and I thought it was funny that there was no real parade and no rain—it was all about her feelings and she was as exciting as a parade, as all-encompassing as a rainstorm. And then suddenly the music stops and a loud, honking horn blows, and you see a light-blue tug boat chugging its way across New York Harbor in front of the Statue of Liberty, and although you can barely see her from this distance, standing at the prow of the tug boat, the sound of her voice fills the harbor and sky. And now the camera flies inexorably toward her, closer and closer, until she belts out the last, breathtaking notes: "*Nobody, no nobody is gonna rain on my parade!*"

What struck me about this scene was, first, its resemblance to the opening sequence in *The Sound of Music,* where the camera zooms in from far away to a close-up of Julie Andrews singing on top of a mountain. Then, it was the way Barbra Streisand sang those final words. Disobeying all the rules of pronunciation, she drew out the first "no" in "nobody" and then took a breath before singing "body"; and she sang all seven syllables of "gonna rain on my parade" on the same note rather than following the notes of the melody as they were meant to be sung — as if, instead of singing a song, she were hammering a nail or firing a machine gun: *pow pow pow pow pow pow pow!* The music was jazzy, unlike the lilting, noble songs of Rodgers and Hammerstein, and Barbra Streisand's singing was unpredictable and unorthodox, unlike the clean, clear, often perky, always proper singing style of Julie Andrews.

The movie that permanently sealed my love for Barbra Streisand, however, was not *Funny Girl,* the film that made her a legend and won her an Academy Award, but *Hello, Dolly!,* one of Barbra's least regarded films, even among her most ardent fans. I had seen it as a child when it was first released in December of 1969, but I don't recall much of that first viewing (except: I couldn't take my eyes off of Barbra Streisand's hair — an elaborate, shiny, thick roll of [fake] red hair, meant to evoke an 1890s topknot, surrounding her head like a halo and bursting, like a surprise, with feathers of green and gold). By the time it premiered on television in the early seventies, however, I was primed for fully self-conscious enjoyment. I already knew every note of the original Broadway cast album of *Hello, Dolly!* starring Carol Channing, and for several years until I saw the film version on TV, it was my favorite album (along with the soundtrack to *The Sound of Music*). I couldn't wait to see and hear the Broadway show brought to life on screen — for so I experienced the movies as more real than "real life."

At first, I was disappointed by Barbra Streisand's portrayal of Dolly Levi because it was so startlingly different from Carol Channing's. In the first number on the Broadway cast album, "I Put My Hand In," Dolly introduces herself in song: "I have always been a woman who arranges things." The music had a rattling, rousing, tin-can, hurdy-gurdy feel to it, and Carol Channing squawked out the notes in her endearing, alternately babyish, baritone voice. But in the movie, Barbra Streisand sang those same words in a smokey, sultry, creamy voice; she quivered on the second syllable of "always" and of "woman" and on the word "things," as if those particular words contained untold richness. Carol

Channing invested the lyrics with the personality of a dottering old lady, bird-brained but warm-hearted, feeding her mangy old cat; Barbra Streisand's rendering of them, however, evoked the image of a seductive, buxom young woman lounging by herself some late afternoon on a cushiony pink-and-yellow-striped sofa in the swank parlor of an elegant French chateau, with thick satin drapes hanging at the floor-to-ceiling windows and expensive flowers bursting from proceline vases on gilt and marble tabletops—all wrong for the character of Dolly Levi, the irrepressible, middle-aged matchmaker of good ol' New York! (Barbra sounded here the way she looked in the film: ". . . her look was designed by Dan Striepeke, head of the Fox makeup department. Striepeke recalls, 'The whole thing that we were trying to create between Ernie Lehman, [director] Gene Kelly, and myself was a John Singer Sargent type of look, the way he painted his ladies of that era. They were very milk white . . .'" [Riese 271]) But then Barbra launches into a song written expressly for the film and for her, "Just Leave Everything to Me," a fast-talking, hard-driving, syncopated list of all the things Dolly can get for you: a husband or wife, girlfriend or boyfriend, or how about a babysitter, couturier, masseur, sex therapist, plastic surgeon, architect, animal breeder, or French teacher? And that's just naming a few. Here was the Barbra I knew from *Funny Girl*—urban, ironic, outspoken, down to earth, a real New Yorker (the shift in tone from her svelte introduction to her staccato song was a jarring one, although it was clear she had a daringly broad range), and quick as a boxer—but still, as different as could be from Carol Channing.

The moment that got me hooked on the film version of *Hello, Dolly!* played another twist on the original Broadway cast recording. Early in the film, Dolly travels from New York City to Yonkers to do some business with Horace Vandergelder, the man she wants to marry. Singing "Put On Your Sunday Clothes," she then escorts Vandergelder's niece, Ermengarde, to the Yonkers train station to catch a train back to New York, where she will chaperon Ermengarde for the day. Dolly, Ermengarde, and Ermengarde's boyfriend Ambrose come out onto the second-story porch of Vandergelder's hay and feed store, descend the stairs leading from the porch to the sidewalk, take another two steps from the sidewalk to the street, and then join a crowd of people dancing along the brick pavement, all heading toward the station. On the Broadway cast album, Dolly and chorus sing, "there's no blue Monday in your Sunday clothes!" But in the movie, Dolly and friends don't just sing that line, they *sell* it: "There's no blue Monday in your Sunday—/No Monday in your Sunday—/*No! Monday! in your Sunday clothes!*" It was exactly at this moment that I let out a laugh. It wasn't the kind of laugh you laugh when someone tells a joke. It was a quieter, more interior laugh, the kind you laugh when all at once you feel complete surprise and exquisite joy. A laugh your heart makes. From then on, whatever differences there were between the Broadway version and the movie version of *Hello, Dolly!*, a big part of the thrill for me of watching the movie was noticing and responding to those differences, always with the certainty that, no matter how unusual, whatever Barbra Streisand did was wonderful—because *difference itself* was wonderful! And it wasn't until *Hello, Dolly!* that I began to grasp just how different Barbra Streisand really was.

The scene that impressed me most of all was the Harmonia Gardens Restaurant scene at the climax of the film, where, after an absence of several years, Dolly is greeted with open arms by her friends, the maître d's, chefs, and waiters. From what I could tell by the photographs on the cast album and in the souvenir booklet my parents bought when they saw *Hello, Dolly!* on Broadway in 1964, the set of the Harmonia Gardens in the Broadway production was good-looking enough: a large, central arch with lights around it (giving a carnival atmosphere to the place, a bit like the Moulin Rouge), a couple of swank booths on either side, and a straight and narrow central staircase at the top of which was a narrow doorway hung with drapes. On the back of the album there was a picture of Carol Channing, her face beaming as she comes down the stairs, her right hand on the railing, her left extended as if expecting it to be kissed, wearing a red dress, and with red feathers in her hair. But in the film, the Harmonia Gardens was more than just another setting—it was a whole world unto itself, a Beaux Arts dream palace so vast, so intricately designed, and so elaborately decorated that, like the old Penn Station or the White City of the 1892 Chicago World's Fair, like the Paris Opera or the second-century Baths of Caracalla, you couldn't take it all in at a glance (fig. 7).[2] When Vandergelder's employees, Cornelius and Barnaby, arrive at the restaurant with their dates, Irene and Minne, like country bumpkins they stand atop the grand stairway all agog over what they see down below: a waiter pushes a food-laden cart along the red-carpeted runway clear across the dance floor on the other side of the restaurant; dignified men and women promenade along the runway and up and down the central staircase; waiters pass through the human traffic holding silver-domed trays aloft on one arm; and crowds of beautifully dressed people sit at tables and mill around the perimeter of the dance floor, where dancing couples whirl around and around the circular space, the music bobbing them along on its friendly current. This was no ordinary interior—in fact, it didn't even feel like an interior. Inside and outside had been gloriously confounded, so that standing at the top of the stairway of the Harmonia Gardens, you felt as if you were breath-

Figure 7. The Harmonia Gardens Restaurant in the film version of *Hello, Dolly!*
(Reprinted by permission of the Museum of Modern Art)

ing the dizzy air on top of a mountain, looking down and all around at the peaceful, shining valley below.

It's true, there were plenty of differences between the Harmonia Gardens scene in the Broadway show and the one in the film that took some getting used to (figs. 8 and 9). For one thing, when Barbra's Dolly finally arrives, she's dressed in gold, while Carol Channing famously wore red: "[The film's costume designer Irene] Scharaff had designed a startling red gown. Michael Stewart, the librettist of the Broadway show, asserted that Dolly's scarlet gown was symbolic of life returning to her. Photographs of Channing wearing the plush, vivid, figure-molding crimson gown had proliferated the media, and she had sung the title song in costume on several television variety specials. Streisand refused to wear a gown of that color and fought onerous battles with Sharaff and Lehman over the design. One day she refused to leave her dressing room unless it was agreed that a new design in gold would be forthcoming. Sharaff

Figure 8. Dolly Levi (Carol Channing) at the Harmonia Gardens Restaurant in the 1995 Broadway revival of *Hello, Dolly!* (Reprinted by permission of Joan Marcus)

compromised and designed a richly beaded topaz dress that pleased Streisand" (Edwards 261). Once I got used to Barbra's gown of gold, the question became, Is there a pattern in it, or is it just solid gold? For there were times when you could see starbursts within the gold material, and so I wondered how intricate and extensive they were.

The other big problem was the staircase. In the film, it was at least twice as wide as it was on Broadway, with low risers and deep treads making one's movement up or down the stairs stately and ceremonial (which would have been fine, except that "stately" and "ceremonial" were not normally the words that would best describe Dolly or the raucous song she and the restaurant staff sing when she arrives). The Broadway staircase had handrailings, just like the railing we had on our staircase at home, but the movie staircase had thick, low, marble, scroll-work balustrades that were only for show, not for holding onto as you came down the stairs. On Broadway, Dolly came down the stairs hold-ing the railing; in the movie, she came down a rather lonely figure, her arms hung down at her sides, not touching anything or anyone. Whereas in the Broadway production the staircase was a discreet thing jutting out from a second-story doorway (not unlike the little flight of stairs they prop up against the door to an airplane to let the passengers out), the imperial staircase in the film sat like a great piece of sculpture

Figure 9. Dolly Levi (Barbra Streisand) at the Harmonia Gardens Restaurant.
(Reprinted by permission of the Museum of Modern Art)

in the middle of a vast open space, fully but ambiguously embedded into the surrounding architecture. And the top and bottom of the stairs that Dolly descends in the film weren't even the real top and bottom; the "top" of the staircase was, in fact, only a large landing, at which point the staircase bifurcates into two staircases going further up in opposite directions (like the staircase in the entrance foyer of the von Trapp mansion); and the "bottom" of the stairs was, in fact, only another landing — actually, a runway around the perimeter of the dance floor — from which the staircase continues six more steps until it reaches the dance floor. (I didn't realize all of this the first time I saw *Hello, Dolly!* on TV; it took several years of looking at movie stills wherever I could find them and several showings of the movie on TV for me to piece it together.)

I found the architecture of the movie staircase somewhat disturbing because the whole purpose, it seemed to me, of having Dolly come down a flight of stairs at the climax of the film was to make the point that whereas before she had been away, now she was unequivocally home. But the set design of the film belied that message by blurring the "before" and "after" of Dolly's return. Yes, Dolly comes down the staircase in the film, but she only enters it midway (at the landing), and then she doesn't come down all the way—she only comes down as far as the run-way, not all the way down to the dance floor. So in a sense, it was as if she hadn't really come home again. Or at least, she hadn't necessarily come home to stay. When she and the waiters sing "Dolly will never go away—/Dolly will never go away—/Dolly will never go away again!," (and then Louis Armstrong shouts out, "*One more time!*" and they do it again), the subtle contradiction between the insistent message of the song and the excessively complicated architecture of the restaurant made me ques-tion, if only half-consciously, the sincerity of the film.

Still another problem was that in the film, Dolly doesn't really make an *entrance* at the Harmonia Gardens so much as an *appearance*. For sev-eral minutes, the restaurant staff dance for joy in anticipation of her ar-rival. But then at a certain point they realize that she has been standing there quietly at the top of the stairs for we don't know how long, wait-ing for everyone to notice that she has come—the camera slowly pans up the stairs, then up her body, then cuts to a closeup of her face as she looks in silent amazement at her friends below. Total silence reigns for a second or two. Then she takes her first step down the stairs and the orchestra beats out the brassy introduction to the "Hello, Dolly!" num-ber. This was okay, but I thought it would have been better if Barbra had made a more emphatic, thrusting entrance—if she had flung open a pair of curtains, say, or if maybe a spotlight had suddenly shone on a door, and there was a sizzling drum roll, and she had suddenly, theatri-cally burst open the door! But there were no curtains here and no door for her to come through. Just vast, untended, rather unframed space.

But the more I thought about the set of the Harmonia Gardens Res-taurant, the more its complexity and ambiguity came to fascinate me. What it didn't give me at first glance I tried to figure out by looking more closely, and what I couldn't figure out on close inspection I made up for myself in my imagination. One day while I was just bouncing the basketball on the driveway and shooting baskets, feeling, as I often did, a little lonely and a little bored, I started thinking seriously about the Harmonia Gardens Restaurant. I tried to figure out how it was layed out: where, for example, did the staircase go, exactly, once it split in two and went up in opposite directions? Was there another circular runway above parallel to the one we see in the film, I wondered? And if so, what was holding that runway up? Pillars of some kind? What would those pil-lars look like? Would they be thick or slender? How many of them would there be? (The youngest of six children, I was always thinking in one way or another about sets of things and the fate of any individual member of the set.) Where would they be placed? Would there be arches con-necting them, like an arcade (like the gallery of arches in the von Trapp foyer)? Or not? Which would be better, right angles or curves? (Curves, definately.) What about the runway down below: from how many places could you enter the dance floor from the runway? Would you have to walk down a short flight of steps to get onto the dance floor? Yes, because, remember, the central staircase continues six more steps from the runway down to the dance floor, so it would have to be like that all around the perimeter of the dance floor. Would there be railings on either side of these tiny flights of stairs? And what would they look like? Would they be kin to the thick, marble balustrades on either side of the main staircase, or should they be a different species altogether? (Was I the offspring of my parents in the same way that my older siblings were their offspring, or was I some kind of different species altogether?) Should I aim for variety or consistency? (Hard to say.) Or could I have both? And what would the dance floor look like? Should it be made of marble? Or perhaps tile? If it was made of tile, what kinds of patterns would the tile make? What if the floor was a *mosaic*?! Wow! A dance floor made out of thousands and thousands of little pieces of colored glass, like a stained glass window—imagine, a stained glass window *on the floor!* And maybe the dance floor could light up, so that at night it would blaze with color and light, like Lite Brite! Imagine hundreds of couples dancing around the dance floor while underneath their feet, rays of colored light flickered, illuminating their feet and the lovely steps they made!

And then what about the red carpet? It shouldn't be just an ordinary red rug—no, it should be richer and more full-bodied and more expensive than that: I decided that if you looked very closely, you could see, woven all over into the red pile of the carpet, a precious second fabric, a blood-red embroidery, an arabesque of deeper red.

III

One afternoon not long after I'd seen *Hello, Dolly!* for the first time on TV, my mom and I were sitting together in the living room—she was doing needlepoint, I'm not sure what I was doing—and she asked me, "Why do you love that movie," meaning *Hello, Dolly!,* "so much?"

I was flattered by the question because rarely, it seemed, was anyone ever curious about the things I took most seriously. Despite the hesitant note in my mother's voice—as if she were afraid to hear the whole Gothic truth about why I loved *Hello, Dolly!*—I paused, and thought for a moment. Scenes from the movie passed through my mind. It occurred to me that there was always something else going on in the background. Early in the film, for example, Dolly stands in front of Horace Vandergelder's hay and feed store in Yonkers, watching his buggy disappear down the road. Before her stretches a tableau of late-nineteenth-century, sun-dappled suburban life: a dalmatian lies contentedly on the summer grass while a man gently prods him with a stick; three boys play with a hoop; a man stands talking to a child; a couple of boys ride by on a bicycle built for two, ringing its bell, ding-a-ling! ding-a-ling!; a man and a woman stroll across the lawn, the woman holding a parasol; a horse and buggy trots past the store; a girl walks by, also carrying a parasol; a sailboat glides quietly by on the Hudson River. All of this is going on as Dolly sings about her plan to "gently lead [Horace] where fortune can find him"—that is, to make him marry her. Every scene in *Hello, Dolly!*, it seemed, overflowed with riches like these.

"I love *Hello, Dolly!* because it's spectacular," I answered my mother. "I love the sets, and all the crowd scenes. I love the restaurant scene. I wish life was like that. I wish I could have lived back then, in New York City in the 1890s."

Not without respect for what I had just said, my mother responded, "You know, I read a great book recently called *The Good Old Days—They Were Terrible!*, and she proceeded to tell me how New York City was never the way they show it in *Hello, Dolly!*—how there were pigs and horse manure in the streets, and women would have had it all over their clothes, their long dresses dragging in it, and there would have been no singing and dancing of course, not like in the movie, and there were no toilets. Can you imagine Dolly wearing that gold dress, with feathers in her hair, and no toilets?!

In *The Good Old Days—They Were Terrible!* (1974), Otto L. Bettmann tries to tear down the myth of a golden past as a way of arguing that the present—the early 1970s—is better than commonly admitted:

> I have always felt that our times have overrated and unduly overplayed the fun aspects of the past. What we have forgotten are the hunger of the unemployed, crime, corruption, the despair of the aged, the insane and the crippled. The world now gone was in no way spared the problems we consider horrendously our own, such as pollution, addiction, urban plight or educational turmoil. In most of our nostalgia books, such crises are ignored, and the period's dirty business is swept under the carpet of oblivion. What emerges is a glowing picture of the past, of blue-skied meadows where children play and millionaires sip tea. . . . we have to revise the idealized picture of the past and turn the spotlight on its grimmer aspects. This more realistic approach will show us Gay Nineties man (man in the street, not in the boardroom), as one to be pitied rather than envied. He could but dream of the Utopian miracles that have become part of our everyday life. Compared with him we are lucky—even if dire premonitions darken our days and we find much to bemoan in our society. Proceeding

from such convictions, this may be called a missionary book, a modest
personal attempt to redeem our times from the aspersions cast upon them
by nostalgic comparisons. (xii–xiii)

"But I guess *Hello, Dolly!* is a wonderful fantasy world for you," Mom
added. She was right. Once I started trying to figure out scenes from
Hello, Dolly! and other movies for myself, I was amazed at how the time
flew by on the basketball court or up in my bedroom or out in the
schoolyard. I would go outside to shoot baskets with plenty of afternoon
light still in the sky, and the next thing I knew the sky was dark and Mom
was calling me in to dinner.

But fantasy set me on the road to a new kind of reality. For in *Hello,
Dolly!* I had found something to occupy my *mind,* not just my imagination. Soon I became preoccupied with the difference between the Broadway stage versions and the Hollywood film versions of several musicals,
Hello, Dolly! chief among them, as well as with the supposed inferiority of
the latter, which I couldn't assent to. I started picking up books on the
subject at Waldenbooks in our local mall (around the same time, I discovered a book of photographs of young naked men called *Les Hommes,*
and I thought that "Les Hommes" was a guy named Les, as in "short
for Lester," but then I couldn't figure out which of the — *incredible beyond
words*—men in the photographs was Les).

I bought *Barbra: The First Decade* (1974) by James Spada (as Nick Pullia has described it, "for many fans . . . the see-Dick-run of Streisand's
career" [34]), an oversized book with lots of pictures, snippets of reviews, and background information about all of Barbra's theatrical performances, records, TV appearances, and movies. There I discovered,
to my disappointment, that not all critics spoke highly of *Hello, Dolly!*
Spada quotes, for example, Pauline Kael's review in the *New Yorker:* "the
songs are dismal affairs, with lyrics that make one's teeth ache, and the
smirky dialogue might pass for wit among not too bright children. . . .
The movie is full of that fake, mechanical exhilaration of big Broadway shows—the gut-busting, muscle-straining dance that is meant to
wow you. This dancing, like the choral singing, is asexual and unroman-
tic. . ." (173). Kael's comments about the set of the Harmonia Gardens,
which Spada does not quote, are even more vicious:

> [T]he interior of the Harmonia Gardens is a gratuitously, vulgarly opulent
> set in beer-barrel rococo—full of upholstery and statues and fountains
> and chandeliers, like a storeroom of all the garbage left over from the
> Alice Faye-Don Ameche musicals. This set, redolent of every bad operetta
> ever written, makes all the action in it look unnecessarily ugly—and the
> director, Gene Kelly, and the choreographer, Michael Kidd, perhaps in-

spired by the set, have staged in it their most tasteless "show-stopping" dance. There were big, terrible production numbers in thirties movies, too, but they had redeeming qualities—a grandiose, crazy frivolity . . . and sometimes, as with Busby Berkeley's ambitious, strange ideas, a native American eccentric's invented form of surrealism, as perplexing in its way as the Watts Towers. It's apparent why Kelly and Kidd decided to avoid trick camera effects and the bird's-eye views that infatuated the thirties choreographers, and stay within the giant-stage concept, but the dancing itself needs some freedom and folly. The excesses of the thirties choreographers were naive and funny (even at the time); the excess here is of anxiety and strain, and it's rather painful. (Kael, "Keep Going" 57)

Further, in a *Mad* magazine lampoon of Barbra that Spada reprints, one cartoon actor on the *Dolly* set says to another, "Isn't this 'Hello, Bubby' set **corny** and **old-fashioned?**" The other actor replies, "That's **nothing!** Wait'll you hear the **score!**" (187; bold face emphasis in the original). And Spada reprints a passage from Vincent Canby's *New York Times* review: "Miss Streisand's obvious youth and real sexuality obliterated any sense of nostalgia in the 'Hello, Dolly!' number and add a curious ambiguity to other aspects of the role, including her speeches directed to Mr. Levi, her late husband. (I had the odd feeling that she must have been married to him at the age of 8 and lost him at 10.)" (173) Tellingly, Canby begins his review (in a passage that Spada omits), "this may be the most superfluous film review ever written, with the possible exceptions of the notices for 'The Sound of Music.' . . ."

Browsing other books about movie musicals, I discovered a wall of critical opinion that said that, starting in the late 1950s, musical films had been suffering from overproduction; impossible pressure to succeed financially; the misguided casting of bankable stars in their central roles instead of the performers most suited for those roles (the casting of Barbra Streisand as Dolly Levi was always mentioned as *the* prime example of this sin); an undue reverence for the Broadway originals that stifled the right kind of creative adaptation to the screen; and the introduction of new widescreen processes that, ironically, seemed antithetical to the proper staging and filming of musical numbers (Sennett 317). I remember that one critic titled his chapter on musicals from the sixties and seventies "Overweight and Undernourished," and there, underneath the title, was a still from *Hello, Dolly!* (The consensus remains the same: at a June 1996 gathering of musical film actresses to raise money for the restoration of classic film musicals, the common wisdom was that "the downfall of the musical was signaled by such box-office disappointments as 'Hello, Dolly!' [1969], 'At Long Last Love' [1975] and 'A Chorus Line' [1985]" [Weinraub 16].)

My mom and I would occasionally talk about the relative merits of Hollywood and Broadway musical productions. Mom thought the movie version of *Hello, Dolly!* was okay but not the greatest. She would often say how she liked Barbra Streisand but really wished that Carol Channing had repeated her stage performance as Dolly Levi on screen. "They always make a mistake when they try to get somebody big to star in the movie, and they do it to make a buck. The same thing happened with Audrey Hepburn in *My Fair Lady*. Now you know I love Audrey Hepburn, but Julie Andrews was so good in that part on stage. Your father still says that was the best night he ever spent in the theater. You came out of that show, and honestly, Pat, you just knew that every song was going to be a hit, and you were just *humming* the songs! They had to dub Audrey Hepburn's singing voice in the movie, and Julie Andrews has such a beautiful voice. Don't misunderstand me, it's not that I don't like Barbra Streisand, you know I do. Now, I thought Julie Andrews was much better in the movie version of *The Sound of Music* than Mary Martin would have been—Mary Martin did it on stage—so I guess sometimes they do make the right choice when they make the movie version."

One time my mom and I almost got into a fight over the issue of Hollywood versus Broadway. Soon after I first saw *Funny Girl* on TV, Mom took me to the mall to buy the soundtrack album. Once we got to the record store, however, she somehow persuaded me that we should get the *Funny Girl* Broadway cast album instead of the soundtrack. "Broadway orchestras are so much more intimate than movie orchestras," Mom said, "because Broadway theaters are quite small. You'd be surprised how small they are, Patrick. I love the feel of a Broadway orchestra. I think you'll be much happier with the Broadway cast album of *Funny Girl*. It's the same music, it's just a much better sound." I took her advice, but when I got home and listened to the thing, I was horrified: it wasn't what I had experienced in seeing the film at all! There were songs I didn't even recognize that they had cut from the film, and on the songs that they kept for the film, Barbra's voice sounded so different—younger, more raw, less pretty, grittier. *Ugh!* I hated it! I wanted to relive what I experienced from seeing the movie; I wanted to feel the exact same tension and excitement when Fanny sings "Don't Rain On My Parade," and I wanted to feel the exact same pang in my heart when she sings "People." I *had* to have the soundtrack album, that's all there was to it. I made my mom rush me back to the mall the first thing in the morning to buy the soundtrack, and as soon as we got home I raced upstairs to my room and listened to it over and over and looked at the pictures on the album jacket and read the liner notes ("A member of the crew told a friend: 'When she did *People* for the first time, I cried. But she came out of the booth and was upset. The phrasing was off and she wanted something else from the orchestra. She, [musical director Herbert] Ross and [conductor Walter] Scharf worked for hours, did it again, and I couldn't tell the difference. But they did it twelve more times and I *could* tell the difference between 1 and 14. Unbelievable!'" [Brodsky]), and tried to recreate the whole experience of the film in my head.

IV

For as long as I can remember, my obsession with Barbra Streisand was more or less tolerated within my family. Typically, I would be playing by myself in the basement or up in my room when I would hear my name shouted—I recall my mother's voice—in a panic: "Patrick! Come here, and hurry up!" I would race to the den where we had the television to see the last ten seconds of an advertisement for the TV premier of one of Barbra's films: ". . . you won't want to miss one spectacular minute of the incomparable Barbra Streisand as the irrepressible, chain-smoking coed Daisy Gamble in the CBS Sunday Night Movie, *On a Clear Day You Can See Forever*, directed by Vincente Minnelli . . ." I was riveted, and counted the days and hours until Sunday night when I would feast my eyes for three luxurious hours on Barbra Streisand. I would always want my mom to watch it with me. At first she would demur, saying that she had some other things to do, she had the wash to fold, and it was such a long movie, tomorrow was a busy day for her. But then, just as the movie was starting, she would come into the den and sit next to me on the sofa, and we would watch the whole thing together, and laugh at all of Barbra's jokes, and then I would race to the kitchen during the commercials to get bowls of chocolate ice cream and orange sherbet mixed, which was one of our favorites.

When I went to see *What's Up Doc?* (1972), I sat between my mom and dad. During the opening credits, Barbra sings Cole Porter's "You're the Top." When she got to the line, "you're a melody from a symphony by Strauss," and started to sing out as the music got louder and the full orchestra chimed in on the word "Strauss," my mom leaned over to me and whispered in my ear with a laugh, "Here she goes!"

Just about everyone in our town who knew my family also knew that I loved Barbra Streisand. For a little while, my sister Sue had a boyfriend named Paulie who was also a Barbra Streisand fan (!), and whenever he would come over to our house somehow the subject of Barbra Streisand would come up, and pretty soon he and I would be trading stories. And when his younger sister, Sandy, graduated from high school, she and all the graduating seniors published their "last wills and testaments" in the school newspaper, and she willed me all of her Barbra Streisand albums. It was an especially remarkable thing for her to have done because most seniors willed things to other members of the senior class or at least to underclassmen, but I was still in seventh or eighth grade at the time, so no one would even have heard of me. All they would have known about me was that I was a Horrigan and that I liked Barbra Streisand.

Not long after I discovered Barbra Streisand, my parents went away on a three-week European vacation, and my Aunt Pauline baby-sat for us (actually, she was my Grandfather Ermentrout's sister, so she was more like a grandmother than an aunt). One night Mary Jo and I were up in my room listening to the soundtrack of *Hello, Dolly!* and for some reason I started lip-synching—and not just to the words but also the instrumentation. Mary Jo almost died laughing and called for Aunt Pauline to come up and see what I was doing. Aunt Pauline thought it was funny too, and pretty soon I was doing it for everybody in the house. As soon as my mom and dad walked through the door upon their return, Mary Jo and Aunt Pauline ushered them into the living room and said, "wait till you see what Patrick can do! Go ahead, Pat, show them!" And I proceeded to lip-synch "Before the Parade Passes By," to the point where I was flat on my back on the living room floor, mouthing Barbra's record-breaking last note (". . . passes byyyyyyyyy!!!!!"), my arms spread out on either side of me, imagining that my position somehow mimicked the crane shot in the film where the camera pulls up and away from Barbra Streisand as she holds that last, long, breathtaking note, while rows and rows of marching musicians and batton twirlers and Civil War veterans stream past her, like waters rushing around the sunken tower of a bridge, down Fourteenth Street.

I have no memory of my parents' response to my performance. I think if they had disapproved of it, I would remember that. I *do* remember dimly, when I was around four years old, dressing up in my sister Mary Jo's grade school uniform—a blue, black, and green plaid pinafore— and coming downstairs excitedly to show everyone. There were a bunch of people in the den watching TV (I don't remember now exactly who was there—for some reason, I seem to recall my sister Mary Jo and my Aunt Pauline, but I may be conflating this incident with the later one during my parents' European vacation), and when I made my entrance, together they shrieked, "Patrick, take that dress off! You'll ruin it! Go upstairs right now and take off that dress and put away those shoes!" So I can only conclude that my performance of "Before the Parade Passes By" for my parents was somehow okay with them. (The only other excitement during the three weeks while my parents were away was when Aunt Pauline was boiling frozen corn on the stove for dinner one night, and the lid got stuck on the pan. When my parents phoned from Europe to see how everything was going, Aunt Pauline shouted in her heavy Pennsylvania-German accent, "I can't get the lid off the goddarn corn!" We always loved Aunt Pauline because she wasn't afraid to say things like "goddarn.")

For sure, it didn't always go smoothly in my family with me and my love for Barbra Streisand. For example, in September of 1979 when I turned sixteen, my sister Betsy bought me tickets to see Carol Channing in *Hello, Dolly!*, which was playing at the National Theater in Washington, D.C. (at the time, Betsy was a sophomore at Georgetown University). It was a perfect birthday gift and I couldn't have been more excited—until I found out that the same night we were supposed to see Carol Channing in *Hello, Dolly!*, the movie version with Barbra Streisand was going to be shown on TV. Of course there was no question of not going to see Carol Channing, but at least I hoped that after the show we could rush back to Betsy's house and maybe, just *maybe* I could catch the last hour of the movie, or at least just see the big production number at the Harmonia Gardens Restaurant (too bad Betsy's TV set was only a tiny, old black-and-white thing—did one of her housemates have a bigger color TV, I wondered?). Betsy was indignant: "I can't believe you'd rather see a stupid Barbra Streisand movie that you've already seen fifty times than go see a real live show! You know something, you are *really* nuts. I'm never gonna buy you theater tickets for anything again, I can tell you that much!"

Another time my brother, John, and I were having an argument over his new stereo system. We shared a bedroom at home, and we didn't always make such a harmonious pair, especially the older we got (for one thing, while I was mostly into Broadway show tunes, movie soundtracks, and Barbra Streisand, John's musical tastes were harder to categorize: he had a couple of Supertramp albums; an Emerson, Lake, and Palmer; one by Todd Rundgren; one by Dan Fogelberg and Tim Weisberg; an Allman Brothers album; and several by Neil Young). The argument may have been over how often I was allowed to use the stereo and how if I wasn't careful with the needle on the record player he was going to kill me—something like that. I started to say, "You know, the way you can test the quality of a stereo system to find out if it's really good is to put on a Barbra Streisand record because the range of her voice—" but before I could even finish my sentence (which, however, John immediately and correctly understood to be an insult to him, his taste in music, and his fancy new stereo), he shouted back at the top of his lungs, "Why don't you shut the *fuck* up, I don't give a *shit* about Barbra Streisand! You don't know what the *fuck* you're talking about!" (Once John went away to college, I learned to like pretty much all of his records and even started branching out into new territory of my own.)

And around the time that *Funny Lady* was released in 1975, my mom and I were at the gas station and she gave the gas station attendant her credit card, and a minute later he came back and said it wasn't the right one, and she said, "Oh I'm sorry, I made a mistake. Here, why don't I just give you cash?" Both my mom and I noticed that the guy seemed annoyed at the confusion. In order to express my solidarity with her while at the same time acknowledging the gas station attendent's frustration, I said as we drove away, "I guess he kind of thought, 'Screw you, lady!'" My mom was aghast.

"Patrick, don't *ever* say a thing like that! Where on earth did you learn that?"

"From *Funny Lady*," I said. It was a long story, but she wanted an explanation, so, I thought, here goes: "When Fanny Brice catches Billy Rose in bed with Eleanor Holmes, at first she's upset, but then she forgives him because she realizes that he was just jealous because she was getting back together with her ex-husband, Nick Arnstein, in Los Angeles. So she tells Billy, 'I figure what happened is I called you from L.A. and told you I was going to see Nick. And you got sore and thought, well, screw her.'"

"Well honey, you mustn't ever say things like that again, *please!* My goodness!" I don't think she explained why I wasn't supposed to say things like that—things like what? What was so bad about "screw you"? Anyway, I never said "screw you" in front of my mom again.

Then things *really* fell apart on Christmas day of 1976, the day Barbra's rock remake of *A Star Is Born* was released. I awoke that morning, as I always did on Christmas, around six o'clock, dying to rush downstairs with the rest of my siblings and tear into all the presents Mom and Dad had bought us. After we finished with the presents (which, for me that year, included three Barbra Streisand albums—*The Barbra Streisand Album, A Happening in Central Park,* and *What About Today?*), I went quietly into the kitchen to look at the entertainment section of the newspaper (quietly, because I didn't want anyone to think that I could be so ungrateful for all my Christmas presents as to wish for something more, even though I *did* want more—I wanted to see *A Star Is Born* as soon as possible); I turned to the movie page to look for the ad for *A Star Is Born,* thinking I might be able to go see it that night, and I froze in horror to find out that it had been rated R: RESTRICTED: UNDER 17 REQUIRES ACCOMPANYING PARENT OR ADULT GUARDIAN. I was only thirteen.

"I'm allowed to go if you take me," I said, hoping against hope that my mom would agree.

"I'm sorry, honey, but we're not taking you to see an R-rated movie."

"But Mom, I've been waiting so long to see this!"

"Patrick, you're not going to see an R-rated movie. Now I'm sorry, but that's final. Barbra Streisand or no Barbra Streisand, you're too young."

I was outraged. My mother continued: "You know, it makes me mad that she did this" ("she" meaning Barbra Streisand). "Why do they have to make R-rated movies? What's so important in the movie that they couldn't cut it out and have it be a PG rating? We'd have no problem with you seeing a PG movie, but no R's."

I protested and pleaded. All pointless.

"I'm really annoyed," she said. "I want to write her a letter and tell her, 'I hope you're satisfied that you just lost one of your biggest fans'" (meaning me—was she *kidding?*). "I think she could lose a lot of support for this." (*A Star Is Born* would go on to become Barbra's top-grossing film, though critically it was one of her most disastrous.)

One day not long after this, I went along with my mom to pick up my sister Karen, who was two years older than me, at the movie theater.

"What movie did you go see?" I asked Karen when she and her friend, I forget who it was, got into the car (for there were three or four movies showing at the theater, including *A Star Is Born*).

"*Rocky*," she said.

"How was it?" I asked.

"It wasn't that great."

"Why not?"

"Oh, I don't know."

"Why don't you know?"

"Just 'cause."

"'Cause why?"

"No reason, just because."

"Because why?"

"Because none of your business."

"Why is it none of my business?"

(Imitating me) "Why is it none of my business?"

"Why not?!" I shouted.

"Hey, that's enough, you two," my mom interrupted.

"Why won't she tell me why she didn't like the movie?" I said.

"Why do you care?" Karen said.

"Karen, don't tease your brother," Mom said.

"I'm not teasing him, he's bugging me."

"He's *interested* in your movie! Can't you be civil to each other?"

"*I'm* being civil, *she's* not," I piped up.

(Again, imitating me) "*I'm* being civil, *she's* not," Karen said.

"Karen, that's enough!" my mom said firmly.

Through all of this, I began to suspect that Karen had gone to see *A Star Is Born* and that she wasn't telling me about it because she knew I would get hysterical if I found out (although I'm not sure why Karen would have been permitted to see an R-rated movie—after all, she was only fifteen at the time). It would, of course, have been supremely unfair if Karen of all people had gotten to see *A Star Is Born* instead of me because she didn't care about Barbra Streisand at all, and she even, on occasion, enjoyed teasing me about my devotion to Barbra, saying, for no reason at all, just to upset me, "Oh, she's so ugly. How can you stand her?" I also began to suspect that my mom was in on the deception. I decided to try and pry it out of them.

"So who was in the movie?" I said to Karen.

"I don't know," she answered.

"Why not?"

"I don't care about who the actors are, you're the only one who cares about all that stuff." (In a mock upper-class British tone of voice) "Oh, the acting was *superb*, darling!"

"Why don't you know any of the actors' names?" I persisted.

"I do know, but I'm not gonna tell you."

"Because you don't know who they are."

"That's what I said the first time. *Duh!*"

"Do you know who played Rocky?"

"Yes, Sylvester Stallone."

"Uh huh, and who else was in the movie?"

"Why don't you go find out for yourself?"

"Why don't *you* tell *me*? Is it because you went to see *A Star Is Born* instead?"

Karen let out an evil laugh.

"What makes you think that?" she said.

"Because I know that's what you saw."

"Well, don't worry, it wasn't very good. You wouldn't like it anyway," Karen said breezily, knowing full well that I *would* like it.

"All right, you two, I said *enough!* When I say *enough* I mean *enough!!*" Mom shouted.

My mom, at least, has pretty much come back around to sharing my interest in Barbra Streisand with me. A couple of years ago she sent me a present—a large, full-color, hardback picture book entitled simply *Barbra Streisand*, by William Ruhlmann—for no special reason other than that she was just thinking about me and wanted to give me something (she's always keeping an eye out for anything that one of her children or grandchildren might like, gift giving always having been one of her favorite hobbies). What really thrilled me, though, was that my mom had gone through the book herself page by page and put Post-it notes with little messages written upon them (all of which I've saved) on all the pictures that she particularly liked. On a March 1992 photograph of Barbra at the Forty-fourth Annual Writers Guild Awards, Mom attached a Post-it that says, "good picture!" In this picture, Barbra's hair looks about the color of my mom's hair, which she disparagingly calls "mouse brown" (Mom says she always wished her hair would turn white, like her Aunt Hilda's, because she thinks it looks so distinguished, but over the years her hair has pretty much stayed the same color, grayish brown). On another picture, Mom has placed a Post-it that says, "a great picture!" This one is an oddly out-of-focus 1963 black and white photo in which Barbra stares coldly straight-faced, with eyes like saucers, into the camera, looking like a visitor from another world. On one page, Mom has flagged two candid shots that might easily have gotten overlooked in a book filled with mostly gigantic glamor photos: one, a picture of Stephen Sondheim hugging Barbra from behind during the making of *The Broadway Album* (1985), both of them smiling warmly (Mom writes, "another favorite"); the other, a picture of Barbra with Leonore Gershwin, the widow of Ira Gershwin, at the 1986 Grammy Awards where Barbra presented Leonore with honorary awards for Ira and his brother George, again both of them looking happy to be together (a lovely woman who looks to be in her seventies, Leonore wears her hair and glasses not unlike my mother: "One of my favorite pix," Mom writes).

V

Barbra Streisand was more to me when I was growing up than an occasion for bonding or coming at loggerheads with various members of my family, and more even than one of the primary touchstones for my blossoming aesthetic sensibility. She was also an escape, my consolation prize for the world's unkindness to me, for everything that made the world an awful place to be. As the 1970s wore on and the closer I got to puberty, in many ways the more unhappy I became. I wasn't well-liked in school; there was always some boy who made me dread going there day after day. And it wasn't just boys; for a while in fifth grade it was fractions. I used to pretend to get sick during math class because I hated fractions, I had a hard time doing things with them, and I was afraid of what Sister Carina would say in that caustic tone of voice if I gave her the wrong answer. My parents eventually became so alarmed by what they considered the poor quality of teaching and the bad attitude of some of the nuns in our Catholic grade school that, in seventh grade, they transferred me to the local public school.

I enjoyed my classes much more in public school than in Catholic school, but the kids in public school were as bad as the ones in Catholic school, and some of them were even worse. My archenemy in eighth grade was a boy who lived down the street from me named Pat Holleran. Now I don't remember if there was some specific reason why he hated me so much—I mean, other than the usual reasons. As a rule, guys hated me because I had female friends, I was a sissy, and I was a top student. There may have been other reasons (something about my family's class status, something about the way I inhabited my body) but I wasn't aware of them at the time. What I *do* remember about Pat Holleran was that he was unkempt, skinny like me, around my height, cute in a mongrelish sort of way, and a mediocre student. He also had a reputation for being a druggie, and he liked to brag about how much sex he had with girls. There was a rumor that a girl in our class gave him a "blow job," and I didn't know what that was, but then someone said that she unzipped his pants and pulled them down and gave him a blow job and so obviously it involved doing something to his penis, but I still wasn't sure what (did she "blow" on it? What was the point of doing that?). One night he and a couple of his friends went down to the bus stop, and he wrote in chalk on the street in big huge letters PAT HORRIGAN YOU FAG and then they all pissed on it. Since I wasn't there when it happened, I'm not sure how I knew that they pissed on it—did Pat himself tell me this afterward? Was Steve, another neighborhood kid, with them at the time, and did *he* report this to me? And if in fact they did piss on it, why wasn't the chalk washed away? Nor do I remember the entire series of events that followed, but there it was at the bus stop the next morning for everyone to see. My mother now tells me that my dad went down to the bus stop the following day before dawn with a scrub brush and a bucket of water and got down on his hands and knees and scrubbed the graffiti off the street. I don't remember my dad or my mom or any of my siblings having any kind of conversation with me about this at the time (although I do have a very dim memory of someone at some point saying to me, "Do you know what 'fag' means?").

I did have a number of female friends, but I knew they didn't count as friends and I felt guilty about having *only* female friends. One evening around the same time as the graffiti incident, I was up the block visiting my two friends named Lisa who lived next door to each other. We were just sitting around on one of their driveways and for some reason I started to feel unwelcome. Eventually and without much of a good-bye (they didn't seem to notice my leaving), I rode my bike back home and went into the garage and closed the doors and sat down on one of the milk crates and started sobbing. I wanted to tell my parents how awful I felt, but I didn't exactly understand what I was crying about and I didn't think there was any way that I could explain it to them to make them understand. And anyway, I figured they would just blame me for my sadness. They were always saying things like, "Why don't you go outside and mix with the other guys in the neighborhood? We know you like to play alone indoors, and that's great; we've always said whatever makes you happy makes us happy. You have a wonderful imagination, you play the piano so beautifully, you love to build things, and we're not telling you to stop that. You're very creative, and God knows your father and I don't have the gifts you have. But you need some companions, or life will be terribly lonely for you."

Barbra Streisand entered my emotional world exactly here. To me, her music and films were always, in one way or another, about being lonely and learning how to cope with it. For example, in *Barbra: The First Decade*, James Spada describes the unanticipated moment when Barbra's voice wins her the recognition that, as yet, her acting talent has not:

> Truly discouraged by all the rejections she had encountered at auditions, Barbra renounced the theatre, saying, "They'll have to come to me." Although she hadn't given much thought to singing, she knew she had a good voice and thought perhaps she could at least make some money at it. In the spring of 1961, primarily due to economic necessity, she entered a talent contest at the Lion, a bar and restaurant on Ninth Street in Manhattan. . . . She chose the ballad "A Sleepin' Bee." After practicing it, she tried her rendition out on several friends. "I was so embarrassed, I couldn't sing in front of them, so I asked if they wouldn't mind, I'd sing facing the wall. When I finished, and turned around, I remember I couldn't understand why they had tears in their eyes." (13)

I could. I used to wonder who those friends of hers were and what they were feeling at that haunting moment when they heard Barbra sing for the first time in their lives. I envisioned three of them: two young women and one rather effeminate young man. They couldn't see Barbra's face, her expressions, so they were free to imagine her for themselves, according to their own needs. They saw what they already knew: the young, skinny, awkward, "homely" girl, lonely, driven, fatherless (Spada maintains that "more than any other event in her life, the death of her father set the stage for the person Barbra Joan Streisand was to become" [*Barbra* 9]), a failure, ambitious, shunned at school (her classmates called her "big beak" and "crazy Barbra" [*Barbra* 9]), facing a blank wall, her voice emerging as the desperate, yearning sound of a

child who longs to be recognized and accepted unconditionally—a voice
that plumbed and pierced the sadness of their souls. When they cried,
they cried for themselves.

Again and again, Barbra Streisand's films uncannily restage this primal
scene. Her entrance in *Funny Girl,* for example, is structured according
to the same drama of concealment and revelation as the "real-life" scene
in Spada's biography. The opening credits end with a shot of New York's
New Amsterdam Theater, with "Ziegfeld Follies" and "Fanny Brice" in
lights over the marquee. Seen only from behind, Barbra/Fanny walks
into the frame wearing a leopard coat and hat, looks up at her name in
lights, and walks away from the camera toward the stage door through
a narrow passageway to the left of the theater entrance. She opens the
door and enters. Cut to a close up, still with her back to the camera, as
she opens another door and walks down a short flight of stairs on her
way, presumably, to her dressing room. She pauses at the threshold of
a hallway leading to the stage area and decides to go in that direction
instead. Walking toward the stage, she pauses again before a mirror on
her left and turns to look at herself in the mirror; the camera turns as
well to reveal her reflection in the mirror. Now we see her face for the
first time: she pulls her collar down from around her mouth and says
to her reflection with a smile and a quiet laugh, "Hello, gorgeous." (In
his review of *Funny Girl* for the *Village Voice,* Andrew Sarris disapprov-
ingly describes this sequence as follows: "Barbra slithers into the very
first frame of the film through a slightly overhead angle shot from the
rear of a creature in a leopard skin coat. The camera follows her with
portentous persistence and suddenly there is a mirror and Barbra-Fanny
greets her reflection with the sardonic salutation: 'Hi, Gorgeous.' Thus
Barbra is allowed to capitalize on the laughter of self-mockery after an
ego-building entrance that would have been considered too gaudy for
Garbo in her prime." [53])

A little later in the film, just after Fanny meets Nick backstage at
Keeney's Music Hall on the night that she has sung her first solo on
stage (and wowed the audience with "I'd Rather Be Blue over You [Than
Happy with Somebody Else]"—*on roller skates!*), Nick invites her to dinner with some friends, but, nervous, shy, feeling she isn't pretty enough
to socialize with him and his attractive women companions, with a lump
in her throat, she declines:

> NICK: Look, we're going to Delmonico's for supper. Won't you join us?
> We'd be happy to wait while you change.
> FANNY: [*turning her self-hatred immediately into a winning joke*] I'd have to
> change too much. Nobody could wait that long.

In a sharp-focus medium shot, Nick leaves through a door, which Fanny closes behind him; cut to a soft-focus close-up shot of the back of Fanny's head, leaning face forward against the door, and we hear *but do not see* her singing, in high-pitched head tones, "Nicky Arnstein, Nicky Arnstein." She turns toward the camera, with an expression of anguish and yearning, and continues singing, "I'll never see him again," then with a shrug abruptly skates away, and the scene ends.

And in *Yentl*, the 1983 musical film Streisand produced, directed, co-wrote, and starred in, about a girl who dresses as a boy in order to study the Talmud, the last scene of the film begins with a shot of an adolescent girl reading the Talmud. The camera moves off to an old woman who appears to be smiling at her, and then it continues to wander through a crowd of East Europeans, sitting in groups, huddled together, some sleeping, some gesturing as if talking to each other, some laughing, some playing chess. It becomes clear that these people are seated on the deck of a steamship, bound, one presumes, for America. All the while we hear Barbra's voice, but we do not see her, singing. The camera floats off the deck, revealing another deck down below, where Barbra/Yentl is now seen, alone, her back to the camera, standing at the ship's stern. The camera approaches her and circles around her from behind, gradually revealing her face, as she sings to the sea and wind

To begin with, these scenes and others like them in many of Barbra's films imbue her with an aura of solemnity (the camera often sweeps around her in 180-degree pan shots as if she were a sacred, sculptural object) and suspense (you never know when she'll turn away or reappear); they insist, first and last, upon the significance of Barbra Streisand as she plays not to her costars but, rather, to her audience—she sometimes looks directly into the camera, reminding everyone that she is Barbra Streisand, despite the encumbrance of the role to which she has been assigned. And they toy with the seeming contradiction that a voice of such power, beauty, and range belongs to such an unconventionally attractive woman.

More importantly, each of these scenes is a little lesson in the anatomy of loneliness. They open it up, examine its constituent parts, and put it back together; but in so doing, they make loneliness dramatic. And once your solitude has turned into drama, in a way you're no longer alone; someone is always bearing witness to you, even when no one else is around, because at least *you* are bearing witness to you. You become your own best friend. You fall in love with yourself (something Barbra Streisand is frequently accused of). You become, finally, like Barbra Streisand, *significant:* "One evening [Barbara's roommate] Marilyn Fried was in the bedroom of their small apartment and Barbara was in the living room with [another friend, Carl] Esser. 'He was strumming a guitar,' Fried recalled. 'I suddenly heard this remarkable voice coming out of the living room. My immediate reaction was to go to the radio and find out who was singing so marvelously. But the radio was not on. I realized there must be someone in this tiny apartment who had this magnitude, this power. I went into the room and asked Barbara, 'Who was singing?' She said, 'I was'" (Edwards 85).

I didn't cry the first time I heard Barbra Streisand sing the way her friends did, but her spirit entered inside of me and changed me nonetheless. After seeing one of her movies, for the next several days I would walk around the house feeling possessed by her. Rarely did I imitate her in any superficial way—I *became* her *on the inside*. She made me feel that nothing I did was insignificant—going to the bathroom, searching through the cupboard for a snack, choosing what I would wear for school tomorrow morning, then making my way down the street to the bus stop, boarding the bus, finding a seat, watching as cars and trees and houses and telephone wires and clouds passed by on the way to school (I always envied people, like my mom, who didn't have to go to school— imagine what it must be like to stay home all day doing everything you liked!), thinking of whatever was coming up today—a test, or gym class (ugh), or art class (Miss Yoh always said I had real talent and hoped I would keep on pursuing it, but all the guys hated Miss Yoh because she was such a "wimp," they said, and they thought art class was bullshit). Soon I began to imagine that my entire life was a movie, a very long movie in which nothing happened except exactly whatever it was I happened to be doing at any given moment, and whatever I happened to be doing, it would be, invariably, *fascinating*—just as everything Barbra Streisand did, no matter how insignificant, seemed fascinating to me. The movie's time scale would follow the time scale of my everyday life, down to the second. So, for example, I would be sitting in church, but in fact it would be a *movie* of me sitting in church. Or I would be walking down the hall at school, holding my books in my arms, wondering what would happen today in the cafeteria at lunchtime, and would somebody punch me in front of all the other kids and would I have trouble finding someone to sit with and if so, what was it going to be like sitting and eating my lunch alone?—It was enough to make me want to skip lunch altogether even though I was so hungry—but in fact it would be a *movie* of me walking down the hall, thinking, wondering, worrying. I made believe that audiences were amazed and alarmed at how long these movies of my life lasted—they went on for years at a time. Imagine an audience sitting in the dark of a movie theater for seven years in a row—but somehow they just couldn't get enough of my life, and so they stayed and stayed and kept wanting more. I liked to imagine at what point the movie would end and the closing credits start to roll. I would pretend that, for example, as I waited inside the car some stiflingly hot afternoon in July while my mom was busy doing something or other at the bank, the camera would portentously begin to rise and pull back from the roof of our station wagon and gravely serious music in a minor key would come up and the credits would start to roll and the audience would suddenly realize that, without any warning, the movie they had been watching for years was over, and they would be angry and cry out in protest, because now they were never going to find out how well I did in the upcoming piano recital, or they weren't going to get to see the big First Holy Communion scene, and it would just be such a disturbing way for a movie to end (but only in vain would they cry, for the screen couldn't hear their complaints, and the movie was beyond their control). But then a whole new marathon-length movie would begin, say, a week later, and things would pretty much pick up where they left off.

One of the reasons *Hello, Dolly!* meant so much during my adolescence was that, as played by Barbra Streisand, Dolly Levi was, like me, young, brimming with life, and lonely. After she has introduced Irene and Cornelius to each other and taught them how to dance, Irene tries to persuade her to join them at the Fourteenth Street parade. Dolly says she'll be along in a minute, but now, for a little while, she wants to be alone. Sitting on a park bench, she thinks of her own life and how lonely she has been since her husband's death. She speaks to him:

> Ephraim, let me go. It's been long enough, Ephraim. Every night, just like you'd want me to, I've put out the cat, made myself a rum toddy, and before I went to bed said a little prayer thanking God that I was independent, that no one else's life was mixed up with mine. But lately, Ephraim, I've begun to realize that for a long time, I have not shed one tear, nor have I been for one moment outrageously happy. . . . But there comes a time when you have got to decide whether you want to be a fool among fools, or a fool alone. Well I have made that decision. . . . I'm going back, Ephraim. I've decided to join the human race again. And Ephraim, I want you to give me away.[3]

Dolly wasn't *overtly* unhappy—her sadness was undetectable ("I have not shed one tear"), but, nevertheless, she was suffering inside ("nor have I been for one moment outrageously happy"). It was as if Dolly had gone numb and needed to do something about it—marry Horace Vandergelder? That wasn't really the answer. Later in the film as she dresses for dinner, she sings that "love is only love"—not violins and fireworks but, rather, a silent awareness of the other person. Though she loved Horace, she wasn't "in love" with him; marrying him was only one part of a much larger scheme to bring herself back to life. She didn't so much need to *do* something about her loneliness as she needed to learn to *think* and *feel* differently about it ("No, it won't be like the first time," she sings as she imagines married life with Horace, but then she affirms that it doesn't need to be).

As a kid, I understood Dolly Levi's predicament. She was in a rut like me. The immediate answer to her problems was to break away and march down Fourteenth Street and sing about how she was going to "raise the roof and carry on" so that she wouldn't have to look back one day and regret all the things she didn't do with her life. In other words, "to be a fool among fools." For me, the solution was just the opposite: I *thought about* the way Dolly breaks away and marches triumphantly down Fourteenth Street, and I thought about it in detail. I became "a fool alone." Feeling cast out in the world, I chose my aloneness in return.

So it didn't matter, say, if I got dragged along to my sisters' high school field hockey games, as I so often did. Once I got bored with just standing there with my mom and watching the game (a game whose rules I neither understood nor cared about), I would drift off to the adjacent track to be, like Dolly, by myself. The track ran the perimeter of the football field and it was divided up into ten narrow lanes. Around and around the track I would walk, all the while imagining, instead of my blue pants and white sneakers, the long, purple dress Barbra Streisand wore when she sang "Before the Parade Passes By," billowing across the pavement; instead of chalk marks on the dirt, iron trolley tracks running stripes down the broad, cobblestoned street; instead of the bushes and trees and chain-link fences of suburban Pennsylvania, billboards, banners, signs, shops, restaurants, bars, apartment buildings with awnings at the windows, a church with its steeples impaling the sky, a train station swarming with people coming and going, horses and carriages rushing, rushing, and city sidewalks filled with people, all kinds of people; instead of the damp, heavy clouds of an October afternoon, the clear, unblocked sunshine of a day in June.

VI

One night in June of 1989, I saw Vito Russo at an ACT UP meeting and I decided to tell him how much I'd enjoyed his essay on Judy Garland in the first issue of *OutWeek* magazine ("The death of Judy Garland in London in the summer of 1969 coincided with the Stonewall Riots in Greenwich Village. It was also the year in which Mart Crowley's *The Boys in the Band* was brought to the big screen, making it the first Hollywood film in which all but one character was gay. These two events symbolically hammered the final nail into the coffin of gay self-hatred, as well as the pre-liberation world of star worship on a grand scale" ["Rebellion" 42]). Nervously—for here was a real live "star," the famous author of *The Celluloid Closet: Homosexuality in the Movies* (1981), which I'd read in graduate school the year before—I said, "Vito? Hi, my name is Patrick and I just wanted to tell you I really loved your piece on Judy Garland in *OutWeek*." And he said, "Oh, you did, thank you," and he turned away, and I rushed off, hoping I hadn't said something stupid.

The following fall at Yale University's third annual Lesbian and Gay Studies Conference, my best friend and then boyfriend Gary Lucek gave a talk entitled "Out on Vinyl: Readings Between the Grooves in Gay Male Pop Music." The thing that most excited me about his talk was its autobiographical aspect:

> My talk today is about culture and about gay men. About expression and transmission and engagement. About gay men talking to gay men—and to other people, like I'm doing right now.
> [. . .]
> But first, let's talk about me.
> I am twenty-eight years old and grew up in an upper-middle-class, Polish-Catholic nuclear family in suburban New Jersey. My parents had and still have a stereo console but have never much used it. The records they had when I was in grade school are pretty much the same ones they have today. They occasionally listened to polka music and my mom went through an Engelbert Humperdinck phase in the early seventies. Together we would watch *The Lawrence Welk Show* (my favorite performer was the token black tap dancer, Arthur Duncan) and even made a pilgrimage once to the Lawrence Welk Estate and Country Club outside San Diego. My older brother and sister shared a box of 45s which included hits by the Beatles, Leslie Gore, the Supremes, Bobbie Vinton, the Shangri-Las, the Dave Clark Five, and Herman's Hermits. Before I could read I associated the songs that I liked with the colors and patterns of the labels.
> I became a full-fledged pop music consumer in the mid-seventies. Already a postmodernist, my first 45 was "Rockin' Robin" by the Jackson Five, which my brother disparaged as "a remake" and hence not "original" and valid. My first album was either a Three Dog Night LP or *The Divine Miss M* by "Betty" Midler (I couldn't say "Bette" yet) which I bought because I loved her single "Do You Wanna Dance?"—another remake. In general, I remember feeling different for liking "black" music (my peers had a worse name for it) and also, God forbid, "disco" music. Liking disco music, I learned, was not an avenue toward popularity in my junior high school. The Rolling Stones, the Who, Paul McCartney and Wings, the

Grateful Dead, Traffic, the Kinks, Rush, Lynyrd Skynyrd, and Genesis were all bands that meant absolutely nothing to me. Indeed, by high school, my sister, her new husband, my brother (who had come out as gay by this time), and I were practicing "The Hustle" in the living room to the tunes of the "First Lady of Love," Donna Summer, Hamilton Bohannon, and Van McCoy. Other late-adolescent formative experiences included seeing Sylvester and Two Tons of Fun on *The Merv Griffin Show* and watching the Village People perform "In the Navy" on a Bob Hope special on board a U.S. naval battleship, two good examples of U.S. culture's propensity to let homosexuals get out of hand. But there I was, soaking it all up. When my friends all got practical things like typewriters or stereos upon graduation from high school in '79, my parents came through for me with the gift of two Donna Summer double-albums, *Bad Girls* and *Live and More*. What better calling card than eight sides of Donna to take with me to New York City, where I was enrolling at Columbia University in the fall of 1979?

I remember thinking during Gary's talk, *This is the kind of writing I want to do*. I could write an essay on Barbra Streisand that captures the pleasure I take in her work and that seeks to analyze her work, situating it in some larger context. I could explore what Barbra Streisand means to me as a gay man. I could try to explain why she appeals to other gay men as well. (Everything else about Gary's talk, however, was a disaster—it was way too long, no one could hear his soft voice beyond the first few rows, the slide projector wasn't working, the room was overheated, and when it was all over I just wanted to get out of there as quickly as possible and go back to our hotel and take a nap, which is what I did. This made Gary justifiably angry with me, and for at least the next year, whenever we would get into any kind of argument, invariably my bad behavior at Yale would come up: "Well, if it was so overwhelming for you, can you imagine how *I* was feeling? *I* was the one giving the talk, I was having to cut out all this important material from my talk because I was going overtime, and all you could think about, AS USUAL, were *your* feelings—how frustrated *you* were! Would you just listen to yourself? How self-centered can you get? It's really shocking to me how insensitive you can be sometimes, Patrick. If things had been reversed, I would have supported you. And if I hadn't, you would have been furious with me. I never would have heard the end of it from you. You at least could have come up to me afterward and told me, 'Hey, Gare, great talk in spite of the technical difficulties,' but you said nothing. You just left. How do you think that made me feel?")

A year later, I again saw Vito Russo at another ACT UP meeting, and this time, now in the midst of writing an early draft of the essay that has become this chapter, I asked him if we could get together or maybe just talk on the telephone at some point about Barbra, about divas, and just about things in general. He said sure, he'd love to, why don't you come over next week? In the meantime, he suggested, I should speak to Larry Kramer, who had recently been negotiating with Barbra in the hopes that she might direct a film version of his 1985 play about the founding of Gay Men's Health Crisis, *The Normal Heart*. Vito said that apparently Barbra had asked Larry, "Why do so many gay guys like me?" and they had had a conversation about it. So Vito gave me Larry's number, and that night I gave Larry a call.

He answered, sounding a little groggy. I figured I had caught him at a bad time. I introduced myself: "Hi, my name is Patrick Horrigan. Vito Russo suggested I call you because I'm writing an essay on Barbra Streisand and her relation to gay men for a course I'm taking in the graduate program at Columbia University, and he said that you—"

"Vito shouldn't have given you my number," he interrupted. "He knows better than that. What is this for?"

"I'm writing an essay about why gay men seem to like Barbra Streisand, and Vito told me that you and she had spoken—"

"Gay men don't like Barbra Streisand. Her fans are a bunch of straight kids out in California."

I wasn't sure at this point if I should just drop it or persist a little longer to find out if he might have something interesting to say. For all his hostility, it seemed like he might in fact talk to me—maybe this was just his usual way of getting warmed up.

"If this isn't a good time to talk, I could try you again some other time," I offered.

"Why are you writing this? What are you, a journalist?"

"No, I'm a graduate student in the English department at Columbia. It's for a course I'm taking on—"

"I can't believe Columbia gives you credit to write about Barbra Streisand. What a stupid subject to write on. Don't you have anything better to write about? Why don't you write about something important? You should be writing about AIDS. You know, there's a war going on—that's what you should be writing about."

I didn't know what to say.

"I don't want to talk to you anymore," he said and hung up.

When I arrived at Vito's apartment, the first thing I noticed was that the entire north wall was made of exposed brick, and the ceiling seemed very high, which made the otherwise tiny space feel like a large elevator or even an empty tower. All around the apartment there were photographs of Vito with this or that celebrity. I wanted to look carefully at each one of them but I also didn't want Vito to think I was interested in his celebrity status instead of in his ideas, so I just stole a glance here and there—wasn't that a picture of Vito and Elizabeth Taylor together?! And it was signed, too, probably by Liz herself, in the way that stars always sign things; you couldn't tell what it said, but there were a few little words at first, then a whole lot of swirls and curls and circles, which was probably supposed to be her name—probably "Elizabeth" for Vito, because he was a special friend, I imagined.

"Did you call Larry?" he asked.

"Yeah, but he wouldn't talk to me. I think I woke him up or something when I phoned."

"You might have. You never can tell with Larry. Was he mean as the devil?"

"Practically."

"Too bad. Sorry about that."

"It's okay . . . your apartment is really wonderful," I said. But Vito acted as if my being there was as natural and unremarkable to him as the huge, steel-framed poster on the wall—a few years old already—advertising a star-studded benefit concert for AIDS with all the stars' signatures scribbled like graffiti from top to bottom: "Liza Minnelli," "Mandy Patinkin," "David Cassidy" (David Cassidy?!), "Dionne Warwick," and what seemed to be dozens more.

Vito said he would show me a few film clips of *The Judy Garland Show* from October 1963 when Barbra was the guest star—one of Judy and Barbra singing a medley of duets ("After You've Gone," "By Myself," "Lover, Come Back to Me"), and then another of just Barbra singing "Bewitched, Bothered, and Bewildered." Vito said he'd never seen her perform more sensationally than this. I expected to disagree with him on that point. Unlike most people I know, I enjoy the late Streisand as much as, sometimes even more than, the early Streisand, partly because I didn't even discover Barbra Streisand until around 1972 when her "early" period was already over; I was only one month old when she appeared on *The Judy Garland Show,* and doesn't aesthetic judgment have an awful lot to do with who you are, when, and where, anyway? Meanwhile Vito was fiddling with the reel-to-reel projector, and after twenty minutes of taking it apart and putting it back together, it was clear the thing was broken. "I'm sorry babe, this is not my lucky day." He told me to come back next Saturday—the Saturday of Gay Pride weekend it turned out—and he'd have the projector all fixed and ready to go.

As I was heading for the door, "Oh wait!" he said, pulling out a large program from a concert Barbra gave in Philadelphia in 1966. Wow! I knew so little about those early concert years. He said the concert got rained out on the first night it was scheduled, but he and his friends—all of them young, starry-eyed gay men—went to her trailer and knocked on the door anyway, not thinking she'd answer but hoping just the same.

And lo and behold, she opened the door and came out.

"Hi everyone!" she said in a friendly, joking manner.

"We love you!" they all shouted.

"Oh thank you! Come back tomorrow night! Did they give you your money back?"

And they all laughed and said yes and that they would come back tomorrow.

"What a great audience you would have been. I'm sorry we couldn't do the show."

And then she said, "Well, I have to go now. Good-bye."

And with that she went back inside her trailer.

I handed the Streisand-concert program back to Vito, but he said, no, I could keep it. "You probably love her more than I do," he said. "You keep it and enjoy it."[4]

VII

Ever since I started loving Barbra Streisand when I saw her on TV in *Hello, Dolly!* my initial reaction to each new album she cuts or movie she makes has been to feel a little let down; she never quite lives up to my dream of how wonderful she might be. But disappointment has never been the end of the story with me and Barbra Streisand. After the initial letdown, I have always pretty much come around to seeing things her way. For example, my sister Karen had told me I wouldn't like *A Star Is Born,* and the shocking thing was, at first she was right. My friend James and I got his mother to drive us to the movie theater where it was playing, under the pretense that we were seeing something else. For some reason, we had no trouble getting in (a number of people assured me that they never check your age at an R-rated movie, unless it's something really rough like *The Exorcist,* but I had always been too afraid to find out), and anyway this time my need to see *A Star Is Born* outweighed my fear of being anything less than perfectly obedient. We arrived late, about twenty minutes into the film (I don't remember why—my punishment for being disobedient?), at the point where Barbra/Esther and Kris Kristofferson/John have already met and they're flying by helicopter to a concert he's giving at a huge outdoor stadium. I felt nervous during the entire film: Barbra had gone bad; so, apparently, had I; and the whole thing left me feeling guilty and dirty.

I could see why the film was rated R, and I wasn't happy about it at all. In one scene, John is pushing Esther out on stage against her will, and she calls him, underneath her breath, a "fucker," a word I'd never heard escape Barbra's lips before. And, even worse, when Esther visits John's mansion for the first time, they start having sex, and while straddling him on the floor, Esther takes off her belt and pulls her blouse up over her head. For a split second, I thought, you could see a few inches of the bottom curves of Barbra's bare breasts. I couldn't believe she would ever do such a thing! (This wasn't the first time Barbra had tried to update her image by playing "dirty." In *The Owl and the Pussycat* [1971], her first nonmusical film, she plays a foul-mouthed prostitute named Doris who goes around wearing an outfit with hands painted over the breasts and a little heart over her crotch. But I never got to see this movie when I was younger. When *The Owl and the Pussycat* premiered on TV, I had the very same fight with my mom that we had over *A Star Is Born*. Forbidden to watch it, I snuck down to the basement TV to see it in secret, but after a few minutes, my mom found me out and made me turn it off and come upstairs.)

Although my first reaction to the partial, fleeting sight of Barbra Streisand's naked breasts in *A Star Is Born* was a negative one, it wasn't long before I started having fantasies about making movies with Barbra in them in which she would show all of both breasts for a long time— in which she did "adult" things like stick her breasts through holes in a wall or where her male costar would accidentally find himself, say, sitting across a restaurant table from Barbra with her bare breasts flopping on the table, and then he'd be so distracted by them that he wouldn't be able to eat his food, and it would all be so funny that the audience would laugh and laugh, the way that I laughed so hard at the sight gags in *What's Up Doc?* Only the sight gags I was now imagining were for grown-ups only, they weren't for kids anymore.

More recently, I felt let down at first by Barbra's Thanksgiving 1997 interview on *The Rosie O'Donnell Show*. Rosie has always been outspoken about her love for Barbra Streisand, and so here was a fan's dream come true: an opportunity, finally, to talk to the star, to tell her how you feel about her, to ask her everything you've always wanted to know, to ask her the things that only a fan would think to ask (I might have asked: Can you name one of your least favorite movies or albums and explain why it's your least favorite? How would you describe the changes in your singing/acting style over the years? What do you think of the myth that gay men have a special affinity for you?). In almost every way, the interview seemed to me a wasted opportunity. Rosie talked too much:

> BARBRA: I wasn't frightened when I was twenty-one. I'm more frightened now. . .
> ROSIE: [*interrupting her*] Really?
> BARBRA: . . . to tell you the truth. Yeah, there's more to live up to now. You know, how do I fulfill your fantasy of me?
> ROSIE: Can I just say this? My fantasy of you is always rooted in truth. With your—with the statements that you make—the speech that you made at Harvard, and—you know, it's not just a kid impression—as I grew into be [*sic*] an adult woman—and your directing and all of those things—it's—it's reality-based, there's no illusion. It's you, you know, as a mom, and as—as—everything.
> BARBRA: Oh that's good.

She asked questions that led nowhere: "Can I just ask you, do you like snacking? 'Cause first of all you're so gorgeously fit. . . . What's your favorite snack? . . . Do you bake, like, cookies and stuff around the holidays?" And even when she asked a question that might have led Barbra to say something interesting ("Do you have a favorite movie of yours?"), she didn't pursue it far enough (when Barbra responded "*Funny Girl, The Way We Were, The Prince of Tides,*" rather than finding out *why* these are Barbra's favorites, Rosie hurried on to another question).

Barbra was inexplicably nervous; throughout the interview, she kept touching her hair and, even more bizarre, pushing down her sweater to reveal her bare shoulders. She also seemed unusually distant. When Rosie asked her, "Is there anyone when you were a kid that you felt this way about?" Barbra paused for a moment and then said, "I don't think so." The answer garnered a laugh from the audience, but that didn't make up for the evasiveness of the answer. (Barbra's adolescent response to movies and actors seems at least to have been more complicated than she let on in the interview; James Spada claims that "by the time she reached her early teens, Barbara began escaping her drab existence more often than just at the Saturday movies. She created her own fantasies at home, usually re-creating the roles she had just seen played out on the screen. 'I was a character in the movie,' she says. 'Not the actress, but the character. Not Vivien Leigh but Scarlett O'Hara. I loved being the most beautiful woman kissed by the beautiful man' " [*Barbra* 9].)

But then I thought some more about the Rosie O'Donnell interview. For one thing, Rosie's clumsy behavior began to seem entirely appropriate given her impossible predicament—having to confront the "reality"

of the star in all her limitations. Also, it must have been a peculiarly unreal experience for a fan like Rosie because, as Barbra says to her early
on in the interview, "You probably know more about me than I do about
me," and it appears, as Rosie listens to Barbra throughout the interview,
that she's heard everything before, that she's speaking to someone she
knows intimately, even though in some ways the opposite is true. I began
to feel touched instead of annoyed at the way Rosie blathered on and on
about herself, even to the point where she serenaded Barbra with her
own rendition of "People." She was nervous; what fan wouldn't put her
foot in her mouth under those circumstances? In a way, Rosie's performance was a stroke of genius: daring to make the star feel the presence
of the fan. There may even have been some anger in Rosie's behavior, as
if she were saying to Barbra, not so much "You have been very important to me, you saved my life" (early on in the interview, Rosie testifies,
"You were a constant source of light in an often-dark childhood, and
you inspired me and gave me the courage to dream of a life better than
the one I knew, and I am profoundly grateful to you in so many says"),
but rather, *You've stood in my way, and now I must be rid of you.*[5]

And I started to appreciate Barbra's aloofness and apparent insecu-
rity. According to Walter Matthau, Barbra's *Hello, Dolly!* costar, "the thing
about working with her was that you never knew what she was going to
do next and were afraid she'd do it. . . . I was appalled at every move
she made" (quote in Edwards 264). Despite his hostility, Matthau has
inadvertantly identified what makes Barbra Streisand such a thrilling
performer. One day she'll come out on stage and sing the roof off (as
she did during her 1994 concert tour), the next she'll act like she's forgotten how to sing (when receiving a Grammy Living Legends award in
February 1992, she sang the words "you'll never know how much I love
you" to the audience in an uncharacteristically breathy, almost Marilyn
Monroe voice—just that much and no more—as if she hadn't sung in a
decade). From one angle she looks gorgeous; from another, not great.
She'll make a spectacular directorial debut (in *Yentl*) and then follow it
up with weaker directorial efforts (*The Prince of Tides* [1991], *The Mirror
Has Two Faces* [1996]). Today, she'll say something smart: in a June 1992
speech she gave upon receiving the Dorothy Arzner Award for women
in film, she said,

> Language gives us insight into the way women are viewed in a male-
> dominated society. Take the entertainment business, for example, though
> I'm sure this would hold true for women in positions of power in any field.
>   A man is commanding—a woman is demanding.
>   A man is forceful—a woman is pushy.

A man is uncompromising—a woman is a ballbreaker.
A man is a perfectionist—a woman's a pain in the ass.
He's assertive—she's aggressive.
He strategizes—she manipulates.
. . . All this to say that, clearly, men and women are measured by a different yardstick and that makes me angry. Of course, I'm not supposed to be angry. A woman should be soft-spoken, agreeable, ladylike, understated. In other words, stifled . . . Come to think of it, a lot of things make me angry.

Tomorrow she'll sound like an airhead: in the liner notes to her rendition of Rodgers and Hammerstein's "Some Enchanted Evening" on her 1993 *Back to Broadway* album, she writes, " 'Some Enchanted Evening,' from the Pulitzer Prize winning show [*South Pacific*], was suggested by my A&R man, Jay Landers . . . and I thought '. . . ehh, I wasn't ever crazy about that song.' But David Foster took it home to see what he could do with it, and came up with a beautiful concept. Then Johnny Mandel did the most incredible orchestration, and I absolutely adore it now. 1993 marks the 50th Anniversary of Rodgers & Hammerstein's collaboration. They gave the musical theater some of its most enduring and heartfelt music" (ellipses in original). (Does she really believe that Rodgers' and Hammerstein's music is "enduring and heartfelt" when, in order for her to sing one of their most famous and, by most accounts, gorgeously operatic songs, she has to have it rewritten for her? And then, in what sense is "Some Enchanted Evening" "enduring" when, in her view, it must suffer such revision?) For these reasons, many Barbra Streisand fans feel abandoned by Barbra. They wish she were just like she was in the mid-sixties—a kooky beatnik, an upstart, a fresh interpreter of B-string standards. They wish she had never gone Hollywood (or at least, never stopped playing Fanny Brice once she got there), never gone frizzy-haired, never gone blond, never tried disco or folk, never bothered with classical, never taken herself so seriously as an actor and director and even, with her two rather self-important return-to-Broadway albums (*The Broadway Album* and *Back to Broadway*), as a singer.

But I'm fascinated by Barbra's unevenness, because in that unevenness there's a restlessness and an irreverence. Often, the irreverence takes the form of a disrespect for the past, including her own past. No doubt some of her revocalizations (her now-classic, slow rendition of "Happy Days Are Here Again") are more appealing than others (the Turkish-Armenian version of "People" on *Barbra Streisand and Other Musical Instruments* [1973]), but what stays constant in her work is the force of revision itself. Take the *Back to Broadway* album: she leaves no standard well enough alone; she turns duets into solos ("Move On" from *Sunday in the Park with George*), solos into duets ("The Music of the Night" from *The Phantom of the Opera,* sung as a duet with Michael Crawford), rewrites harmonies ("Some Enchanted Evening"), adds salsa to what was once simply up-tempo ("Luck Be a Lady" from *Guys and Dolls*), restores long-discarded verses and bridges ("Children Will Listen" from *Into the Woods*), creates medleys where there were none (she synthesizes "I Have a Love" and "One Hand, One Heart" from *West Side Story*), expands and contracts at will. She's acting here on some of the same impulses (call it "bad taste" if you must) that made her put a shoe in her hair at the Lion in 1960, that made her sing "nobody is gonna rain on my parade" against the melody, and that made her so entertainingly, refreshingly unconventional. In an article on Barbra's recent album of spiritual music, *Higher Ground* (1997), the *Village Voice* critic Simon Frith argues, correctly I think, that "as Streisand's voice swells one can hear the thought in it, her consideration of one sound rather than another. There's an intellectual arrogance in Streisand's music at its best, a contempt for too easy melodic indulgence" (87). After all, it's precisely this kind of "arrogance"—this tendency toward aberrant interpretation—that ultimately attracted me to Barbra's film version of *Hello, Dolly!,* which was so different in so many ways from the famous and beloved Broadway original.

And Barbra's sometimes crass self-ignorance about her complicated, upstart relation to the past can seem, I think, somehow life-affirming. In her 1986 "One Voice" concert, for example, she prefaces her spectacular rendering of "Over the Rainbow" (in which she sings "somewhere" as a seven-syllable word!) with this faux-offhand disclaimer: "Recently I've been doing some research for an album that I'm planning to do, and I came across what is one of the finest songs, I think, ever written. But I thought I couldn't sing it because it's identified with one of the greatest singers who ever lived. But the lyrics felt so right, so relevant tonight, that, what the hell, I decided to sing it." It's as if she's saying, Judy Garland's life and death were wonderful and horrible, but they weren't the end of the world. Not only is tomorrow another day, but so is today.

It's too easy—too easy for me, at least—to feel abandoned by Barbra Streisand. And too easy to abandon her in return. So I've learned how to keep on forgiving her, to keep coming back to her, to let her change her mind, let her slip, go fuzzy around the edges, and then come back like a locomotive. Fearing abandonment myself, I've refused to abandon Barbra Streisand. It's a good partnership.

The day after the release of *Just for the Record . . .* (1991), Barbra's four-disc, thirty-year recording retrospective, including a good deal of never-before-issued material, I was describing the CD set to my therapist. At first, I hesitated to bring it up. Why talk about Barbra Streisand now? I wondered. Don't I have more important things to worry about? (For example, problems with my Herman Melville professor—how we were always disagreeing, and how I was thrust into the role of devil's advocate although I was saying things that I believed, I wasn't just saying things to get him angry, and how it was clearly a contest of wills. I would go into the class with a lot of ambitious ideas and with the hope that this time it would be different, but it wouldn't be long before I felt utterly abused and reduced by his narrow agenda and his ability to fein ignorance and the way he forced people into silence and cut them off. And the thing he hated the most was whenever I would try to produce any kind of gay interpretation of the text—and I mean, come on, *Herman Melville!* Wasn't it staring him right in the face? But I worried that my participation wasn't encouraging other students to speak who may also have felt silenced by him for their own reasons and that I was, instead, just creating more and more animosity in the classroom. And then there were all the problems with my roommates—the drinking and fighting and all the mess they made whenever they would get into a fight, and how I hated to be in the middle of other people's arguments. And problems with Gary, who by this time had left New York and moved to San Diego and wasn't speaking to me because I had gotten furious with him the week before when he told me he had just tested negative for HIV, and how he'd said what a relief it was because he had been practicing unsafe sex and now he knew that everything was okay. And he said, "Why aren't you happy for me?" and I said, "Gary, what you're telling me is that you've been having unsafe sex. How can you expect me to be happy about that? Why don't you take better care of yourself? Do you want to be alive or don't you?" And what would my life be like, I wondered, if something should ever happen to Gary? How would I survive without my best friend? And all the problems with my family—my sister Suzanne was getting married, and why did I have to go to the wedding? Why must I be subjected to another heterosexual wedding? What would my family think of me when I told them that this time I wouldn't attend? Would this be the last straw? Would they cut me off forever, never speak to me again? Would Suzanne understand that it wasn't because I didn't care about her? It was hard for me to explain why I couldn't go to the wedding; all I knew was, I just can't do it, I can't go, I can't put myself through that.)

But *Just for the Record . . .* had been on my mind a lot since the day before, and there was something I wanted to say about it, I wasn't sure what—something I needed to feel. The best two things about it, I said, are the first and last cuts. The first is the earliest extant recording of Barbra's voice, made in 1955 when she was thirteen, where she sings

Figure 10. Mom and me, April 1966.

"You'll Never Know" to the accompaniment of a simple, plaintive piano. Then on the last cut, the fifty-year-old Barbra sings the same song as a duet with the recording of her thirteen-year-old self, now accompanied by a full, lush orchestra. I began to recite the words of the song: "You went away and my heart went with you. / I speak your name in my every prayer. / If there is some other way to prove that I love you. . ." I started to cry. ". . . I swear I don't know how." I wept now wholeheartedly and couldn't understand why. Except that my tears told me, there must be a reason. My therapist whispered consolingly, "Patrick . . . it sounds like a lovely duet . . . the voice breaks in a child that age . . . so there's a forgiveness in the duet . . . and granting the child her own voice at the same time . . . think of a bar mitzvah, where the child is thirteen, and he

Figure 11. Barbra Streisand and her nineteen-month-old son, Jason Gould, on the set of *Hello, Dolly!*, July 1968. (Reprinted by permission of UPI/Corbis-Bettmann)

becomes a member of the community for the first time . . . or the First Holy Communion rite, where it's as if the child is alone before God, and receives the host on his tongue . . . I remember when you told me not long ago how your mother once said to you that one of the happiest and most important and memorable days of her entire life was the day of her First Holy Communion, as important as the day she got married, and the times she gave birth to you and your sisters and brother . . ."

"You'll never know if you don't know now," the adult Barbra sings, holding, at last, her former, broken, bewildered, unknowing thirteen-year-old self close in her arms, collapsing the distance between them with the power and still-fresh innocence of her soaring, keening voice; "Darling, you'll never know if you don't know now . . ."

OUTTAKES II

The Carpenters (1969–1983)

"[Derek] Green [the managing director of the British branch of the Carpenters' record company, A&M], a song lover, admired [the Carpenters'] quality if not their bag. 'My God, Karen's *voice!* People have got to dislike *music* to dislike those Carpenters' records,' he says now. But back then, it was certainly uncool to like them. 'Record company staffs are young, and young people want to be hip. Those in the company who did like the music were very much in the closet' " (Coleman 96).

I had a crush on Karen Carpenter. I have an image of her in my head wearing a frilly white gown, her long brown hair done up in big curls (the kind my sisters used to wake up with after sleeping in curlers the night before a prom or a bridal shower), sitting next to her brother Richard, looking more like his girlfriend than his sister—although the "love" they emanated for each other reminded me of the love I felt for my siblings, or at least the love that we were supposed to feel for each other and that seemed to exist in family portraits. Karen and Richard Carpenter looked like they were sitting for a family portrait. It must have been a shot of them as they were being introduced as guests on a Bob Hope TV special or some other kind of variety show. When they performed, Karen sat at the drums, which was so unusual for a girl. There was a masculine quality in her occasionally low voice and her handsome face—something in her thick, dark eyebrows and wide mouth, the lines around her mouth and across her forehead, and the way her hair was often combed in bangs over her forehead as if she were a boy ("Recalling her childhood once she became a globe-trotting singer, Karen said: 'While Richard was listening to music in the basement, I was out playing baseball and football, and playing with my machine gun! I was very tomboyish, quite a character, I hear!'" [Coleman 37]). Her voice was enveloping and smooth and soothing, but with the slightest scratching sound every now and then, suggesting a twinge of pain, eating away at the edges. Meanwhile, Richard sat primly at his piano ("Developing their friendship, [Richard's collaborator John] Bettis was surprised to find that the staid appearance of Richard did not match his inner self. 'His sense of humor and wit, his outlook on life, his image, is the farthest thing from the way people perceive Richard,' Bettis says. He identified a strong streak of irreverence" [Coleman 61]).

"Talking to myself and feeling old. . . ." I used to listen to that song ("Rainy Days and Mondays") on my record player and feel guilty that Karen was singing about my life and how I had nothing to do much of the time and didn't have many friends—how could anyone have known so much about the way I felt inside? (". . . at the war's end [Karen and Richard's parents] Harold and Agnes made plans to buy their own house. The pleasant environment they chose would significantly shape the lives of the future Carpenter family. New space for solid, detached, large-roomed properties with twin lawns at the front, spacious garden at the rear, and a garage" [Coleman 34]—sounds like the house I grew up in.)

I wonder if one of the reasons I felt so close to Karen Carpenter was because I had a sister, Karen, who sometimes seemed kind of boyish and whom I was often paired with because I was closest in age to her out of all my siblings—even though most of the time we hated being with each other and drove each other crazy by teasing each other. We knew exactly how to get each other mad: all she had to do was call me a girl, and all I had to do was suggest that she wasn't girlish enough.

Mame (1974)

My mom took me to see the movie version of *Mame,* starring Lucille Ball, at the old Majestic Theater in the Mount Penn section of Reading, not far from where she grew up. We arrived about fifteen minutes late, just at the beginning of the scene where nine-year-old Patrick enters his Auntie Mame's bedroom the morning after she has thrown a big party for no reason in particular ("I know that this very minute has history in it—we're here!" she had sung the night before). He wakes her up out of a groggy, hung-over sleep, and they have a conversation about what life with Auntie Mame will be like (his parents are dead and Mame is his only living relative), what kind of school he will attend, and how, whenever he hears a word he doesn't understand (like "bastard"), he should write it down on a little pad of paper and every now and then Mame will go over it with him. Mame chides him for looking so dreary, all dressed in gray, as if he's just come from a funeral (he has), and she promises to make his life sunny again. She even asks him what he thinks about her and the circumstances he finds himself in, which was so exciting to me because I always loved it when my mom or some other adult would ask my opinion about something, as if I, too, were a real person: "Do you think it's so terrible coming to live with your Auntie Mame? Don't answer that. Your coming here is the best thing that ever happened to you. . . . We're going to make up for everything that you've missed. I'm gonna show you things you never dreamed existed!"[1] Then Mame launches into a song, "Open a New Window," that, if I hadn't already been completely won over by the characters and the situation, drew me deep into the heart of this musical about the liberation of a prim little boy through the vehicle of his gutsy, fun-loving, unmarried, unembarrassed aunt. Taking Patrick by the hand, Mame flings open the drapes (two sets of floor-to-ceiling drapes, actually), throws open the French doors, goes out onto the balcony, and proudly presents the glistening East River, the Fifty-ninth Street Bridge, and all of Queens, spread out before them, just waiting to be seen and tasted:

MAME: Look at that!
PATRICK: At what?
MAME: *At everything!*

In song, Mame urges Patrick to become "three-dimensional," "unconventional," and to thumb his nose at anyone who doesn't like it. (It wasn't all that different from what Dolly Levi says when Ermengarde is shocked to discover that Dolly has "acquaintances," as Ermengarde calls them, at the Harmonia Gardens Restaurant: "Not acquaintances, Ermengarde," Dolly assures her, "friends, dear friends from days gone by. My late husband, Ephraim Levi, believed in life, any place you could find it, wherever there were people, all kinds of people. And every Friday night—even when times were bad—every Friday night, like clockwork, down those stairs of the Harmonia Gardens we came, Ephraim and I. Not acquaintances, Ermengarde, friends"; in their different ways, both Dolly and Mame believed in the immense variety of life.) As Mame and Patrick sing "Open a New Window," they ride a pony down Beekman Place; visit the Natural History Museum; participate in a feminist rally in front of a courthouse (picketers' signs read MATERNAL WELFARE and CONTROL BIRTH); watch a Burlesque show; dress up as firemen, ride a fire engine (but just for fun—not to a real fire), and ring the fire engine bell; go parachuting; perch themselves on one of the rays of the Statue of Liberty's crown, dangling their feet high above New York Harbor (I knew that was fake); visit the "progressive" school in which Mame plans to enroll Patrick (where nudity is condoned and where the children run wild, pull each other's pants down, break things, play pranks on the mailman, and just basically raise hell); visit a Christian church; visit a Jewish synagogue; drink and dance at a nightclub; ride in the paddy wagon when they and all the other nightclub patrons get arrested; and file briskly into court where Mame is friends with the judge and everyone sings in triumphal chorus, "Open a new window every day!"

Because my mom and I were late in getting to the theater, we stayed to watch the beginning of the next showing (you could still do that at most theaters in the mid-seventies). I wanted to stay and watch the whole movie all over again. From then on, I had fantasies about making *Mame* bigger and better than it already was. I felt the film needed re-making because of the peculiar shape of its narrative. The first half is full of song and slapstick (like Lucy zooming around a department store wearing only one roller skate because she can't get it off), consisting mostly of Patrick's initiation into the frantic, colorful world of his aunt and of New York in the late twenties and early thirties. The second half, however, takes place years later when Patrick has graduated from col-lege and is dating a rich girl, Gloria Upson, whom Mame quickly takes a strong dislike to (by this time, too, Mame's new husband, Beauregard, has died tragically in a skiing accident). There is less singing and danc-ing in the second half of the film, and Mame seems lonelier and more depressed than she had earlier in the film. Finally, she sings the heavy, dramatic ballad "If He Walked into My Life," about how she made mis-takes in raising Patrick, whom she thinks has changed for the worse, become shallow and much less fun-loving than he was when he was a little boy. I was disturbed at the way everything turns sour in the sec-ond half of the movie, but at the same time, I liked it because it seemed true to life. I began more and more to like the idea of this musical com-edy turning into a murky, gut-wrenching drama, although I had a hard time coming to terms with the fact that the shape of the story, there-fore, had to be somewhat imperfect, and it seemed that one day I would be okay about it, and the next day I would be all upset by it and dis-satisfied and I'd want to rewrite it with a happier ending. (In fact, *Mame* does end happily, with Patrick marrying, finally, a much nicer, Irish girl, and with Mame taking their son Peter under her wing the way she had Patrick years before, but all of this is really a coda to what feels like a long, slow slide into depression, which is appropriate since the events of the second half of the film follow on the heels of the Great Depres-sion.) I experimented with combining elements of *Mame* with elements of *Hello, Dolly!*, a happier film, pairing Barbra and Lucy as friends, a combination, however, that only intermittently seemed to work, despite their commonalities. Basically, I was stuck with the hard truth that life often starts out happy and ends up depressing. Eventually, I came up with a solution whereby *Mame* would be considered one of the all-time great movies in Hollywood history (it surely wasn't in real life) largely because Lucille Ball's spellbinding performance (an Oscar winner, I de-cided) encompassed such a breathtaking range of emotions—from the heights of comic exuberance to way down deep in the shadowy valley of tears. Critics would agree that this was an unusual feat for a musical-comedy actress, but after all this was the 1970s and the Hollywood musi-cal had come a long way since its heyday at MGM, and so it was time to inject some hard-core seriousness into what had always seemed more or less a light, utopian, simple-minded genre. (That same year I had seen *That's Entertainment,* a documentary about the history of MGM musicals, with my mom and Aunt Pauline at a movie theater on the boardwalk in Ocean City, New Jersey, so I knew a little about where the Hollywood musical had come from and where it seemed to be going.) The way I came to terms with *Mame* and all that had happened to the Hollywood musical by the 1970s was so different, for example, from Ted Sennett's snobbish, patronizing, typically dismissive attitude; in *Hollywood Musicals,* a book I got for Christmas in 1981, he argues, "Misguidedly cast as the irrepressible, indestructible lady of print, stage, and screen, Ball worked gamely, handling the slapstick portions with ease and croaking out the merely average songs. But she was not an actress who could carry a musical comedy on her shoulders, and her performance mostly conveyed a sense of desperation rather than high spirits" (348).

3

The Wreck of the Family

At midnight on New Year's Eve,
the S.S. POSEIDON, en route
from New York to Athens, met
with disaster and was lost.
There were only a handful
of survivors.
This is their story . . .[1]

I

The second time I saw *The Poseidon Adventure*, I was so frightened after the first half hour that I had to call my parents from a pay phone in the lobby of the movie theater and ask them to please come get me and take me home.

In the film, a luxury ocean liner gets hit by a giant tidal wave and turns upside down; ten people climb their way up through the hull in a desperate attempt at escape. Of those ten, only six survive.

I had seen the film for the *first* time without any serious problems several weeks before (this was in 1972; I was nine), and though shaken, I had emerged all in one piece from the darkness of the movie theater into the dreary light of a Sunday afternoon in December, with my fourteen-year-old sister, Suzanne—much like the handful of exhausted survivors in the film when, after hours of tortuous climbing, crawling, and swimming, they are lifted out of the capsized wreck of the *Poseidon* into the blinding, anomie-inducing light of day. That night I couldn't sleep for visions of tidal waves and windows shattering; for a day or two after, the sound of a toilet flushing made me dash out of the bathroom

106

for fear that something was chasing me or that somehow I'd get sucked down into the hole. But it was my first PG film, and I had survived it.

The second time around, however, *The Poseidon Adventure* was a different story. I knew as soon as the lights went down in the movie theater that I had made a big mistake. I trembled at the sight of the ship unknowingly, inexorably making its way through the rough ocean waters. The names of the actors, as they spanned the screen one after another, seemed like the roll call of the dead: GENE HACKMAN, ERNEST BORGNINE, RED BUTTONS, CAROL LYNLEY, RODDY McDOWALL, STELLA STEVENS, SHELLEY WINTERS, and on and on. As each character was introduced during the first half hour of the film, before disaster would strike, I hated to think of what lay in store for them; and yet I had no choice. Now I knew everything, and the knowledge was unbearable. I knew how Reverend Scott (Gene Hackman) would take it upon himself to lead a handful of passengers through the twisted wreckage of the capsized ship but would die at the last minute before the final escape. I knew how teenage Susan (Pamela Sue Martin) would develop a crush on Reverend Scott and then have to live the rest of her life with the memory of his horrible death, which happened right before her eyes. I knew that Mrs. Rosen (Shelley Winters) would reluctantly join Reverend Scott's band of adventurers, lighten the atmosphere with her warm sense of humor (while climbing the Christmas tree as a means of escape from the dining saloon, she quips, "Mrs. Peter Pan I'm not!", and everyone in the audience laughed, grateful for a moment's relief from the terrible suspense), but in the end suffer a heart attack and die. I knew that for all his fastidious health consciousness, the middle-aged bachelor and haberdasher, Mr. Martin (Red Buttons), would have to roll up his sleeves and use his muscle and act like a man if he intended to save his life (at New Year's Eve dinner, he explains to his dinner companions the Rosens, "I'd like to be married . . . I just can't seem to find the time. I mean, I get down at the shop at eight, I open at nine, I close at seven, and I go home at eight. Except on Wednesdays and Fridays, and I go home at ten"—none of which would amount to a hill of beans when the ship turned over). I knew that, despite the way Mike Rogo (Ernest Borgnine), the cop, and his wife, Linda (Stella Stevens), the former prostitute, liked to argue, they really cared for each other, and so when Linda suddenly gets thrown off a catwalk into a pool of fire and dies, Mike is devastated and momentarily blames Reverend Scott, as if Reverend Scott's insistence that people keep moving and try to save themselves, that they not look back and dwell on the dead, could in fact be interpreted as cruel and insensitive. I *liked* Linda Rogo! I *liked* Mrs. Rosen! I didn't want them to die!

Figure 12. Robin and Susan Shelby (Eric Shea and Pamela Sue Martin) in *The Poseidon Adventure.*

And not only did I like all of these characters; I could identify with nearly every one of them at some point during the film. For example, I was the precocious preadolescent boy, Robin Shelby (Eric Shea), when he feels both ignored and infantilized by his older sister, Susan (fig. 12):

ROBIN: [*reading a book*] Hey, did you know this? The engines on this ship have more total horsepower than all the cavalry Napoleon used to conquer Europe. How 'bout that?

SUSAN: [*looking at herself in her mirror while combing her hair; bored*] That's heavy, Robin. Real heavy.

[*A knock is heard at the door.*]

ROBIN: The ship's generators create enough electricity to light Charleston, South Carolina and Atlanta, Georgia.

STEWARD: [*enters with a telegram*] Shelby?

SUSAN: That's right.

STEWARD: Cable.

SUSAN: Thank you.

ROBIN: Hey, it's my turn to open the cable!

SUSAN: Don't be so childish. "Mother and I waiting impatiently your arrival. Our thoughts and our love are with you on this New Year's Eve. Dad."

ROBIN: We should have sent them a wire.

SUSAN: I did.

ROBIN: [*jumps up and down on the bed*] Then how come you didn't ask me for my ideas?! I mean what to put in it!

SUSAN: Why couldn't I have had a brother that's a little easier to live with? Stop jumping up and down on my bed and go take a shower.

ROBIN: What shower?! I'm going to the engine room.

SUSAN: You're going to church service.

ROBIN: On my vacation?

SUSAN: Will you get in that bathroom?

ROBIN: The third engineer promised to show me the propeller shaft.

SUSAN: You can see the propeller shaft later.

ROBIN: Why don't you just shove it!

SUSAN: Don't you ever say that to me again!

ROBIN: Shove it! Shove it! Shove it!

Like Susan and Robin, whose always-simmering antagonism toward each other boils over at the prospect of parental dispensation (here, the telegram bestowing affection and good wishes), my siblings and I were always vying with each other in different combinations for my parents' attention. We fought a lot (fig. 13). But my brother and sisters' motto was, "whenever there's a fight in the house, it's always between Patrick and somebody else"; they thought that only *I* was spoiled, that only *I* wanted attention. They needed me to play a predictable role in family squabbles (as in different ways each of them did), so I became known as "the Screamer." And my brother, John, repeatedly told me, "if my friends' younger brothers mouthed off to them the way you mouth off to me, they would kick their teeth in!" Susan Shelby could never threaten Robin with physical violence the way John threatened me, but I found her scoldings all too familiar.

At the same time, I identified with Susan when she scolded Robin. I spent hours, like Susan, staring at myself in the mirror, pretending I was an actress, wrapping my head in a towel to make me look more like a girl with long hair, like my sister Suzanne, or like a nun; I resented my effemininity and hated the masculine entitlement other men and boys seemed to flaunt at my expense. Smart-mouthed boys like Robin were always making my life (like Susan's) miserable: they said vulgar and insulting things ("you faggot!") and were completely insensitive to their power to hurt me. I sought revenge in being an excellent student, and I comforted myself by playing the piano with aching sensitivity. But in the tough world of boys and masculinity, those things counted for almost

Figure 13. My sister Karen and me, September 1970.

nothing. Likewise, with no apparent interests of her own (or no interests that counted as worth representing in the film), and with no occupation other than her prescribed familial role as "the older sister," Susan had every reason to be furious with Robin, who at the very least got to read interesting books (the brochure describing the ship) and enjoyed a degree of mobility (he bounces rambunctiously on the bed and has an invitation to go sight-seeing in the engine room). Susan's verbal abuse of Robin ("Don't be so childish"; "Why couldn't I have had a brother that's a little easier to live with?") and her power to thwart his desires ("You can see the propeller shaft later!") are only the signs of her own more profound *dis*empowerment by the familial, social, and cinematic regimes that reduce her full humanity to an abject stereotype of sexual vulnerability (Robin says to her, "Why don't you just shove it?") and banish her to her mirror, narcissistically combing her hair, thinking nothing.

And I was Acres (Roddy McDowall), the young waiter, staring half-absently at Nonnie (Carol Lynley), the singer, and her band as they rehearse one of their numbers, "The Morning After":

> NONNIE: [*sings; looks lovingly at the guitarist, her brother*] "There's got to be a morning after. . ."
> WAITER: [*looking askance at Acres as he, Acres, looks at Nonnie and her band*] Where'd that lot come from?
> ACRES: They boarded at Gibraltar. They're on their way to Sicily—a free trip for free music. They're going to a jazz festival.
> WAITER: [*in a mocking, singsong tone of voice*] "Morning after"—oh, I can't take this stuff. Give me a Strauss waltz anytime.
> ACRES: I rather fancy it.
> WAITER: You? You'd even fancy bagpipes.

Like Acres, I could be mesmerized for hours listening to my Barbra Streisand records (which, to certain of my siblings, might as well have been bagpipes). Unconsciously, I understood that when Acres looked at Nonnie, he wasn't feeling the conventional kind of love for her; his wasn't the classic cinematic male gaze. He was probably thinking about himself—some boy he was in love with; he may even have *identified with* Nonnie as she sang sweetly and ruffled her brother's long, pretty, brown hair.

I definitely had a strong identification with Nonnie. She frightened me perhaps most of all the characters. She seemed the least equipped to handle catastrophe, to face the future; all she had, it seemed, was her brother, and now he was gone. She was always ready to retreat, to stay back and let the others go on ahead. I could feel all of her fragility and incomprehension, later in the film, when she is reminded that her brother, Teddy, is dead, while she must remain among the living:

> NONNIE: My brother, Teddy, has lovely hair. He's really dead, isn't he? [*she lies down, cuddling herself*] I can't go on without him. I can't.
> MR. MARTIN: Nonnie, you will go on. We do, you know. We have to. At first we don't think it's possible, but in time—believe me, in time, you'll find other things—other people—someone else to care for you, you'll see.

Despite Mr. Martin's kind assurances, the thought of living without *my* parents and siblings terrified me and made me, like Nonnie, whose name meant, essentially, "nothing," want to curl up like a baby and stay that way forever.

It's true, despite my strong feelings for all the characters, I craved to see again the tumultuous spectacle of the ship's rolling over, the tidal wave engulfing everything, sending cups, plates, forks, champagne bottles, tables, chairs, pianos, and bodies flying through the air. But there were other things I just couldn't face again—like the hideous corpse sitting upright in the ship's galley with his face charred and blood-covered, the hair half burned off of his head, his eyes ghoulishly open; poor Susan Shelby wept at the mere sight of it! The second time I saw *The Poseidon Adventure,* I knew that every minute I spent with the characters would only mean one minute closer to the hour of their darkest night. Everything they said and did, every meaningless gesture, every trite comment, every careless expression of affection or disdain, now radiated within the shadow of their final fate. No longer could I live life never thinking of tomorrow. (My mom always said you should never go to bed angry with someone because you could wake up the next morning and they could be gone.) It was bad enough to love someone and never to know, Will they be alive tomorrow? Bad enough to wonder, Will I live to see my sixteenth birthday? Will I be married someday? Will I ever have children? Will I live in a nice house? What will I do with the rest of my life? Will I be happy? Oh God, will I die a painless death? Please let it be painless. Let me die in my sleep, let me *not* die from fire or ice. But if I have to choose between the two, which will I choose? It's such an awful choice. I would choose freezing to death over burning to death. All of this was bad enough, but it was altogether worse to have to live your life in the full awareness of everything that was to come. *The Poseidon Adventure,* at that point, became unbearable.

Once the ship turned over, I knew I had to get out. As I rose from my seat in the dark and walked up the inclined aisle of the movie theater toward the doors at the back—the doors with round porthole windows like the windows in the cabins of the SS *Poseidon!*—as I rushed (but not so quickly and nervously as to conjure up in my mind the ghost of that corpse from the horrific galley scene pursuing me) to the pay phones to call home and ask to be rescued, I felt as if I were walking the slanted decks of the *Poseidon,* as though the floor were moving beneath me. I thought the floor was actually tilting—tipping—up!—making my escape more difficult!—as I struggled to get out through the back doors.

The incident, however, only increased my fascination with *The Poseidon Adventure.* Yet rather than attempting to see the film a third time, I confined myself to meditating upon the movie poster, which, because the movie was showing at our local mall, was easily accessible to me. The image on the poster helped me reexperience in my head what I'd seen on the screen: "HELL, UPSIDE DOWN" the poster bellowed in all-capital letters! The picture is less a scene from the film than a fantastic composite of several different scenes synthesized into one mind-blowing image (fig. 14). We see the grand ballroom of the capsized *Poseidon* full of terrified passengers running hysterically in every direction because the sea has just exploded like a bomb through the back wall of the room (in the film itself, it comes gushing through a floor-to-ceiling smoked-glass window, but the poster makes everything look more pumped up and fast paced). A powerful, sharply delineated starburst of white water hurls people through the air, some of them rear-end first, toward the viewer, while in the foreground Gene Hackman, Ernest Borgnine, and Stella Stevens struggle to run clear of it. Behind them, Red Buttons appears to be reaching down to help Shelley Winters to her feet, Eric Shea and Pamela Sue Martin emerge from the wreckage of dead bodies and overturned tables, Carol Lynley frantically reaches out her arm as if to grab hold of something steady, and Byron Webster (who plays the ship's purser) and an unidentifiable actor cry out in pain. On the ceiling, people hang and in some cases fall from tables that, when the ship was right side up, had been bolted to the floor.

I was particularly intrigued by this picture because it gave you some sense of the lavish architecture of the ballroom, which I was always trying to resurrect in my mind. The main attractions of the room, of course, were the huge, art nouveau, oval-shaped, stained-glass windows in the ceiling. I say "of course" because it was impossible to forget the scene when, during the capsizing of the ship, some poor son of a bitch crashes through one of these windows, flat on his back, causing an electrical shortage. But I'd either forgotten or just never realized from seeing the film that (as the poster image revealed) the ballroom was divided like a cathedral by rows of widely spaced pillars into three airy sections, one larger central space with two narrower spaces, one on each side of it. Also, the picture suggested that both the floor and ceiling were carved up by interesting level changes (this reminded me of the complicated interior design of the Harmonia Gardens Restaurant).

On the one hand, *The Poseidon Adventure* satisfied my appetite for images of carnage, destruction, and familial and social disarray. On the other, it dwelled on the scenes of individual and collective reconstruction that follow and redeem those moments of calamity. For example, in June of 1972, Hurricane Agnes blew into Reading and flooded our basement with six inches of water. Whatever my parents felt, I was only too happy to see the red shag carpet completely ruined, to help move the furniture, to throw out the stacks of books sopping wet, and to spend two

Figure 14. Poster for *The Poseidon Adventure*.

114

Figure 15. (*Clockwise from left*) John, Mary Jo, Suzanne, Patrick, Betsy, and Karen, fall 1972.

whole days with all of my siblings taking turns sweeping out the water and repairing the damage. Not only could I experience the thrill of seeing Home and Family disarranged, but I could reinsert myself into those structures in a new, nonstereotypic way that made me feel, for a change, needed and equal, not impertinent and a failure (fig. 15).

Likewise in *The Poseidon Adventure*, disaster united and gave purpose to an otherwise fragmented group of people (fig. 16). The passengers, who

Figure 16. In *The Poseidon Adventure,* the survivors watch Reverend Scott and Acres enter the fiery ship's galley: Linda Rogo (Stella Stevens), Mike Rogo (Ernest Borgnine), Manny Rosen (Jack Albertson), Belle Rosen (Shelley Winters), James Martin (Red Buttons), Robin Shelby (Eric Shea), Nonnie Parry (Carol Lynley), and Susan Shelby (Pamela Sue Martin). (Reprinted by permission of the Museum of Modern Art)

just prior to the moment of catastrophe were heedlessly ringing in the new year in the ship's grand, three-story-high dining room, now quarrel bitterly over whether they should wait to be rescued from the outside or whether they should try to save themselves. Reverend Scott insists on the latter: they must climb upward through the overturned ship toward the portion of the hull that, young Robin assures him, is only six inches thick. But the door that leads from the dining room to the galley, and hence farther into the hull, is now three flights above them on the "floor" of the dining room. To reach it, they must upend the huge, steel Christmas tree, which had fallen soon after the ship's capsizing, and climb its green branches. Like Jesus dragging his cross to Calvary, Reverend Scott lifts the heavy trunk of the tree and, with the concerted help of several other men, carries it forward. The surrounding, awe-struck assemblage of passengers parts, like the waters of the Red Sea, as Reverend Scott and company shoulder the tree through their midst and, mustering all their strength, slowly and precariously raise it once more.

The sequence is unforgettable for several reasons. First, references to the New and Old Testaments commingle here (as elsewhere) and saturate the film's text; this too obviously overdetermined Biblical allusiveness gives the sheer impression of significance, whatever specific interpretation we might proffer. We are made to feel, these scenes *must* mean *something!* Second, its heroism is endorsed by the film's swelling, Wagnerian score. Third, our bird's-eye view gives us the full benefit of its gargantuan physicality and irresistible suspense. Fourth, and most importantly, we witness, as in every other disaster film of the 1970s beginning with *Airport* but in few Hollywood films since, the dramatic interconnectedness of an entire society of ordinary people (or its synecdochic equivalent) as it responds to a crisis.[2]

Once the tree is in place, Reverend Scott nominates Robin, the smallest and most fleet-footed of the passengers, to be the first to climb the tree. When Robin reaches the top, he shouts triumphantly, flush with the pride of having made a significant contribution to the collective survival, "It's a cinch!"

Around this same time, my two-year-old cousin Rebecca was ill with spinal meningitis. I secretly hoped that she would die, since that would surely create the kind of excitement around the house I'd come to associate with *The Poseidon Adventure;* and I was relieved when she did. (Whenever I'd be up in a room by myself, I would bend over and look at it upside down and try to imagine what it would look like with all the furniture falling down onto the ceiling; this was fun, but it wasn't as thrilling as having *real* problems!) And when my Uncle Tom died unexpectedly, my Aunt Peggy packed up her five kids and flew down from Boston to our house for Christmas that year. It was the most chaotic holiday I'd ever experienced. My parents were so busy consoling and accommodating people that they didn't even have time to wrap our presents.

The Poseidon Adventure was like that—innocent people got killed, holidays turned into funerals, heterosexual couples got torn apart. But then new alliances formed (Mr. Martin promises Nonnie he isn't going anywhere without her), and the death of one ensured the life of someone else (though she hasn't swum in years and is too fat to risk trying now, Belle Rosen heroically saves Reverend Scott from drowning, only to suffer a fatal heart attack herself from the strain of doing so—Mrs. Rosen it was who "cried for a week when they tore down the Third Avenue El," as her husband Manny reminds her near the beginning of the film, and somehow she was like that gloriously rickety late-nineteenth-century dinosaur: charming, inefficient, neighborly. And when the El had finally been torn down, the *New York Times* headline read, "Third

Avenue Blossoms As El Disappears" [Stetler 116]). As a preadolescent spectator of the film and participant in the real-life catastrophes that befell my family, I was free to explore what seemed an unusually wide range of identifications, just as, within the film, catastrophe makes people free to discover capacities within themselves that were, until then, unimaginable.[3]

Despite her debilitating grief over the death of her husband and the strain it inevitably put on our relationship, my Aunt Peggy and I did share one euphoric moment when, having finally managed, after several failed and increasingly comical attempts, to light the fuse on the miniature rocket I got for Christmas, together we raced frantically across the snow-covered lawn, away from the rocket's threatening blast, laughing triumphantly, hysterically, tears coming to our eyes, as the rocket shot with a loud *whoooooosh!* into the cold white sky.

II

When my mother brought me home from the movie theater after my second, aborted viewing of *The Poseidon Adventure,* she asked me worriedly, "What's the matter?"

She had a way of asking "what's the matter" that let you know (or so it seemed to me) that she was asking mainly because she was forced to ask because of the drama of your tears or because of your towering silence. She preferred not to know, it seemed, the answer to the question, but hoped that the whole thing would be quick and painless and something she could smooth over with a few words about how "we all feel those things once in a while and it's really nothing to get all bent out of shape about." Apart from her general aversion to the apparently unquietable turmoil of my inner life, my mother *did* have good reasons for being suspicious about my emotional involvement with this film. Besides wishing I hadn't gone to see it a second time, she was confused by my attraction to *The Poseidon Adventure* because she knew that my grand passion during these years was musical comedy—to the exclusion, it seemed, of everything else.

My five favorite films in 1973 were (1) *The Sound of Music;* (2) *Hello, Dolly!;* (3) *Funny Girl;* (4) *My Fair Lady;* (5) *The Wizard of Oz.* I kept a running list (secret of course) that could be modified only with great fanfare and difficulty; I *was* open to the possibility that a new film could conceivably come along and disturb the ranking, although it certainly would have to be a very special film, as, for example, *Mame,* in 1974, turned out to be. In that year, *Mame* displaced *My Fair Lady* for the number 4 spot, putting *My Fair Lady* at the still-respectable number 5 (anyway, there was something about Audrey Hepburn as Eliza Doolittle that turned me off—I didn't like her voice, which was dubbed, and her body was too much like a boy's, or so my mother always said, although that was one of the things she loved about Audrey Hepburn). I decided that by then I had really outgrown *The Wizard of Oz* (or at least I was asked so often by my parents and siblings "Aren't you sick of that movie *yet?!*" that I used my mature age—eleven—as an excuse for demoting it), so I put it at number 10, a kind of "honorable mention." The next year things got even more complicated with the release of *Funny Lady*, and the year after that I saw *Cabaret* for the first time on TV—two films whose eligibility for one of the top five spots had to be given deep consideration. Actually, *The Sound of Music* and *Hello, Dolly!* were, barring catastrophe, untouchable in the number 1 and number 2 positions (but what kind of catastrophe could ever be so mind-altering?), so all we were really talking about here were the number 3, 4, and 5 spots. Not incidentally, I was so moved by *The Poseidon Adventure* that it eventually became the one and only nonmusical film in my top-ten count. I was a builder of canons.

This was also not the first time my parents had to come rescue me from a situation that was making me unhappy, and it wouldn't be the last. I was always a very homesick child. One of the reasons I refused to go to summer camp—apart from my dislike of the outdoors and my fear of being cooped up for any length of time with a bunch of boys—was that I hated the thought of being away from home. About a year before I saw *The Poseidon Adventure,* I went to visit Aunt Peggy and her family up in Boston. I think we all thought this was a good idea because I liked to play with my cousin John, who was a couple of years younger than me, I liked Aunt Peggy, I liked their house and their toys, and it would just be for a long weekend. But no. After the first day and night, I'd had all I could take. I imagined everyone in my aunt's house was mad at me. I saw unfriendly looks in people's eyes. I heard unkind words being said to me. When Aunt Peggy said "no" (it might have been, "No, you can't eat those cookies now, we're having dinner in fifteen minutes"), the world came crashing down around me. I missed my toys and I missed my parents and my brother and sisters and I wanted to go home. So Mom and Dad made arrangements to fly me home two days earlier than planned.

And again: In the early summer of 1985, just after I graduated college, I went to Oxford for a six-week summer school program to study modern British fiction. I decided to spend a month prior to the beginning of classes in London, where I had spent my junior year of college. I got a room in my old dormitory and tried to spend my days reading, visiting museums, and my nights going to the theater. It was a disaster. I didn't know anyone anymore at the college, and the one or two faces that looked familiar seemed strangely off-putting instead of inviting. I've never been the type to strike up a conversation with strangers, so I felt adrift. To make everything worse, I was haunted by memories of my friend Ludwell, the boy I had an unrequited crush on all during my junior year in London: here we lay on the grass that unseasonably warm day in March, while our friends threw a Frisbee and Ludwell and I listened to Glenn Gould playing Bach's Goldberg Variations on my roommate Al's boombox; there, across the path, I watched Ludwell talking and laughing with Ian, and I felt jealous, certain there was something going on between the two of them. I couldn't stand being here again and reliving the whole cycle of hope and dejection day after day. So after three days in London, I called my parents and asked them to bring me home—I would still go to summer school in Oxford in three weeks, but in the meantime I would stay at home with my parents in a place that felt safe and far, far away from my feelings about Ludwell. Bewildered (for I couldn't tell them the real reason I needed to leave London now), weary from trying to understand my emotional ups and downs, they said, yes, of course, if it's what you want. We want you to do whatever will make you happy.

"So, what happened?" my mother asked when she picked me up from the movie theater. "Was it something Tommy did?"

I had gone to see *The Poseidon Adventure* this second time with a younger boy, Tommy Wagner, who was about seven or eight, and some of his friends and siblings. Probably my mother and I were *both* embarrassed (I know *I* was) that only I, among the oldest of the group, and a boy, had to be taken home in the middle of the film. But we couldn't openly acknowledge that to each other. One source of constant tension between my parents and I all during my childhood years was the kinds of people I chose for friends and their presumed effect on my gender socialization. Either I played with girls, which meant that I was growing up to be more like a girl than like a boy; or with cousins, which seemed like incest; or with younger boys, which, I take it, smacked of pederasty—though my parents' persistent wish that I find a boy of my *own* age and with *like* interests to play with now seems as homophilic as any desire I might have been nursing for little Tommy. I think the ideal boy for me, as far as my parents were concerned, would have been someone like Robin Shelby in *The Poseidon Adventure:* normal, boyish, about my own age, maybe not so athletic, a little nerdy perhaps, but *normal* (and only once in the film—when Reverend Scott dies—does he cry). So Tommy Wagner fell into the third category of friends I had that were unacceptable—he was too young for me.

When my mother asked me what was wrong, why I couldn't watch *The Poseidon Adventure* straight through, I began to cry. They were crocodile tears—or at least I *thought* they were, because I had learned to think of my own feelings as fake. Tommy *did* have something to do with my re-action to the film. He wasn't paying much attention to me that night, for one thing, what with the excitement of the film and the other friends who came along. And then there was his sister, Julie, who was my age or a year younger at the most—Julie, who my siblings sometimes liked to pretend I had a crush on: "Patrick, I saw Julie Wagner today!" And they would drag out the syllables of her name to suggest that I liked her. But I couldn't talk to my mom about my mixed feelings for Tommy and Julie.

Nor could I have explained then, though it seems plausible now, that I was having a hard time articulating my response to the film because the film itself permits virtually no catharsis and, therefore, encourages little self-reflection: no sooner do the six survivors exit through the ship's hull and board the rescue helicopter awaiting them, than the film abruptly cuts to the final credits, seen against a flat, blue background; we get no detached outsider's view of the upside down ship, no good taste of the characters' deliverance, and no vision of what their relation-ships with each other might consist of now that they're free, all safely huddled together in that helicopter bound for—we never know where.

My tears probably confirmed my mother's suspicion all along that *The Poseidon Adventure* would be too intense for me. I already had a history of being traumatized by scary TV shows. There was an episode of *Dark Shadows* that gave me nightmares for months afterward in which a veil was torn from a woman's face only to reveal the hideousness and bloody distortion underneath. And there was a similar episode of *Mannix* called "The Deadly Madonna" in which a grotesque face would be seen sud-denly peering into someone's living room window and the poor unsus-pecting person inside would see the face at the window and scream! Sometimes even the merest *preview* for a TV program sent me into hys-terics. One late night my mom and I were quietly watching TV when a preview for an upcoming broadcast of *Dorian Gray* came on, a 1970 film version of Oscar Wilde's notorious 1890 novel, *The Picture of Dorian Gray*. I remember my mother groaning, "Oh *that* thing" not five seconds into the preview. (What did my mother know of *Dorian Gray*?[4]) I was strangely, instantly drawn into the scene in which a handsome young man stares at his likeness in a painting and ponders, half absently, "How sad it is! I shall grow old, and horrible, and dreadful. But this picture will remain always young. It will never be older than this particular day of June. . . . If it were only the other way! If it were I who was to be always young, and the picture that was to grow old! For that—for that—I would give everything! Yes, there is nothing in the whole world I would not give! I would give my soul for that!" (Wilde 26) If anything, the dismissive tone of my mother's voice ("Oh *that* thing . . .") gave me a false sense of security in watching the commercial. For I knew that tone of voice well. It was the tone my parents used in order to pooh-pooh anything they didn't approve of—it might be a risqué sitcom like *Love American Style* or *Maude* (they had a fit over the episode where Maude gets an abortion), or an adults-only variety show like *Saturday Night Live* or *Monty Python's Flying Circus.* They would say things like, "You kids may want to watch this, you may even think it's entertaining, but we don't want that kind of crap on in our house. You'll either watch something else that's more suitable or you won't watch anything at all, is that clear?" My siblings and I used to joke that my parents could find something objectionable in *The Waltons* if they wanted to.

But their "tsk tsk" was sometimes hard to read. For example, they regularly groaned and sucked their teeth over the nightly news, but they weren't simply disturbed by what was happening in Philadelphia (corruption in city government, a public transit strike) or around the country (Watergate, the Patty Hearst kidnapping, campaigns for the Equal Rights Amendment); they also seemed to disapprove of the fact that those things were being talked about on TV in the first place. And yet that never stopped them from watching Action News on channel six every night.

When my mother muttered "Oh *that* thing" as the preview for *Dorian Gray* came on, if anything I thought, "oh, I'm probably gonna *like* this! This is probably gonna be for *me!* Oh yeah, look at that pretty boy and that pretty painting and the pretty room with all the old furniture and the purple drapes with the thick chords holding them in place and the chandelier—wow, it's really great!" But when the announcer continued, "while day by day the portrait grows more and more hideous as his vices become more and more unspeakable," and then the image of the horrible, oozing, ragged face flashed suddenly upon the screen, just like the face of the corpse sitting bolt upright in the awful galley scene in *The Poseidon Adventure,* I gasped, buried my face in my hands, and burst into tears!

Finally, when my mother asked me what scared me so much this time about *The Poseidon Adventure,* I said that it was because I couldn't bear to see all of those people dying.

"Oh but Patrick, it's just a movie! It's not real. All those people are actors. They don't really die in the movie! I mean, they die in the movie but they don't die in real life. They're all still alive today. They make those movies in Hollywood!" She looked at me with incredulity. "Why, *you* know that . . . don't you?"

No, I didn't really know that, I said.

My mother was annoyed with my histrionics and wanted to withdraw herself from me—partly, I imagine, out of fear, for she often experienced her children's pain as her own, and there's only so much pain you can bear as the mother of six, let alone of one like me whose emotional needs seemed so great and so unpredictable; I felt rejected (both by Tommy and my mother), confused, and alone. Our discussion of *The Poseidon Adventure* didn't go much further that night.

III

At some point in the late 1980s, my mother called to tell me that a friend of our family, Brad Mayer, died of AIDS. I hadn't thought about him in years.

The Mayers were among the first people my parents became friendly with when they moved from their small two-bedroom house to the larger, four-bedroom house where I grew up. We all belonged to the same church, Caroline Mayer became one of my mom's best friends, Dr. Mayer and my dad played tennis together, and the Mayer boys— Reggie, Randy, Brad, and Kevin—would sometimes join us at the beach during our annual summer vacation in Ocean City. Kevin was the one we got to know the best. He baby-sat for us on occasion, and whenever he did, something wild would happen. One night he filled a bucket with chemicals and exploded it in the backyard; another time, he let me stay up until dawn to watch the milkman pull up in his truck. Kevin played a really strange game called "Uncle" in which he would contact the spirit of his mysterious dead uncle. He would sit in a corner, cross his legs, close his eyes, and sit very still and quiet, and then he would start to hum and then moan and then he would start shaking until his entire body was convulsing and he was shrieking and it was supposed to be the spirit of his uncle now entering his body. Suddenly he would jump up and race downstairs to the basement and grab one of the ping pong balls and—here's where my memory gets fuzzy—either he would put the ping pong ball in his mouth and his eyes would roll back in his head, or he would talk to the ping pong ball and the ping pong ball would talk back. Somehow, he would receive a message from his uncle, and the message was usually a command to play Parcheesi or Twister or some other kind of game next.

Kevin gave all of us nicknames that my siblings never tired of teasing each other with, even years after Kevin had gone off and married and had kids of his own. I don't remember all of our names, but one of the girls was "Wednesday" (after Wednesday on *The Addams Family*), my brother, John, was "Jean-Claude" (after Jean-Claude Killy, the famous downhill skier), and for reasons I never understood (although everyone else seemed to get the joke), I was "The Hunter," which had to be pronounced in an ostentatious, mock-Oriental accent.

Although I liked Kevin, often the games we played when he was around would end up in a fight or, more likely, with me in tears. One time he taught us a game called "Scissors," in which you sat on the floor and passed a pair of vegetable scissors around from person to person in a circle, and when it was your turn to pass it, you had to say, "I, Patrick" or "I, Kevin"—"I [so-and-so]—receive the scissors from [the name of the person who passed them to you]," and now you had to say either "crossed" or "uncrossed," and then you would say, "and I pass them to [so-and-so] 'crossed' or 'uncrossed.' " Now the trick was figuring out what "crossed" and "uncrossed" meant. Naturally, I thought "crossed" meant that the scissors were open and "uncrossed" that they were closed, because when they were open they did sort of look like a cross or an X. But sometimes somebody would pass the open scissors to their neighbor and say, "I pass the scissors uncrossed," and other times they would pass them closed and say, "I pass the scissors crossed," and sometimes (this was *really* confusing) they would say that they received them crossed and then they would hand them onto the next person in the same position but say that they were *un*crossed! Well, I didn't get it. Soon everybody started laughing and telling me that they were trying to make it as obvious for me as possible. I noticed that they were doing stupid things with their arms and legs—and I wasn't sure if maybe the joke had something to do with their eyes as well—but I just couldn't figure it out. Eventually I got so frustrated and angry that I ran out of the room crying. Somebody—I forget who, probably Mary Jo—had to come and tell me that it had nothing to do with the scissors; it all depended on whether or not you crossed your legs. (Oh *brother!*)

Then there was "Killer," a game whose rules I at least understood even though I wasn't very good at it. We all sat at the kitchen table, which was big and round, and we turned out all the lights except for a single candle in the middle of the table. Everybody was dealt a playing card, and the one with the Ace of Spades was the "killer." The killer's job was to wink at somebody on the circle without being seen doing so by anyone else. So you had to be a quick and subtle winker. Really, you had to be able to just blink with one eye. (I could never do tricky stuff like that—I couldn't snap my fingers or whistle or blow big bubbles, although I could curl my tongue into a perfect U.) If the killer winked at you, you had to wait a few seconds and then say "I'm dead." I forget the exact object of the game, but the fun of it for me was getting to sit in the dark with all my siblings and with Kevin (like we were all in this together—like the band of survivors in *The Poseidon Adventure*), knowing that even though we were pretending to kill each other and were sitting in the dark, really there was nothing to be afraid of.

Kevin taught us tricks we could do with our bodies. Like sitting in the lotus position and then pulling one leg up behind your neck. (None of us could do it, but he could.) Or turning your eyelids inside out. (That was so gross, we never wanted to try it, but we always wanted him to do it.) Or, he taught us to stand in a doorway and push out really hard on the door frame for about three minutes and then come out of the door frame with your arms down at your sides, and then watch what happens: your arms rise all by themselves without your having to lift them! (How did it do that?!)

Kevin liked to tease my brother, John, which was a nice change of pace for me since I was usually the one to get picked on. One summer at the beach, John had fallen asleep on a chair in the living room and while he was sleeping, Kevin inserted Monopoly playing pieces in between his toes, put an unlit cigarette in his mouth, and took photographs of him that way. (Although he tried to hide it from my parents, Kevin smoked cigarettes openly around us kids.)

When he baby-sat for us, Kevin would often bring his guitar along and sing Rolling Stones songs and even a few songs he made up himself, like "Flockanicka": "I got a girl named Flock-a-nick-a, / She's so beautiful, she's so fine, / She's six-foot-three with lips like wine"—stuff like that.

When Kevin baby-sat, we knew we were going to have fun (so much fun that eventually my parents stopped asking him to baby-sit). When his older brother Brad baby-sat for us, however, the atmosphere was different. Whereas Kevin was generous and outgoing and zany, Brad was aloof, cool, hard to interpret. One night I remember noticing the way Brad listened. He was sitting at the kitchen table with his face resting in the cup of his hands, his fingers making a double-V pattern across his face, listening, expressionless, as someone was talking—it might have been Mom or Dad or one of their priest friends visiting from out of town. It was the blank but steady look in Brad's eyes that impressed me. I had never before seen that kind of expression on anyone's face when they listened; I'd never even thought about listening as a discreet thing. It never occurred to me that there were different ways to listen, or that some people listened and some people didn't. You couldn't exactly tell what he was thinking when he listened (though I suspected that he didn't agree with or didn't like most of what he heard), but you could tell he was taking it all in.

Brad told stories that hung in the air and left you with an uneasy feeling. He had just taken a trip to Mexico, he told us—I don't remember now why he went there or with whom. It was wonderful, he said. There was a school—a village full of children—and one day he and all the children and all the grownups went swimming, and no one had a bathing suit. They just took off all their clothes and went naked—there wasn't a swimming pool, just a pond—and everyone was dirt poor. They stripped on the shore and dove right in. The thought of going naked in public with other people around—other boys—was beyond anything I'd ever imagined. All I could think was, I could never do that. And: you could see their penises?! (And: you could see *Brad's* penis . . .)

Brad was a movie buff. One night as we sat around the kitchen table eating popcorn with too much melted butter on it, he told us the story of *The Thing,* one of his favorite horror movies from the 1950s (I didn't realize that other people had "favorite" movies too and that it was OK to have favorite movies). It took place in the North Pole or some place frozen like that, and there was a team of scientists who discover a creature frozen solid in a block of ice (I'd never been particularly frightened by cold weather, but somehow Brad made it sound worse than hell). So one night, one of the scientists is sitting in the greenhouse where they kept the monster to thaw out, and he's reading a book or the comics or maybe the weather statistics. He's reading by candlelight, and the camera closes in on the page that he's reading, with the light of the candle casting shadows across the page (Brad noticed things like that in a movie —camera angles and compositions of shadows and light), when gradually another shadow creeps across the page. For a second the scientist wonders—looks puzzled—then—Oh my God! It's the monster! *It's alive!* Standing up behind him! Reaching out its horrible, long, bony fingers!

Brad's hands were long and slender. Everything about him was like that—he had long, pretty, straight brown hair, parted in the middle like a girl's. Sometimes he wore it in a ponytail, sometimes in a bandana. He was tall, nearly six feet. And for some reason, he always smelled like chemicals.

Another night while my parents were away, Brad told us in excruciating detail about a new film he had just seen in which a luxury cruise ship gets hit by a giant tidal wave and turns upside down! I was spellbound.

Brad knew all about ships and the disasters they met with at sea. Over the years, he built a series of incredibly beautiful models of the *Titanic,* he hung over his bed a framed reproduction of a 1912 news clipping about the famous disaster, and he turned his basement (which Hurricane Agnes would later flood recklessly to the ceiling) into a photography studio where he made simulated photographs of the sinking of the ship: first, he spread a large, green garbage bag over a table top; next, he applied shaving cream to look like choppy waves and sea spray, then cut up chunks of white Styrofoam to look like pieces of the iceberg. He would position his *Titanic* on blocks behind one end of the table so that, looking at the ship from the other end of the table, it appeared to be "floating" on the water. There were tiny lights inside the ship that he turned on, and he turned off all of the basement lights: nighttime. To the endless sound of George Harrison singing "While My Guitar Gently Weeps," he took a series of snapshots with the nose of the ship pointed deeper and deeper into the water (behind the table). These black-and-white pictures looked uncannily like the real thing—as if Brad had actually been out there on the ocean with his camera that tragic night in 1912 when suddenly he saw the *Titanic*, not two hundred yards away, go plunging down into the freezing Atlantic.

During the years that Brad and Kevin baby-sat for us, the two oldest Mayer boys, the twins Reggie and Randy, got drafted into the Vietnam War. Dr. Mayer was against the war and was prepared to move his family to Canada if it ever came to that. I remember hearing something about how Reggie and Randy starved themselves in order to fail their physical examinations. Recently my dad told me that around the same time, Brad announced that he was going to enlist in the navy. He was eighteen and old enough to do what he wanted, he said, and what he wanted was to go out to sea. Dr. Mayer tried to dissuade him, but Brad was determined. My dad says now that Dr. Mayer and Brad were always fighting, always on opposite sides of every debate; Dr. Mayer loved all of his boys, Dad says, but he and Brad were like day and night. So Dr. Mayer asked my dad if he would talk to Brad (it seems that people were always turning to my parents in times of crisis—they still do). Accordingly, Dad took Brad out for breakfast one morning and talked with the boy. He has never told me the details of their conversation, but I imagine it went something like:

"Now Brad, why do you want to go and join the navy?"

"I want to go, I want to get away, I want to get out of here."

"Brad do you know what it means to enlist in the armed forces? When I was your age I enlisted in the Korean War, my brother Dick and I, and they sent us to boot camp down in South Carolina, and I tell you Brad, we were lucky because neither of us went into combat—we both were given desk jobs. But do you realize that you might have to fight, and if you fight, Brad, you might get killed? Now you don't want to put your life in danger for no reason, do you?"

"I want to get away from here."

"Brad, do you know that your parents love you very much? And the last thing in the world they want is for something to happen to one of you boys. I know you and your father don't see eye to eye on a lot of things, and I'm not here to say who's right and who's wrong—that's none of my business, and you'll work that out with your dad someday, in your own way, in your own time. But one thing I do know for sure, and that is that if anything ever happened to you, your mom and dad would be crushed. They would do anything in the world for you, Brad. They would sooner lay down their own lives than see you get hurt. I know because I would do the same thing for any one of my children. Your mom and dad love you dearly, Brad, I promise you."

And so, presumably, went the conversation. Eventually my dad talked Brad out of enlisting and, instead, arranged for him to spend a long weekend retreat with Father Mike. "He was just a kid," Dad tells me, "and he was angry, and he was hurt. I'm sure there were a lot of hard times in that family. Dr. Mayer was a rigid man in many ways, but a good man. He could be tough on those boys. But what a mistake it would have been if Brad had gone into the navy. He was just a dreamy kid. He didn't know anything about the navy. He would have been eaten alive.

"You know, Pat, those were tough years for everybody. This country was in a state of upheaval and you didn't know who or what to believe. I don't know if I ever told you this, but your mother and I were in San Francisco, it must have been in 1967 or '68, and we were riding one of those trolley cars, and all of a sudden a whole group of—hippies, I guess that's what we called them—just came rushing onto the trolley and they were shouting at us and giving up buttons or stickers—I don't know if they were peace signs—but that's what it was like. And we were a little frightened 'cause you didn't know what they were gonna do next. And they looked at us and thought we were 'squares', I'm sure that's what they thought we were. But, you know, one day I was sitting out in George McDonald's backyard—all you kids were there, you were playing together, we were having a big cookout; you know, we used to get together with the McDonalds about once every month. And George and I were talking about the hippies and the war, and I said to him, 'George, we've been dumb. These kids'—and I was referring to the hippies—'these kids are right. We've been offended by the wrong thing.' We didn't like their long hair and their bad manners and their filthy language, 'but *so what!*' I said. 'We have no business being in Vietnam!' And the kids were right. I give them credit for that."

When my mother called to tell me that Brad had died, I felt the way I always did during the late eighties whenever she would mention anything having to do with AIDS (it might be the prospect of a new vaccine; or an ACT UP demonstration she happened to see on the news, and was I in it? And was I in danger of getting arrested?). I felt angry and defensive. I felt what she really wanted to say, but didn't know how, was, "I know that your life and your choices are different from mine . . . but . . . I am thinking about you . . . I worry about you . . . I miss you . . . I love . . . I need . . ."

We had already gotten into a huge argument a couple of months earlier over an editorial in *Time* magazine in which the writer argued that AIDS activists had unfairly monopolized the media's attention, and so other worthy causes—like cancer research—were being ignored. This came in the mail with a Post-it from my mom that said, "I found this very interesting." "Interesting"? I wondered. What was she trying to tell me? She knew that I was involved with ACT UP at the time and that I felt strongly that direct action was the only way to shock the system into paying attention to AIDS and to the way that homophobia was preventing people from responding intelligently and compassionately to the epidemic. When she wrote that she found the article "interesting," was she saying that she agreed with it? Did she want to know what I thought of it? Did she honestly think I would feel anything other than outraged and insulted at the idea that *too much* time and money were being spent on AIDS? I thought about it for a few days and decided to ignore it and not respond and to just let it drop rather than getting into a fight over it. But when she called me several weeks later and asked if I'd gotten the article, I said curtly, "Yes, and I really didn't appreciate it."

"What didn't you appreciate?" she asked.

"I've heard that argument before, that AIDS has become this celebrity cause and that it's really not as bad as AIDS activists make it out to be. I find that really offensive. And I didn't like having you shove it in my face out of nowhere."

"I didn't shove it in your face, I sent it to you because I thought it was an interesting argument."

"What are you talking about, 'interesting'? What's interesting about an argument that's basically saying that people like me shouldn't be doing what we're doing and that we're selfish and that we're trying to promote our 'gay agenda' under the guise of AIDS activism? Don't you find that offensive? I do! As if homophobia has nothing to do with the AIDS crisis!"

"Well, I don't know about the part about the gay agenda, I merely thought—"

"Well if you don't know about it, then why are you sending me articles about it?"

"I thought we could have a dialogue about—"

"You know, I would never send *you* an article advocating abortion, because I know that it's not something that you're open to discussing. I think it was really insensitive of you to send me this article."

"Well you know something? I *do* think these AIDS activists can sometimes go too far."

"What do you mean 'these AIDS activists'? Mom, you're talking to one! *I'm* an AIDS activist!"

"So what you're telling me is that you're not open to discussing what you do."

"It's not that I'm not open to discussing it, it's just that I don't think you have any idea of what we're trying to do, and I really don't think you have any idea of what it's like to be a gay man and live through all the bullshit that people say about AIDS and about gay men and how they deserve it and—" I was starting to cry and trying to pull myself back.

"Patrick, I never said that gay men deserve to get AIDS *and you know it!* Don't you put words in my mouth! Every time I say something you jump down my throat. I'm trying to understand ACT UP, but you won't even give me a chance."

"Oh, so this is your way of trying to understand—sending me a hostile article about—"

"It wasn't a hostile article! I merely thought it made a good point and I wanted to know what you thought about it, that's all. You are free to agree or disagree, and I'm open to hearing whatever it is you have to say. But not when you yell at me and accuse me of things. You know, sometimes I think I'm your whipping boy. I'm not perfect and there's a lot of things I don't understand, and I don't understand a lot of things about the homosexual community, I freely admit that."

"You know, a couple of years ago, I suggested that you and Dad attend one of those Parents and Friends of Lesbians and Gays meetings and you—"

"Patrick, we don't need to go to a meeting for parents of lesbians and gays."

"I think it would really help you—"

"Patrick, we don't need any help. We're fine. We don't have any problem with your being gay, and you know that. We're fine."

"What are you afraid of?"

"Afraid?! What are you talking about?"

"It's like you're embarrassed to go because—"

"Patrick, your father and I don't need to get up in front of a whole group of people and talk about having a gay son. We don't have anything to say about it. We're fine. And that doesn't mean that we're ashamed of it. We aren't the kind of people who join groups like that. I think it's *you* who have the problem."

"Me!" I shouted. "What problem do *I* have?"

"You're so angry, would you just listen to yourself? No one can talk to you. I think we should just end this conversation right now."

"Oh great, just run away as soon as we really get to something important."

"I'm not running away. You can't be civil, and I won't have you speak to me that way. So, I'm sorry I sent the article. You can be sure I'll never send you another article about AIDS again."

I was still fuming.

"I'm saying good-bye now."

I hoped we could avoid an argument this time. We were silent for a moment, dwelling on the double thrust of the news: Brad died of AIDS; Brad was a gay man. My mother broke the silence by mentioning, "he was with a Jesuit when he died. I'm thankful for that. I know that makes his mother and father feel better. You know he never quite found himself when he left home — he just wandered. It's tragic."

Sometime in the late 1970s, Brad rode his bicycle out to San Diego and was hardly talked about in my family again. Now and then someone would mention something about how Brad owned a bicycle repair shop out west, but there was hardly more news than that. Not until my mother telephoned to give me the news of his death did I begin again to think about Brad, and to discover that we seem to have had much in common — our mutual fascination with disaster; our shared sexuality; our loving, uncomprehending, suffocating families of origin; our adolescent withdrawal into the consolations of culture; our search for some place else, as adults, in which to be ourselves (for Brad, I presume, it ended up being San Diego; for me, for now, it is New York City). As my mom told me what little she knew about the circumstances of Brad's death, my mind went elsewhere. I began to wonder what Brad's life was like in San Diego. I wondered if he had a boyfriend, a whole circle of friends and lovers. When did he know that he was gay? Did he know back when he was baby-sitting me and my siblings? What kind of relationship did he have with his brothers? What was it like for *him*, growing up gay in Reading?

My mother couldn't answer any of these questions, and I couldn't ask them. We said good-bye after one or two minutes of the routine questions: "How are you doing otherwise?" "Fine, and you?" "Fine." And the expressions of love: "Are you eating well?" "Yes, Mom." "I love you, Patrick." "I love you too." And the promise to write or call soon.

IV

The Poseidon Adventure has not (not yet) become a classic of gay male culture as have, say, certain Broadway musicals or *Mommie Dearest*. But I've discovered that a gay affection for *The Poseidon Adventure* and other disaster films is bigger than just me. In the fall of 1989, the Tunnel Bar, an East Village gay bar in New York (now gone) hosted a "*Poseidon Adventure* party" that featured an imaginative transformation of the bar into the boiling, upside down engine room of the *Poseidon*, reenactments of boat passengers hurtling through the air, refreshments, and repeated showings of the film. One of the party's organizers and the Tunnel Bar's then manager, William Bonney, told me that *The Poseidon Adventure* is not particularly one of his favorite films, that he prefers comedy ("it makes me laugh") and science fiction ("I love the future; I wish I was there"). William thinks *The Poseidon Adventure* "is camp," that it "tries to be dramatic and isn't."

Ironically, some of the very people who show the most "queer" interest in *The Poseidon Adventure* disavow that same interest. But look again: When the ship turns over, Reverend Scott (often described in promotional literature for the film and in reviews as an "activist" priest) engages in a furious debate with the purser and other passengers over how best to respond to the crisis. Read the following dialogue metaphorically instead of literally—not as a debate over whether to wait for help or to try to save yourself, but rather, in light of gay activism, as a debate over the merits of coming out ("climbing out") versus assimilating into the larger straight society ("staying here till help arrives"); or, read it as if it were a debate among AIDS activists: should we work with the medical establishment to lead us through the epidemic ("staying here till help arrives") or should we try to make the establishment respond to the epidemic on *our* terms?

PURSER: For God's sake, Reverend, what you're doing is suicide!
SCOTT: We're cut off from the rest of the world. They can't get to us; maybe we can get to them. You've said enough, now get out of the way.
PURSER: Pray for us, but don't do this! Climbing to another deck will kill you all!
SCOTT: And sitting on our butts isn't going to help us either! Maybe by

climbing out we *can* save ourselves. If you've got any sense you'll come
with us.

[. . .]

SCOTT: [*pointing up*] That's the way out; that's our only chance.

PURSER: Don't listen to him! We've got to stay here till help arrives!

SCOTT: Help from where? From the captain? He's dead. Everyone is dead
who was above us before the ship turned over, because now they're
underneath us, under the water.

PURSER: That's not true!

SCOTT: Of course it's true, you pompous ass! There's nobody alive but us.
And nobody's going to help us, except ourselves. It's up to each one of
you. It's up to all of us. Now for God's sake, come with us.

PURSER: I order you not to go! He knows nothing about this ship!

A WOMAN: The purser's right!

A MAN: [*to Reverend Scott*] Why don't you mind your own business?!

[. . .]

SCOTT: I want to appeal to you for the last time.

ANOTHER MAN: You don't know what you're talking about!

SCOTT: I know this much: the sea's going to keep pouring in. We're going
to keep settling deeper and deeper. We may even go under before we
get up to the bottom to cut our way out. But it's something to try. It's a
chance; we might make it. If you stay here you'll certainly die.

A THIRD MAN: We are staying with the purser.

However inadvertently, *The Poseidon Adventure* may appeal to gay audiences because its drama of being trapped in a vessel underwater with no
guarantee of escape to the outside, without the assurance that there is
even going to *be* any outside to escape to, and with no inkling of what
lies in store on the outside *should* there be an escape, resonates powerfully with the life-denying experience most of us have had of growing
up and living some part of our adult lives in the closet. And *The Poseidon Adventure* may appeal to gay audiences, living today in the midst of
a global health crisis, because it dramatizes the internal dynamics (the
disagreements over strategy, the fear of the unknown, the fear of death,
the brief hiatuses of humor and pleasure) of a community of friends,
acquaintances, lovers, and strangers shocked by catastrophe and determined against strong resistance (from within and without) to nurture
itself, to survive—indeed, to flourish.

The Tunnel Bar's *Poseidon Adventure* party took its place in a series of
more overtly queer and AIDS-activist-related events, all hosted by the
bar around the same time, including: "Xmas in Outer Space"; a "Dys-
lexic New Year's" party; "The Death of Disco"; *Rocky Horror Picture Show*
parties; beach parties; "Life Is Hell So Let's Drink and Fuck" parties;

and fund-raisers for God's Love We Deliver (a food program for people with AIDS), the annual Wigstock festival (a popular drag fest and queer community-building event), and Gay Men's Health Crisis (the first and largest AIDS service organization in the world).

V

Just before the six survivors are lifted out of the wrecked *Poseidon,* a close-up shot of each of them—Mike Rogo, Manny Rosen, Susan, Robin, Mr. Martin, and Nonnie—shows the mixture of grief, numbness, and relief they feel now that their journey through hell has come to an end. Mike Rogo turns to look back one last time at the flames that consumed his wife, Linda, then faces the camera again with tears in his eyes, looking up as his rescuers from the outside blowtorch a hole through the hull. He will survive, but survival has become indistinguishable from tragedy.

On the night of Gay Pride Day a few years ago, I decided to call my friend David to see how he was doing. I'd seen a close friend of his walking alone at the march—I knew that David had recently entered the hospital (again) with some kind of HIV-related brain disorder. Too afraid to face the reality of his impending death, too embarrassed by my habit of paying close attention to certain friends only when they are in trouble, I hadn't visited David in the hospital this time around. But the spirit of Gay Pride made me feel that I had nothing to be ashamed of—David was my lovely friend, I had begun to think of him as part of my alternative, extended gay family, and I wanted to talk with him. I called, and his boyfriend, Philip, told me that David had died three weeks ago and that his ashes had been scattered on the Hudson River that afternoon. It was a nice ceremony with a few friends, Philip said. He was sorry he had to tell me this. There would be a memorial service for David at the Gay Community Center in September. Again, he said, I'm sorry to have to tell you this.
    Survival.

OUTTAKES III

The Snow Goose (1971)

When I saw *The Poseidon Adventure* in 1972, I didn't know that the person who wrote the 1969 novel upon which it was based, Paul Gallico, also wrote *The Snow Goose*, a BBC movie based on his 1940 short story, which I had seen on TV in 1971. Yet my reactions to *The Poseidon Adventure* and *The Snow Goose* were similar. In some ways, they're the same story. Set on the wet, moody coast of southeast England in the late 1930s, *The Snow Goose* is the story of a lonely, hunchbacked lighthouse keeper named Philip Rhayader and an orphaned girl from the local fishing community named Frith who, together, rescue and nurse back to health a beautiful white goose that has been shot down by hunters. A delicate friendship grows between Philip and Frith, and as the snow goose leaves and returns periodically to Philip's lighthouse, so does Frith, until the summer of 1940 when Philip is killed by German gunfire while assisting, against Frith's wishes, in the evacuation of British soldiers from Dunkirk. The film left me feeling empty and hurt. Like Reverend Scott in *The Poseidon Adventure*, who sacrifices himself that the other passengers might live to escape the capsized ship, Philip Rhayader, knowing, it seemed, that what he was about to do was risky and foolish because of his poor health, nevertheless threw himself, Christ-like, in the path of death to help his fellow human beings: "These men are lost," he told Frith, who was in tears at the thought of losing him, "like the snow goose we found in the marshes and we healed. These men need help now. They need me. And I must go because I can. No one can stop me this time. Now, Frith— Frith—for once, Frith, I can be a man and play my part."[1] I understood that Frith was upset not just because she had come to like Philip, but because, more important, he had become her family. For Frith had lost her parents in a bad storm years ago, and when the snow goose returned one spring, Frith wondered if maybe the bird, like Frith herself, must cling to whatever family, however unconventional, she can find: "Perhaps she never did find her family again," Frith speculates, "perhaps they were lost in a storm too—perhaps that's why she came back to us."

The Snow Goose was also a painful movie for me because it spoke about loneliness, about the ways that people try to compensate for feeling lonely, and loneliness was a sore subject with me (as my Grandmother Horrigan told me around this same time, "You know, Pat, you're a loner"). When Frith says to Philip that it must get lonely living in a lighthouse so far out on the coast, Philip replies, "I'm not alone. I have my

135

paintings, my birds, and my boat, and with my boat I can sail away unseen from those people that I appear to bother." Philip was a "loner," then, like me, not just because the things he did (painting, tending his birds) required hours of patience and solitude (my parents would always compliment me on how patient I was; whenever I would proudly present to them one of my plastic model houses or paintings or string art pictures or Lego buildings, they would marvel, "Oh Pat, you do such beautiful work, and you have such patience—the hours it must have taken you to do that. I don't know where you get your talent from; you certainly don't get it from me!"). Philip was a loner because he was running away from people who (he suspected) didn't like him, from people who were bothered by his sheer presence. His art, and the "independence" that went with it, then, was his hiding place ("I can sail away unseen"). And it didn't make him happy—not really. For when Frith leaves, he spends much of his time painting her picture, wishing she would come back to stay. And when Philip is gone, all Frith is left with is Philip's painting. The film ends with a shot of Frith sadly walking away from the empty lighthouse carrying the painting, the only remains, now, of her relationship with Philip. The bleak, depopulated English landscape now expressed the way Frith, and I, felt.

Once when I was mowing the lawn (my least favorite chore when I was growing up), I came across a dead bird in the grass in front of our house. For some reason, no one else was home. I had the entire place to myself. I knelt down and, using a piece of cardboard, lifted the bird up and placed it gently into a trash barrel filled to the top with freshly mown grass. I wept bitterly and couldn't bring myself to put the lid on the trash barrel—such indignities do the dead suffer. I remember not understanding why I was crying so hard—why the bird's death, and the lowly circumstances of its burial, affected me so powerfully. The more I cried, the deeper and harder my sobbing became. I don't remember, now, when or how I stopped crying, nor do I recall how, finally, I disposed of the poor, dead bird.

Sybil (1976)

I watched every minute of *Sybil* when it premiered on TV in 1976, and when it was all over the merest thought of the music by Leonard Rosenman, played over the opening and closing credits, gave me a frightened, sinking feeling. The musical theme began as a contrite, childlike melody, as if by Schumann or Schubert, played simply on a piano, accompanied by children's voices; but soon it was scarred by piercing violin sounds that had nothing harmonically to do with the melody—as if, before you knew it, a pretty peach had started turning rotten, and when you picked it up to take a bite, you saw blemishes and festering holes and mold spreading and little bugs crawling all over its underside.

Sybil was the story of a nice though extremely troubled young woman, played by Sally Field, who as a child suffered abuse at the hands of her schizophrenic mother and now, as an adult, has developed multiple personalities (about sixteen of them) to cope with her trauma. I loved Sybil; I felt so sorry for her. I felt I understood her, even though nothing like what she went through as a child ever happened to me. Early in the film, she worries that she might have done someone harm during one of her blackouts: "Have I hurt somebody? Have I done something bad?"[2] Apparently, she, like me, was accustomed to blaming herself for her own unhappiness.

And not unlike the relationship between Maria and the Reverend Mother in *The Sound of Music,* the relationship that develops between Sybil and her psychiatrist, Dr. Wilbur (played radiantly by Joanne Woodward), was miraculous. Dr. Wilbur calmly and lovingly accepted and forgave Sybil for everything that had ever happened to her and everything that had become of her. When Sybil says, ashamed of her multiple personalities, "Nobody knows," Dr. Wilbur says reassuringly, "Somebody knows now." "Do you believe me?" Sybil asks her, and she replies, "Sweetie, I believe that you believe." This seemed so different from the way that Dorothy's family and friends, for example, react when she tells them about her journey to Oz: "Doesn't anyone believe me?" she pleads, but Uncle Henry only murmurs without conviction, "Of course we believe you, Dorothy," which wasn't true, and Aunt Em bluntly contradicts her: "Oh, we dream lots of silly things" (Langley 68–69). I would have understood, of course, that Sybil's mental disorder and Dorothy's dream were not to be confused—one, the cause of excruciating pain, the other, as Dorothy tells it, sometimes "not very nice," sometimes "beautiful," but all in all the most authentic, the most plentiful experience in the entire film. Still, the virtuosity of Sybil's illness was impressive and entertaining (one minute she was urbane, self-confident Vicky; the next childlike, scared-to-death Peggy; the next lovely and talented Vanessa; the next her own monstrous mother) in the same way that Dorothy's Technicolor dream, replete with green-faced witches and blue-gowned midgets, talking trees and weeping tin men, fireballs and floating bubbles, was wilder and weirder than anything back home in Kansas. And when Sybil thinks that "something awful is going to happen—I can feel it—it's going to fall apart or blow up or there's going to be an earthquake or a tidal wave or a glacier or something—I don't know what, just something awful is going to happen," Dr. Wilbur makes perfect sense of her "crazy" ideas:

"Sweetie, that bad end of the world feeling is not the end of the world. It's just the coming of your own anger." Sybil was "crazy," had imaginary playmates and alter egos (not unlike me) because she was angry at her mother, and that anger was beginning to burst into Sybil's consciousness, and the coming of that self-consciousness was so frightening to Sybil that she thought of it as a disaster. I knew all about the pleasures of disaster and the peculiar relief it could bring (*The Towering Inferno* was my then-most-recent favorite disaster movie, even though it petrified me): no more same old family, no more unbreakable rules, no more boredom, no more stifling good taste and good manners and good faith.

And even if I couldn't completely match my story with Sybil's, she at least had friends who were somehow like me—for example, her childhood friend Danny. At one point in the film, she tells her friend Richard, "[Danny and I] were children together. He was an outcast like me, only in his case it was because he danced. . . . Whenever I feel especially warm toward somebody, especially grateful, I think of Danny. He had kind of a holy forbearance at the age of nine or ten. How he got it in that benighted [Wisconsin] town I'll never know" (during this speech, the camera cuts to a flashback of Danny—already, like me, at age nine or ten, a "show queen"—entertaining Sybil as he dances on top of a steamer trunk, singing "Cheek to Cheek").

Sybil begins with close-up shots of what looks like a child's abstract painting. But eventually the camera pulls away from the painting, revealing a skillful rendering of Manhattan. The painting then turns into actual film footage of Manhattan—a lengthy, spooky, aerial shot of the city, set to Rosenman's sinister music (the 1961 film version of *West Side Story* opens in almost exactly the same way), hundreds of skyscrapers jutting up into the air like a bed of nails—a metaphor of sorts for Sybil's jagged, impossibly mixed, dangerously diverse, ever-seething, ever-changing personality. But Sybil's New York is also a place of freedom, however self-destructive that freedom tends to be—an uninhibited place. At one point in the film, Richard (played by Brad Davis) asks her to kiss him while they ride the subway: "It's New York," he assures her, "nobody cares."

4

Like Home

I

Sometimes I think I should have been an architect. When I was little I loved to build things—blocks, Lincoln Logs, Lego, and later, plastic model houses. My passion was for domestic architecture, not municipal buildings, not skyscrapers. *Home*—that's what I was always trying to re-create with the materials, however recalcitrant, at my disposal. I would always reach the point where the wooden blocks became too blunt to evoke, say, a dormer in the roof, or the Lego set didn't come with elegant enough windows and doors, so I was prevented from building a mansion in the grand style I dreamed about; or the Lincoln Logs never looked enough like smooth, white, aluminum siding or handsome grey stone walls, no matter how much I squinted at them and tried to pretend differently. But I never gave up trying to make a perfect home.

In *The Wizard of Oz*, Dorothy wants to escape her dull, black-and-white Kansas home by going someplace over the rainbow. "What she expresses here," Salman Rushdie argues in his stunning book-length essay on the famous 1939 film starring Judy Garland, "what she embodies with the purity of an archetype, is the human dream of *leaving*, a dream at least as powerful as its countervailing dream of roots. At the heart of *The Wizard of Oz* is a great tension between these two dreams; but as the music swells and that big, clean voice flies into the anguished longings of the song, can anyone doubt which message is stronger?" (Rushdie 23)

In a way, I was just the opposite of Judy Garland's Dorothy: I dreamed of creating my own home within the home I grew up in. I was more like Dorothy in *The Wiz*, the 1978 film version of the black Broadway musical. As played by Diana Ross, Dorothy is not a child anymore but a young woman in her twenties who likes living at home with her Aunt Em and Uncle Henry, likes her job as a preschool teacher, never ventures outside of Harlem and, for reasons unknown, shows no interest in men (she rolls her eyes when Aunt Em tries to set her up with a guy in the neighborhood). But she's a misfit. When all the members of her extended family sing about the good feelings they have for each other at a holiday dinner party, Dorothy sits alone in the kitchen and confesses in song, "I don't even know the first thing about what they're feeling." Not exactly fulfilled at home, she is committed to it nonetheless.

Both films, of course, devote most of their energy to an elaboration of the fantasy of going, as Rushdie calls it, "Elsewhere" (23), and *The Wiz* in particular loses all interest in Dorothy's homecoming by the end of the film: from across the street, we watch her walk through the front door of her dear old apartment building, but then the movie ends and the closing credits start to roll. We're treated to none of her joy at seeing her aunt and uncle again, and we're given no idea of how she'll fit into her former life now that she's been to the Emerald City and back. But the fantasy of home remains alive. In the end, we never really learn what makes Dorothy so ambivalent about home.

A remake (a film version) of a remake (a Broadway musical) of a remake (the 1939 MGM film) of an original (a children's book), *The Wiz* became one of my top ten favorite movies in the late seventies because it seemed to capture, however indirectly, my mixed, inarticulate feelings about where I came from and where I was going to . . .

One of my favorite pastimes as a kid was to explore the houses under construction in and around my neighborhood. This was one of the many things I did alone as a child, and I don't recall feeling guilty or sad or lonely while doing it as I sometimes did, for example, when I listened to my Barbra Streisand records or when I shot baskets on our driveway while privately fantasizing about my favorite movies. I would climb or sometimes just walk right through windows, enter a room and try to figure out which one it was supposed to be depending on how much progress had been made on the house. I'd stand at the edge of an abyss (a stairwell, perhaps? or maybe it had some utilitarian purpose, a shaft of some kind—I couldn't say what for—that would get hidden, eventually, underneath the final, cosmetic layers of bricks and siding) and walk the gangplank to the lower level or descend the ladder if there was one or just jump (*yikes!*), free falling, to the next, lower landing. I would imagine staircases not yet put in place, or I'd ascend and descend staircases whose railings hadn't yet been attached, pretending I was Barbra Streisand as Dolly Levi, coming down the red staircase of the Harmonia Gardens Restaurant. I would try to figure out how some odd space, not quite big enough for a family room but not so small as a closet or storage space, suspended, say, halfway between the first and second story, might reasonably be made use of by the strange new occupants to come. I wished the house I lived in had odd, out-of-the-way spaces like the ones I found in these houses.

Sometime in the late 1960s, my parents took us down to Ft. Lauderdale, Florida to visit my Nana and Granddaddy Horrigan, who spent some portion of each winter vacationing there, in a hotel-condominium called Ireland's Inn. We stayed at the Mark 500, a hotel nearby, which to me was an amazing place. It was three or four blocks long, and each of its several buildings was connected by a system of bridges, stairs, balconies, and walkways. One night after dinner, I ran up and down and all over the ramps and bridges, not just because I was bored (we had dinner at Ireland's Inn with Nana and Granddaddy that night, and not only did the service take forever, but we didn't even sit down until around 8 P.M.—that is, not until after Nana and Granddaddy enjoyed their before-dinner cocktails. Never again, said my parents, will we delay the children's dinner just so Mom and Pop can have a drink! Imagine how hungry those poor kids must have been! Why, they probably didn't even have any appetite left by the time the food came! [I ordered spaghetti and meatballs]), but also because the space produced feelings in me that no architectural space had ever done before. The Mark 500 was my discovery of architecture as space. (I vomited up all my spaghetti later that night.)

During that same trip to Florida we took a nighttime river cruise, with dinner and live music on the boat, and we sailed past one big, beautiful house after another along the shore. These houses were extraordinary because every one of them was a "trophy," a unique architectural statement, probably designed by "name" architects, and they were modern: huge glass picture windows and spiral staircases; indoor swimming pools, seemingly right in the middle of the living room where a coffee table or a sofa should have been; flat instead of gabled roofs; surprising terraces and balconies, some off second-story bedrooms; roof gardens with umbrella tables and chairs; spotlights calling attention to the cars parked in the open-air garages (the weather was so perfect all the year round, no need to protect the cars at night from the cold wind and wet rain like you had to do in Pennsylvania); and grand double-door front entrances with doorbells that chimed an entire melody before the pert butler or maid answered the door and said, who may I say is calling? For the lucky people who lived in these modern pleasure palaces, there was no difference between inside and outside. Everything was on display, everything visible, nothing secret, nothing shameful; everything was made, proudly, to be seen and enjoyed as a thing of beauty.

Figure 17. The house I grew up in, Reading, Pennsylvania, January 1987.

I think what I missed in the house I grew up in was a sense of spatial perspective. The house, built around 1960 (fig. 17), is a sturdy, two-story colonial with four bedrooms upstairs; a den, living room, kitchen, and dining room downstairs; a big two-room basement; four bathrooms (two upstairs, one downstairs, one in the basement); a two-car garage with two garage doors and a driveway that goes straight from the house to the street (no elegant crescent-shaped driveways as some people had in my neighborhood); a path from the curb to the front door, also straight, which we rarely used, and a cement area connecting the driveway to the kitchen door on the side of the house. (The distinguishing feature of this cement square was a pair of baby shoe prints, which my brother, John, had made when he was a little boy of two or three and the cement hadn't dried yet and, impetuously, John just walked right onto the wet cement while my dad was smoothing it over; years later when we had the cement redone, my parents decided not to pave over the shoe prints but to leave them there for all to see as a kind of little concrete welcome mat.) There's an attic with a crescent window at each end (after I'd

grown up and moved away, after I'd seen Europe—seen how four-square
London looked after Paris, how new and straight and plain everything
in the U.S. looked after London—I realized with some feeling of wonder, wow, those windows in the attic are almost beautiful! I had taken
them for granted all those years, but there they were: beveled glass, window panes in the simple shape of a starburst or a peacock's tail fan, and
they opened out on hinges instead of sliding up and down like all the
other windows in the house). And a single brick chimney on top.

In addition to the crescent windows in the attic, there were a few special features here and there: a cupola on top of the garage, crowned by
a weather-vane; brick on the first floor, aluminum siding on the second;
a street-side lamppost with a glass-paneled chamber on top; small built-
in bookshelves on either side of the fireplace in the living room; bricks
around the fireplace and large, grey flagstones at its hearth; a large built-
in wall of shelving in the den with a discreet, narrow door on one side
that opened onto a space behind the shelves and which could be used to
store card tables, or other unwieldy but flat objects; a bay window in the
den looking out onto the backyard, though without quite enough room
in the window seat to sit or recline comfortably; wood paneling waist-
high in the dining room; an outdoor stairwell in the back of the house
leading down to a door in the basement—all of these, minor, diverting
touches in what seemed an otherwise unremarkable house.

The main experience of being inside the house was one of disconti-
nuity in space. When you were in the kitchen, you couldn't see the den
or the living room. And while through one kitchen doorway you caught
a glimpse of the stairway down the hall, and through another you could
see into the adjoining dining room, both doorways had doors in them
(these weren't graceful, ceremonial thresholds), and if you closed the
doors, you'd feel as if you were in the only room in the whole world. And
it was like that in nearly every other room in the house as well. The house
wasn't cramped exactly, or at least it didn't feel cramped, but I guess it
was designed for maximum room size and so it minimized in quantity
and quality the passage from room to room. That was one of the wonderful things about the houses in Ft. Lauderdale: attention had been given,
it seemed, to the transition from room to room, to the relationship between rooms, to all the rooms together as an aesthetic ensemble. There
seemed to be an awareness on the part of architects and inhabitants alike
that living in a house consisted not just in being in any particular place,
but, more importantly perhaps, in *moving* from place to place within, in
looking from a particular vantage point, in *being seen* from another. The
person who designed my family's house seemed to have thought of none

of this; the architecture of our house was driven neither by the special needs of its eventual inhabitants nor by the unique, overarching vision of its designer.

The modern architecture I saw in Florida, however, was not the only architecture that came as a relief from the unimaginative efficiency of the house I grew up in. During roughly the same period as our trip to Ft. Lauderdale, my parents took us on a trip to Chicago to visit our friends, the McDonalds, a big family with six or seven kids, who had lived in our town for a few years but then had to move to Chicago because of Mr. McDonald's work. The McDonalds lived in an enormous old Victorian house in suburban Chicago unlike anything I'd ever seen. This house had six floors! (Our house only had two floors, plus an attic, which didn't count as a floor because we only used it for storage, and a basement.) There wasn't just one upstairs floor of bedrooms like in our house, but *three* of them, and each floor had its own unique plan, different from the others. The staircase was twisty and irregular, with several cozy little landings (our staircase at home was just one straight shot, nothing fancy); there were fireplaces in some of the bedrooms (imagine bothering to make life in the bedroom so pleasant!) and stained-glass transoms above some of the doors. There was a big front porch with a flight of stairs leading up to it (we had no front porch at our house, just a narrow porch area elevated by only a single step from the driveway, and you couldn't really fit tables and chairs on it the way you could on the McDonalds' front porch, and you would never visit people on our little porch area the way the McDonalds could entertain people on their front porch, all day if they wanted to).

What I discovered, then, in the Mark 500 and in the mansions along the river in Florida and in all those unbuilt houses going up in my neighborhood and in the McDonalds' rambling old Victorian funny house was a feeling of self-consciousness made possible by the structure, or lack of structure, of the space itself. It was the same feeling I had when seeing and imagining what it would be like to inhabit the high-ceilinged entrance foyer of the von Trapp family villa, or the opulent Harmonia Gardens Restaurant, or the grand, ill-fated ballroom of the SS *Poseidon:* the feeling of being out in the open air even as you stayed indoors—open interior space; a feeling that no matter what you did and no matter how insignificant it was, you were visible—that all the various parts of the house were not only physically connected with each other but were, somehow, *aware* of each other. *Sentient space.* A feeling that there had been an aesthetic intention, not simply a functional one, in the arrangement of space. Space designed to meet the individual needs of its inhabitants, rather than the inhabitants forced to adjust their needs to the constraints of the space. (Some years later, as a college junior in London, I would again feel this way—not, however, about a style of architecture, but, rather, about a style of writing: the high, woman-centered modernism of Virginia Woolf's *Mrs. Dalloway,* with all of its dynamic tension between interiority and external reality. It was *Mrs. Dalloway* that made me realize how much it was possible to love to read, and eventually to write.)

But you could also get lost in all of this architecture old and new, built and unbuilt, and that was its other main attraction for me. Because for all the internal fragmentation of the house I grew up in, somehow it always seemed there was never enough privacy. I always seemed to be getting caught doing something I didn't want anyone else to know about. Once, my cousin Jimmy caught me lip-synching to the original Broadway cast album of *Camelot.* I had just seen a local high school production of the musical that spring and was busy imagining a multi-million-dollar film version starring Barbra Streisand as Guenevere. (I hadn't yet seen the actual film version starring Vanessa Redgrave, but I'd just started listening to my parents' copy of *The Second Barbra Streisand Album,* on which Barbra sings "Who Will Buy?" from *Oliver,* and she did that so beautifully that I figured she would be a good choice to play Guenevere because, after all, playing a medieval queen would be no more of a stretch for a modern Brooklyn girl like Barbra than singing the song of a nineteenth-century London orphan boy.) And another time, some years later, my sister Suzanne's friend Tom, who came home with her on their spring break from college, caught me masturbating in my room, which I had to share with him during his visit. (I might have been caught jerking off many more times if my room hadn't been right at the top of the stairs so that the sound of people's knees cracking or their pocket change jingling as they climbed the stairs served as a warning for me to pull up my pants, smooth out the covers, and resume whatever it was I was supposed to be doing—studying, playing records, or sleeping.)

I lacked privacy, however, not only because there were eight of us living under one roof, and then the house was always full of visitors and relatives and friends milling about. I felt perpetually exposed because the walls were so thin you could hear conversations in the kitchen when you were upstairs in the bedroom. You couldn't block out the sound of the TV in the den when you were in the living room, even if you shut the door between the two rooms. Mom and Dad's snoring could be heard all the way down the opposite end of the hall (what a drag). The rooms were bunched up and piled in on each other. Intimacy and beauty had been sacrificed for volume and economy.

My dad says that when they bought the house in 1961, it cost $40,000, "which seemed like a ton of money then," but it was worth the invest-

ment because they had been living in a smaller ranch-style house where
everything was on one floor, and it was so hard once you put the kids to
bed to watch a little TV or even just to have a conversation because the
noise would wake them up—and of course the family kept growing, so
they needed a bigger house with a bigger yard.

In *The Feminine Mystique* (1963), Betty Friedan argues that "the contemporary 'ranch' or split-level house" is part of what keeps women from
realizing their full personhood beyond the spousal and maternal duties
enshrined in "the feminine mystique": these kinds of houses "give the
illusion of more space for less money. But the women to whom they are
sold almost *have* to live the feminine mystique. There are no true walls
or doors; the woman in the beautiful electronic kitchen is never separated from her children. She need never feel alone for a minute, need
never be by herself. She can forget her own identity in those noisy open-
plan houses. The open plan also helps expand the housework to fill the
time available. In what is basically one free-flowing room, instead of
many rooms separated by walls and stairs, continual messes continually
need picking up. A man, of course, leaves the house for most of the day.
But the feminine mystique forbids the woman this" (245–46). I doubt
that moving from the smaller ranch-style house to the larger colonial-
style house gave my mom a sense of freedom to transcend her roles as
wife and mother, and I'm not sure that the differences between the two
houses in terms of their organization of space had much of an effect,
in the long run, on my family's quality of life. Over the years my family
made relatively minor adjustments within the overarching dome of suburbia (even now, my parents are busily engaged in building a bigger
kitchen and a new den onto the house), but the larger, deadening fact
of suburbia, and its attendant architectural ethos of mass production,
never changed.

For all the ambitiousness of my architectural wishes, I did have one oddly
small-scale idea for a house that I would return to in my mind again
and again over the years, especially as I grew into my teens. I imagined
a modest one-story dwelling with a simple front door—no fanfare—that
opened into a rather dark foyer. The house consisted basically of one
not very large rectangular space. As you entered the house through the
front door, you immediately faced a large, plain wall. The wall in my
mind was always a dour shade of blue (I hadn't forgotten about the wall
that Barbara Streisand faced as a teenager, with her back to her friends,
singing the sad song that made them cry). It seemed to have no struc-
tural function; it didn't reach all the way to the ceiling, nor was it flush
with the right-hand or left-hand walls of the house. It was almost like a

screen for projecting things onto, or a blank canvas ready for painting. Or it was like sculpture: you could walk around the wall to the other side of it. The wall existed tentatively, as if it was on the verge of not being a wall, but it was and remains to my mind the single most striking and important feature of the house.

I also imagined two coach lamps, one at either end, attached to the wall, casting a dull glow, and against the wall in the center, a small table for the placement, perhaps, of letters (like the letter that Maria left on the side table in the von Trapp family foyer—the letter that said, "I'm leaving, farewell") or keys or cards or flowers or some other small, ordinary objects. Behind the wall my mind went cloudy—there would be some kind of kitchenette, and a bedroom, or maybe just a bed. I didn't envision much of a living space here, although there did seem to be something quite self-sufficient about the place, sufficient for one lonely person, at least.

For attaching to the place was always that peculiar feeling of loneliness, sadness, sterility—of being bereft. Increasingly I would imagine this place as the setting for a movie; it would be the kind of place to retreat to when you are old and alone, or when you've just had a miscarriage, or an abortion, or when you've just gotten married but still you feel awkward with your partner, and the life you are about to embark upon holds little promise, hardly any flavor, or your husband (or your wife) is still a mystery and a stranger to you after years of marriage and you feel like you're entering a void. The place looked neat and well-kept, but it was in so many ways an impoverished place, a place without windows, without much air to breathe. In a way, it was a place of death, a funereal home. A house nowhere.

I can think of two possible sources for this architectural fantasy. One is a part of the downstairs hallway, a wall maybe eight feet long, in the house I grew up in. Against the wall there was a bulky wooden bench that doubled as a toy chest, but kind of a crappy-toy chest—I mean, the toys we kept in it weren't the ones we used much because the bench was cumbersome to open and close. On the wall above the bench two sconces were hung (fig. 13, in chapter 3).

The other source is my hometown church, Sacred Heart. Behind the altar and the priests' and altar boys' chairs there was a large, freestanding wall, papered in gold. It provided a backdrop to the altar and (its main function) concealed the entrance to the sacristy directly behind it. For years until I became an altar boy, I was fascinated by the thought of what went on behind that wall—where did they disappear to when they went behind there after the mass was over? What did it look like on the other side of the wall?

My imaginary wall and the melancholy house that contained it may have first come to me when I heard Carole King's "It's Too Late" one summer in the early 1970s while visiting my Aunt Rita's house at the Jersey shore. I may have been thinking (as I often did whenever we went to someone else's house) how much more comfortable *our* beach house was, and then the song was so honest and true about a relationship gone irreversibly lifeless, and for some reason I felt as if I had lived through the kind of trouble Carole King was singing about: "Something inside has died and I can't hide and I just can't fake it."

I had all kinds of architectural ideas growing up, most of them gigantic, and, increasingly, implicated in fantasies about making movies. I would always have major architecture fantasies when I would be taking a bath. I loved baths better than showers because you could wallow in them, and they were the perfect occasion to practice stroking my cock. They went on for forty-five minutes, sometimes an hour at a time, until someone else in the house lost their patience and shouted for me to get out. At some point around the same time as stroking my cock started to feel *really* good (but before I had my first orgasm), I found that running water from the spigot in the bathtub plus liberal helpings of shampoo made lots of slippery soap suds, and they were great for cock-stroking (what a waste, my mother would say if she only knew how much shampoo I was using!). As I lay in the water up to my ears, playing with myself, slowly lifting my leg out of the water and pretending it was some great and terrible sea monster breaking the surface, I transformed in my mind the porcelain sides of the tub and the tile walls of the shower into acres and acres of luxury high-rise apartments and office buildings. The tub would often become a kind of spectacular apartment building/hotel/shopping mall/entertainment complex with mile-long escalators (the outside surface of the rectangular tub was carved with sleek, diagonal lines) and an occasional, fanciful roof garden or grand balcony (the soap dish, carved into the inside surface of the tub). I imagined thousands of people enjoying this mega-complex, with long lines of them waiting to get in to see a movie. (In his history of suburbia in America, *Crabgrass Frontier*, Kenneth T. Jackson describes the advent of the "super regional mall," not unlike the one I fantasized about while soaking in the bathtub: "During the 1970s, a new phenomenon—the super regional mall—added a more elaborate twist to suburban shopping. Prototypical of the new breed was Tyson's Corner, on the Washington Beltway in Fairfax County, Virginia. Anchored by Bloomingdale's, it did over $165 million of business in 1987 and provided employment to more than 14,000 persons. . . . Most elaborate of all was Huston's Galleria, a world-famed setting for 240 prestigious boutiques, a quartet of cinemas, 26 restaurants, an Olympic-sized ice-skating pavilion, and two luxury hotels" [260].)

Movies and architecture converged again in my mind for my famous deluxe movie theater/convention center, which was so massive a structure that it couldn't be envisioned in an urban context as a series of skyscrapers but had to be built in the suburbs instead. You had to drive at least two hours from anywhere to get there (the way, for example, we had to drive two hours or so to get to Hersheypark in Hershey, Pennsylvania, which, along with New York City, was one of my favorite destinations growing up). The main attraction of this place was a huge movie screen several stories high with an incredible sound system (inspired by the several-stories-high movie screen at the Smithsonian Institution's National Air and Space Museum in Washington, D.C., which I'd visited sometime in the early seventies), and they even gave you a *program* when you came in, like they did when you went to a Broadway show (I always wished there was more fanfare associated with going to the movies, like my mom said there was when she was a kid).

But that wasn't all. The place was such a labyrinthine city-in-miniature that you needed a special color-coded map to find your way around (I wasn't exactly sure what the complex contained besides the cinema, but I knew that whatever it was, it was of great importance — maybe a hospital—certainly nothing so common as the shops at our local mall). I learned this, I'm pretty sure, from watching a *Medical Center* episode, or some kind of doctor or detective show on TV, in which the path to any particular part of the hospital was indicated by a painted stripe along the floors or walls. So, for example, if you wanted to go to pediatrics, you just followed the blue line—kind of like Dorothy following the Yellow Brick Road to Oz right from the very beginning in Munchkinland. Likewise, in my fantasy movie theater/convention center, there was a bewildering network of variously colored stripes on the floor, and you were given special cards that got punched by machines every so often (I'm not sure exactly what all of this was for, but it reminded me of driving along the highway and every so often going through a toll booth and receiving a card with numbers and hole punches all over it—who knew what all those numbers and hole punches meant?—or dropping money in a bucket or giving it to the attendant).

The point was, it all felt very serious and off-putting, and that's what I was reaching for with my complex: it was a place where you could easily get lost, you frequently *did* get lost, and when you did, boy, were you in trouble. I even had police squads in residence to go in search of poor lost souls, as well as an emergency room for people who got lost and were so overcome with panic and fear that they needed special medical assistance. I loved the idea of entertainment shading into nightmare—learned partly from disaster movies, partly from reports of audience members fainting or otherwise going into hysterics over *The Exorcist* and having to be carried out of the movie theater on a stretcher or in a wheelchair, and partly, I think, from having to endure the uncontrollable bodily changes brought on by puberty, like getting an erection every morning at the bus stop for no reason at all and not knowing where or how to stand so that people wouldn't see it. So I imagined audience members going into convulsions and needing medical assistance over, for example, the movie version of *Mame*—obviously not because there was anything horrific about *Mame* or movies like it, or about Lucille Ball, but because the audience would be so overstimulated by the spectacle of New York City in the Roaring Twenties and the wrenching sadness of the Depression that abruptly followed and the profundity of Lucille Ball's performance that encompassed it all that they would need to lie down and take a nap.

People always used to say to me, when I'd usher them into the den or down to the basement to see the finished product of my afternoon's labor, a great pile of blocks in the form of a spiraling, turreted, gabled, pinnacled estate, "You're going to be an architect someday." For some reason, that felt like an accusation. I felt embarrassed and mildly insulted by the suggestion. For one thing, architecture sounded somehow like a man's job, and I didn't like to see myself in the burdensome role of manhood. Secondly, I thought what I really wanted to be when I grew up was a priest. I may have perceived on some level that designing buildings meant that you would eventually have to let them go, whereas being a priest meant that you were always up there on stage, at the center of everyone's attention, talking and singing and leading everyone in prayer.

But at the same time, architecture and religious life had something in common. Sometimes when I built blocks I had an inkling of infinity: I would look at the structure I had just made, and think, in this house (the house I lived in) lives a boy (me) who builds blocks, and in the house of blocks he builds there lives a boy who builds blocks, and in that house there's a boy who builds blocks, and in that house a boy who builds blocks and in that house . . . and in that house . . .

I loved dollhouses and probably would have developed a lifelong interest in them if it hadn't been impressed upon me so forcefully that dollhouses were for girls. My sisters had a simple dollhouse in one of their bedrooms which eventually I had to play with in secret. At a certain point during the day, my mom would notice that I wasn't in the basement or on the first floor, and I hadn't gone outside, so where could I have gone? I wasn't in my bedroom—wasn't in any of the bathrooms—she would call my name:

"Patrick, where are you?"

"I'm up here."

"Where's 'here'?"

"In Mary Jo and Sue's room."

"What are you doing?"

As if she didn't know. And *now* what was I going to say? Should I lie and say that I had lost something and I was looking for it in the girls' bedroom? But she would never believe that—what could I possibly have lost in the girls' bedroom? And anyway, what would I have been doing there in the first place? There seemed to be no way to keep up the deception, so I had to give up playing with dollhouses.

But not before I tried to get a dollhouse of my own. I wanted a Fisher Price dollhouse which, however, my mom said wasn't appropriate for me because the package said it was for children ages three to eight, and I was nine. But I knew the real reason was, I was a boy and dollhouses were for girls, even though there was a picture of *both* a boy *and* a girl playing with it on the box—though it's true, the boy looked to be about four years old or even younger, while the girl was more like seven or eight, the implication being, look at the little boy trying to join in playing with his older sister's dollhouse, he doesn't quite know what he's doing (he's not invested in domestic fantasy and interior design like she is), isn't his unself-consciousness cute! Whereas if I had gotten a dollhouse, I would have known exactly what I was doing.

My dad would often tell the story of how, when he was still living at home as a young man with his parents and younger siblings, one of his sisters had made a new dress and was proudly showing it off to everyone. He said to her, "Why, that dress is big enough to fit a house."

"Oh Jack, no it's not!" she cried.

"Oh yes it is," he said, "I'll show you." And he took the dress and put it over the girls' dollhouse and said, triumphant, "See? I told you it was big enough to fit a house!"

"Oh Jack!" she cried.

Every year from around the time I was seven years old until I went to high school, my father and I would build a miniature train-yard at Christmas. We would begin discussing the layout for the train-yard sometime in late October. One year Dad took me out to breakfast after church on Sunday morning—we went to a diner (I loved diner breakfasts: pancakes, sausage, juice, and hot chocolate, and sometimes a sec-

ond and even a third cup of it!)—and after we'd eaten, or while we were
waiting for the food to come, Dad took a napkin from the silver dis-
penser on the table and started sketching possible ways to lay out the
train tracks this year. The usual platform we used was eight feet by four
feet, but, I wondered, couldn't we make it bigger this year, say in an
L shape, by adding another four square feet to the platform? Well that's
getting quite elaborate—do we have enough train track for that? Dad
asked. No, but couldn't we buy some more? I asked in return. We'll see.
How about a figure eight? Possibly. Then there were the years when we
got more proficient and added mountains, and even an elevated train
track and a tunnel. Dad would say, now we know better than last year
how to construct a mountain. We know we have to lift the entire track
on pilings; the train can't make it up any steep inclines. But how will
we prop it up? Oh, I'm sure they sell some kind of thing for that—they
have all kinds of stuff for really fancy track work, but, as you know, your
father is somewhat limited as to what he can come up with, but we can
certainly give it a try. The possibilities seemed endless. I couldn't conceal
my excitement about all the things we would try this year—this year, I
knew, it would be the best train-yard we had ever done.

Every night when Dad got home from work I would hound him to
come downstairs to the basement and work on the train-yard with me.
Some nights he didn't have time or could only give me a couple of hours,
or maybe just a half hour, but then other nights it would be all evening,
and then he would spend all day Saturday or all day Sunday with me
as well. I would often hear my mom or someone else say, "Okay, now,
leave your father alone! He spent *how* many hours with you on that train-
yard yesterday, and now he's going to rest!" Or, "and now he's going to
play some tennis with your brother and sisters!" or, "he's going to spend
some time with *me!*"

"You can do it by yourself, you don't need me, you know what you're
doing," my dad began to say more and more, the older I got. But that
wasn't the point.

One night Dad and I were doing the lighting for the train-yard. This
was always a backbreaking job for my dad (I watched but didn't completely understand what he was doing): you had to run two wires from
the generator underneath and across the length of the platform. Then
you had to attach all the other lights in the train-yard—the tiny lights inside each of the houses, street lamps, traffic lights, train signals, and so
on—to these two main wires. It was a tough job, requiring Dad to lie on
his back underneath the platform, and I'd have to shine a flashlight on
what he was doing and adjust the pillow under his head and sometimes

even mop the sweat off his forehead. And every year my mom would worry that it was too much of a strain on him and that he would injure his back doing it, and why didn't he teach me how to do it myself?

Mom came downstairs to see how things were going. I was completely absorbed in what we were doing, but I was also thrilled that she showed an interest in the train-yard because it was something that no one else in the family shared with my dad but me. Wanting to show off, I told her, "Stick around, you might learn something!"

Suddenly my dad barked at me, "*Don't* say that to your mother!"

"I just meant—"

"Jack, *that's enough,* it's been long enough, it's almost eleven o'clock. You'll miss the news."

"Okay, Peg." Then to me, "I think you owe your mother an apology."

I vaguely remember one conversation I had with my dad about girls while we were working on the train-yard. I asked him if he ever had any girlfriends when he was my age (nine or so), and he said, yes, there was a girl he liked named Virginia, and this surprised me because I'd never heard him talk about any other girls or women in his life besides Mom. I forget if he asked me if *I* had any girlfriends—at that time it would have been a new girl in school named Elizabeth Hoffman—and I'm not sure, if he had asked, how much I would have said about her.

I learned a lesson in delayed gratification working on the train-yard with my dad. This was the first year we decided to try building a mountain. We started with blocks as a base (my wooden blocks, which I had long ceased playing with—the ones that made everyone think I should become an architect), then we molded and stapled chicken wire around them (I wondered, but never asked, what is "chickeny" about "chicken wire" anyway?), then applied layer upon layer of paper towels soaked in plaster-of-paris (another strange term I never openly questioned—"of Paris," as in the city?) on top of the wire. Finally we spray painted it green and added miniature shrubs, trees, and houses. As we were just beginning to apply the plaster-coated strips of paper towel, I created what seemed to me a perfect and realistic mountain ridge out of the ripples and folds of the paper towels. Already I could see my mountain taking shape! Dad, working fast and, I thought, sloppy, indelicately

plopped down on top of my beautiful little mountain ridge a whole wad
of soaking-wet paper towels, thereby obliterating it completely.
"*Nnnoooooo!*" I protested. "I *wanted* it like that!"

Again exasperated, he said sharply, "Pat, this is only the beginning!
We're gonna have to put *multiple* layers of this stuff on to make it strong.
You're not even gonna *begin* to see what it'll look like when it's finished
until we've done all the plastering and then the painting. *Then* you can
start fussing about how you want the trees and shrubs, or what have you,
to look, but we're nowhere near that stage yet. Okay?" (plop!)

"Okay." (tsk)

My favorite part of building the train-yard was putting on all the finishing touches—designing the system of (cardboard) roads, deciding which
end of town to put the three little houses under construction, placing
the trees and hedges, fencing in the lawns with little plastic white picket
fences, positioning the little people-figures here and there (always a cluster of them in front of the church, and another bunch milling around
the train station). And then the ultimate thrill was announcing to my
mom that it was finished and she could come downstairs now to see it.

Wait, wait! First I had to turn off all the basement lights, then I turned
on the train-yard lights—a perfect sparkling little world—and set the
train steadily, slowly, peacefully in motion (fig. 18). I stepped back and
said, "All right, you can come down now."

My mother always reacted to the sight of my completed train-yard
with wonderment and surprise: "Oh, Pat!! It's *beautiful!* Oh my goodness, how do you do it! It's just wonderful, honey. You are so talented,
you and your father."

Then, after a few minutes, "I've got rolls in the oven. I must get upstairs. This was great, honey. Jack, will you come slice the meat? As soon
as you're ready. Dinner should be on the table in half an hour."

"Okay, Pat, I'm going upstairs to help your mother."

I could have sat staring at the train-yard, the train sadly making its
way around and around the tracks—into the tunnel, out of the tunnel, around and around in its small world without an exit—dreaming of
another world for another hour and another hour after that.

II

I love living in New York. The feeling has deepened over the fourteen
years that I've been here. I went through a period of not liking it, which

Figure 18. The train-yard, ca. 1976.

roughly coincided with graduate school. I'd gotten to the point where I almost couldn't be out in public—crowds on the sidewalk drove me crazy, the mere presence of other people, at home or out of doors, made me angry. I feel differently now, the way I felt when I first moved here in the fall of 1985, which was a kind of perpetual "I can't believe I live here all the time!" I walked everywhere—to work, to the Village, to Times Square, to Central Park, to Penn Station when friends arrived from out of town for a visit. At the beginning of Virginia Woolf's *Mrs. Dalloway,* Clarissa Dalloway says to Hugh Whitbread, blithely, "I love walking in London. . . . Really, it's better than walking in the country" (6). I felt like that about New York.

In fact, one of the reasons I loved *Hello, Dolly!* so much as an adolescent was that it captured so well, I thought (though I didn't learn the
word until years later), the *flaneur's* ecstatic submission to the tidal wave
of city life. The brilliant precredit sequence opens with what looks like
an authentic photograph of late-nineteenth-century New York City. It's a
brown-and-white shot of the movie set, a stupendous replica of New York
circa 1890—but then it begins to change into color: green first, then
blue, then full color. Then, the picture gradually comes to life (a thin,
curved line expands from the upper-right-hand corner of the screen,
setting the image into motion as it moves from right to left). Next,
images of feet—walking, hopping, strutting, skipping magically, "accidentally" in time to the music: a horse's hooves clip-clopping along the
street; a man sweeping the gutter with a broom; a woman walking along
the sidewalk (is it Dolly?—apparently not, because the camera moves
away); a boy rattling a stick along a fence; a man and a small girl coming
out of a doorway, the girl skipping, past a tall, skinny man who, after
getting his shoe shined, struts along the sidewalk (watching the movie
with me recently, my friend Tom said, "well there's a big queen!") until
he bumps into a young woman, at which point they change course and
walk off in a different direction together; a girl playing hopscotch, and,
beyond her, three girls playing jump rope, until a horse-drawn street-
cleaning car sprays water on the sidewalk, shooing them away; a man
flanked by two women, proudly strutting down the street, then dodging
the street cleaner's hose; a kid zipping by on a scooter; a woman carrying groceries, climbing the front stairs of an apartment building (could
this be Dolly?), and passing at the top of the stairs another woman, wearing a colorful reddish-brown dress and swinging her handbag—a chorus
of male and female voices sings "call on Dolly . . ." (now we know, *this is
Dolly!* though we haven't yet seen her face) ". . . if your neighbor needs
a new romance"—and the camera pulls away from her feet, as we watch
her, from behind, strutting down the block, her arms stretched out on
either side of her, as if to embrace the day, the sunlight, the music, the
whole of New York City itself!

Shot only from behind or, in one instance, from above, Dolly now
swims through the city, here on foot, there on top of a street car, like a
fish in her element, handing out her calling card—first to this woman,
then to that man; then to a policeman, a workman hanging upside down
from a street lamp, a man in a sewer, and a fat woman riding on top of a
trolley. In a breathtaking overhead shot, two white-capped street clean-
ers push their carts along the cobble-stoned street as Dolly passes between them in the opposite direction, extending her card generously to
each one. And now, a shot of what at first looks like a somewhat abstract

arrangement of turkey feathers—the camera begins to circle around it—we have been looking, it turns out, at Dolly's hat, and the hat, we now realize, is on top of her head. Finally, we see Barbra Streisand's face come into full view. She smiles warily at the camera, gently snickers as if sharing a little private joke with us, as if she's known us for years and is glad to see her old friends again; she sings, "I have always been a woman who arranges things . . ."

The message of the opening sequence of *Hello, Dolly!* seemed to be that Dolly was somehow a part of all those anonymous people whose feet we saw going about their daily business and to whom she extends her card. Dolly struts through the city with her arms outstretched because, in some important sense, she *is* the city. She encompasses everything she sees, she sums it all up in herself—in her spirit, her sense of humor, her variegated speaking style, her rhythm, her generosity.

In his 1863 essay "The Painter of Modern Life," Charles Baudelaire says of the painter Constantin Guys what might also be said of Barbra Streisand's Dolly:

> [T]he crowd is his element, as the air is that of birds and water of fishes. His passion and his profession are to become one flesh with the crowd. For the perfect *flaneur*, for the passionate spectator, it is an immense joy to set up house in the heart of the multitude, amid the ebb and flow of movement, in the midst of the fugitive and the infinite. To be away from home and yet to feel oneself everywhere at home; to see the world, to be at the centre of the world, and yet to remain hidden from the world—such are a few of the slightest pleasures of those independent, passionate, impartial natures which the tongue can but clumsily define. . . . the lover of universal life enters into the crowd as though it were an immense reservoir of electrical energy. Or we might liken him to a mirror as vast as the crowd itself; or to a kaleidoscope gifted with consciousness, responding to each one of its movements and reproducing the multiplicity of life and the flickering grace of all the elements of life. (9–10; emphasis in the original)

Seeing Barbra Streisand as Dolly Levi walk the streets of New York, I came to think of urban life as infinitely generous; it turned me into the kind of "passionate spectator" of urban life that she herself was and that Baudelaire called "the perfect flaneur": ". . . he hurls himself headlong into the midst of the throng, in pursuit of an unknown, half-glimpsed countenance that has, on an instant, bewitched him. Curiosity had become a fatal, irresistible passion!" (7)

The depiction of urban life in *Hello, Dolly!* was different from anything I'd encountered before. When I was in grade school, for example, I learned about city life from reading and rereading Virginia Lee Bur-

ton's *The Little House*. In this classic children's story, written in 1943, a
little pink house, comfortably situated "way out in the country" (1), suf-
fers the transition from an agricultural to an industrial society but in
the end manages to return to a preindustrial, pre-urban, prelapsarian
way of life. The house is a typical mid-twentieth-century ticky-tacky box,
but the time period when the book opens is marked as the preindustrial nineteenth century—the mother figure wears a long hoop skirt; the
father a pair of checked trousers and a Byronic head of hair and beard;
and a horse-drawn carriage, cart, and sleigh dot the landscape. Little by
little, a booming, dirty, overcrowded city mushrooms around the poor,
sweet house. Finally, it is rescued by "the great-great granddaughter,"
now grown and married with children of her own, "of the man who built
the Little House so well" (32) (throughout the book, the house is gen-
dered female—the cover illustration bears the subtitle "HER-STORY").
The house is carefully and easily lifted off its foundations and towed out
of the city, like a patient on a stretcher, to a still-undeveloped spot in the
country: "Never again would [the Little House] be curious about the
city . . . Never again would she want to live there . . . The stars twinkled
above her . . . A new moon was coming up . . . It was Spring . . . and all
was quiet and peaceful in the country" (40; ellipses in original).

Looking now at *The Little House*, I think that one of the exciting things
about it is watching the city, as the pages turn, grow and grow from a
paved road to rows and rows of suburban tract housing to block after
block of tenement buildings, and then a trolley system, an elevated train,
and a subway, one after another, burst on the scene. Meanwhile skyscrapers have risen all around and eventually supplant the tenements;
lights blaze at night, crowds of people—pedestrians, shoppers, tourists,
businessmen, construction workers, little families—point and shuffle,
gape and hurry by, as traffic rushes, rushes night and day!

A smear of browns, grays, and blacks, the city as Burton rendered it
wasn't meant to be pretty—certainly not as pretty as the house in the
country enjoying the colorful change of seasons (my mother often says
that she prefers living in Pennsylvania to places like California or Florida
because "I love the change of seasons. I'd hate it if it were always summer or always winter. I love seeing the leaves turn color in the fall—the
fall, really, is my favorite season of the year. I guess if I had to choose just
one climate, it would be a fall climate"). But I can't imagine that I didn't
enjoy each successive, methodical cutting away of the countryside, each
spurt of urban growth, loud, chaotic, and violent though it was. And no
child, I would think, could miss the visual pleasure of Burton's masses
of city dwellers, strips of little watercolor strokes in purple, brown, yellow, pink, blue, and green, sweeping right and left—as pleasing and as

abstract as the arc of thirteen orange and yellow suns with happy faces
tumbling and laughing their way across the sky at the beginning of the
book, the Little House at peace with all the world ("She watched the
sun rise in the morning and she watched the sun set in the evening. Day
followed day, and each one a little different from the one before . . . but
the Little House stayed the same" [2; ellipses in original]), or the rows
and rows of "white daisies cover[ing] the hill"—precisely drawn white
circles amid innumerable strokes of kelly green—during "the long Summer days" (8). Still, the return of the Little House to the countryside
came as a relief to me when I was a child. I liked Burton's city, but it was
at best an exciting place to visit, never a place to call home.

III

My parents took me to my first Broadway show, *Annie*, in the winter of
1977, and in the spring of 1978 I went to New York to see *The Wiz* on
a high school day trip. From then on, I visited New York with family,
school groups, and eventually with my friends—especially my friend
Beth, who shared my love of New York and Broadway theater—as often
as I was allowed (two or three visits per year). I loved everything about
the experience of going to New York, including the smell of bus exhaust
at six or seven o'clock in the morning, before the bus pulled out of the
Reading Bus Terminal in downtown Reading, and then the sun coming
up and the morning fog lifting over the rolling brown and green farm-
lands between Reading and Kutztown, which was the first stop on the
way to New York.

I didn't automatically think, however, that because I loved New York
so much I could or should live there when I grew up. I had to dwell
on the *idea* of New York before the desire and, more, the determination to live there overtook me. And it wasn't the idea of New York
City enshrined in a Broadway musical that enabled me, eventually, to
make it my new, second Home (for example, the image, however lov-
able, of 1930s New York in *Annie*: "NYC! You make 'em all postcards!");
rather, it was the idea of New York elaborated in a *Hollywood* musical
that changed my mind: the dream-vision of New York City as Oz in the
1978 film version of *The Wiz*. (Director Sidney Lumet prefaced a new
edition of L. Frank Baum's *The Wonderful Wizard of Oz*, which coincided
with the release of the film version of *The Wiz*, as follows: "The last line
of Frank Baum's original story reads, 'And oh, Aunt Em, I'm so glad to
be at home again.' The last line of the superb movie that MGM made
with Judy Garland was, 'Oh Aunt Em, there's no place like home, there's
no place like home.' The last song in *The Wiz* that Charlie Smalls wrote,

the curtain song, is called 'Home,' and its last word is 'Home.' To me, in essence, this is what the movie *The Wiz,* is all about" [vii].)

Not long before I saw *The Wiz* on Broadway, I heard or maybe read somewhere that the upcoming film version of the musical was going to be set in New York City. This was all I needed to know for my imagination to flare up with ideas for how the movie would look if I were making it myself. I loved *The Wiz* on Broadway, but I'm sure that even my initial experience of it in the theater was filtered through my desire to see it done on screen—what I saw on stage was a sketch, merely, of the movie version to come.

The first scene that came to me was the Winkies' joyous celebration after Dorothy kills Evillene, the slave-driving, sweatshop-ruling Wicked Witch of the West. Luther Vandross's anthemic "A Brand New Day" was the best, most immediately stirring song in the show ("Can't you feel a brand new day?"), and I recognized its big-screen possibilities immediately. I felt that there needed to be many more singers and dancers than were used on stage, and that the number should feel not just like a "day of independence" (as the Munchkins call it when Dorothy's house lands on the Wicked Witch of the East in the 1939 film) but full-scale national liberation—the second coming! Armageddon! May Day! The dawn of a new era, at long, long last, the Kingdom of Heaven here on earth!

It seemed only natural, then, to stage this production number on the roof of the tallest building in New York City, the World Trade Center, which had been used so stunningly in the 1976 remake of *King Kong,* although, it was true, Kong never straddles the twin towers in the film as he is pictured doing in the movie poster (if only they had pulled off *that* special effect!). I'd already heard that the World Trade Center would stand in for the Emerald City in the film, and so I figured that the celebration of the witch's death would not happen there but, rather, somewhere nearer her lair—which, being a sweatshop, I had trouble visualizing, since I didn't even know what a sweatshop was. I had some notion that it was a factory, but why "sweat"? Because the working conditions were so awful or the work so strenuous that it made you sweat? Because they made sweatshirts and sweatpants in this kind of factory? Or you had to *wear* sweatpants and sweatshirts in this place? The point is, not knowing enough about what a sweatshop looked like and how to stage a big production number in it, I felt that the World Trade Center was the best place to send up fireworks about the witch's death.

I figured we could shoot parts of the scene on a soundstage made to look like the top of the World Trade Center (although I knew there were two towers, I only imagined the scene taking place atop one), but for the really big effects, we would actually have to get the entire cast up there on the roof somehow and shoot the scene with swooping helicopters, which would fly toward the top of the building so close as if they were about to crash right into the side of the building, but just at the last split-second, they would glide right over the top of it, over all the actors' heads, showing, as in a Busby Berkeley production number, the elaborate, abstract patterns they made as they danced.

I had a few precedents for this aerial photography. First, the camera work at the beginning of *The Sound of Music*, which culminated in a zoom-in shot, via helicopter, of Julie Andrews on top of a mountain; second, the climax of "Don't Rain on My Parade" in *Funny Girl*, where the camera flies across New York Harbor and zooms in on Barbra Streisand as Fanny Brice, standing at the prow of a blue tug boat, singing; third, the shots of Yves Montand in *On a Clear Day You Can See Forever* singing "Come Back to Me" to Barbra Streisand's Daisy Gamble (he's her psychiatrist; she doesn't know it but she's the reincarnation of a nineteenth-century English noblewoman, Melinda, with whom he has fallen in love, only Daisy finds out inadvertently by hearing the tapes of her sessions with him, so she runs away—it's a long story), as, again, the camera, suspended from a helicopter, floats toward him (I always thought it should have been *Barbra* up there on the roof of the Pan Am building, singing a song!); and fourth, the image of a lone helicopter in *The Towering Inferno* (all about how the tallest building in the world burns down), underneath the opening credits, flying over sea and mountains (of all things, *The Towering Inferno* most resembles *The Sound of Music* at this point), making its bumblebee way toward San Francisco and the roof of a gleaming, unnaturally tall skyscraper; and again later in the film, when a helicopter tries to land on the roof to rescue a group of women stranded in a restaurant on the top floor of the building as the fire rages below them, but as the poor mechanical bird nears touchdown, something goes wrong, and it bursts into flames!

I also imagined, in my movie version of *The Wiz*, huge banks of floodlights—possibly tinted green—shooting off the roof of the World Trade Center as hundreds of people sing and dance and the camera buzzes around the top of the building. (Hollywood is slowly catching up with me: there's a scene very much like this in *Independence Day* [1996].) We would shoot the scene at night, so you wouldn't be able to see the ground, except maybe for a splattering of lights; you'd feel, instead, as if you were rocketing through space on a flying beam. (My love of spectacle often carried over into my real life during the late seventies and not always with the best consequences. For example, as editor in chief of my senior yearbook in high school, I wanted to have a hand in planning the school mass on the day the yearbooks were distributed. I had ideas for hymns and readings that would be particularly appropriate for this special mass, ideas about how the yearbook staff [with me at the head] would process into the gymnasium along with the priest and the altar boys, how maybe I or one of my sub-subeditors could read select passages from the yearbook after communion but before the recessional hymn [or maybe we could have a slide show after communion featuring photos from the yearbook!], ideas about how we could all be wearing our official yearbook-staff pins or perhaps corsages bought especially for the occasion [were funds available for such things? I wanted to know]. One day a bunch of us staff members were standing in the hallway discussing all of this with the principal, whose permission we needed, and Mrs. Kreisel, the yearbook faculty advisor. Now, Mrs. Kreisel and I had battled it out all year over the yearbook. I felt that she was only doing her job as faculty yearbook advisor for the little stipend she got for it at the end of the year but that, otherwise, she had no real interest in, and certainly no real aptitude for, making a book; I, on the other hand, was supercommitted to every detail of every phase of the book's production and reveled in the responsibility and the authority vested in me as editor in chief [this was another thing I had in common with Barbra Streisand—both of us were perfectionists, and the older we got the more important it became that we controlled as many aspects of our work as possible]. But it was late May, the book was finally finished, nerves were frayed, and Mrs. Kreisel, frankly, had had it up to here with my big ideas. As I proposed to the principal all the things we might do with the yearbook mass, Mrs. Kreisel, now out of all patience, raised her voice at me, right there in the middle of the hallway, in front of everyone: "Patrick! We'll have none of your Cecil B. DeMille productions! We're not doing anything fancy for this mass! It'll be just another mass like any other mass, yearbook or no yearbook, and that's final!")

The next major cluster of images that came to me for the film version of *The Wiz* that I was developing in my head—images that were partly inspired by something I'd heard about the making of the film (that the avenues and bridges of New York were being paved with golden linoleum, called "Congoleum," representing, of course, the Yellow Brick Road)—involved Dorothy and her companions dodging and darting their way through the carnival of New York City street life. It was a combination of ethnic pride parade and noisy, bustling New York traffic— taxis, cars, buses, trucks, pushers, peddlers, pedestrians, strollers, vendors, dancers, acrobats, people on skates and people on skateboards, bicycles, unicycles, tricycles, and bicycles built for two, even a fleet of horse-drawn carriages—all merrily making their way on a pilgrimage across the Brooklyn Bridge toward some promised land, which, however, was nothing more or less than midtown Manhattan (for that was the only part of New York that I was really familiar with). In other words, their destination was the place where, at least in my mind, they already were. I could see Dorothy and her friends caught in a (wonderful!) traffic jam, having to climb over the hoods of cars and buses, weaving through rows of stalled traffic, running the red lights. Just getting around New York City, never mind the nitty gritty of the Wizard, the Witch, and the Winkies, was dreamworld enough. It gave you enough to do, to see, and to remember for a lifetime; it was all the initiation into the real world, into adulthood, that you—or Dorothy, or anyone—would ever need. Imagine *living* there! Imagine waking up and seeing all of that outside your window. Life would be one continuous production number after all!, not unlike the New York City of 1890 in *Hello, Dolly!*, where one production number—"Dancing"—flows seamlessly into another—"Before the Parade Passes By"—and where the narrative is *advanced*, not impeded, by singing and dancing! Street life in New York City was wall-to-wall musical comedy. I couldn't think of anything else for Dorothy and her friends to do there other than, simply, to *be* there. No going back to Kansas after that.

(Years later, on a bright sunny Sunday in June of 1986, my parents came to New York for a visit. We were walking down Fifth Avenue from the Guggenheim Museum to the Plaza Hotel when we accidentally intercepted the annual Gay Pride March—at that moment, the gay square dancers' contingent was turning the corner at Fifty-ninth Street and Fifth Avenue. I didn't realize that it was Gay Pride Day and I'd never seen the march before. I had to watch. But my parents were ambivalent: "The sun is too bright on this street, it's hurting my eyes; let's walk over one block to Madison Avenue, okay?" my mom said.

"Okay, if you want to," I said, "but I'll catch up with you in half an hour, how does that sound?"

Okay, they said and departed. I stood on the corner and watched in utter amazement, as if I'd stumbled upon the cast and crew of *The Wiz* filming "A Brand New Day." I was out to myself and to my family, but I still hadn't come out in the world—as yet I didn't know anyone in New York who was gay. This must be why I'm here, I thought, this is what I've been searching for, as hundreds of gay people streamed past in broad daylight. I had never felt so happy to be alone in a crowd.)

Little by little my appreciation for the *actual* film version of *The Wiz* crowded out my fantasy of what the film should be. It's too bad, in a way, because I think if they had followed my instructions, they would have made a better film. I learned about the film in bits and pieces, through

advanced notices; feature stories on members of the cast; the new paper-
back edition of Baum's *The Wonderful Wizard of Oz,* which I bought not
because I wanted to read the book but because it had (as the book jacket
proclaimed) "32 full pages of exciting, colorful scenes from the spectacular hit movie plus Director Sidney Lumet's account of how Baum's
Kansas fantasy was transformed into the Manhattan extravaganza of Universal's great new motion picture"; and a large souvenir book about the
making of *The Wiz.* I even bought the November 1978 issue of *Ebony* with
Diana Ross as Dorothy on the cover—the first time I ever purchased a
"black" magazine, though I don't remember what I thought about the
rest of the magazine. All that mattered to me, I suspect, was that I was
getting what I craved: information about *The Wiz!*

My first major exposure to the film, before actually seeing it at the
Berkshire Mall movie theater in December of 1978 (the same place I
had seen *The Poseidon Adventure* six years earlier), was an article on the
film that appeared in the October 1978 issue of *Life* magazine, the first
issue since it had ceased publication some years before. I bought the
magazine when my family was visiting Boston College for parents' weekend (my brother John was a freshman and my sister Suzanne a junior). I
still associate that big, beautiful, brand new issue of *Life* with the leaves
falling and the crisp air and Boston and the feeling that nothing was so
exciting or so important to me as the arrival of *The Wiz.*

There was a photo of hot air balloons on the cover (the caption
read, "Balloons are bustin' out all over!"), along with the headlines
" 'Godfather' Puzo's New Novel," "Spectacle in Rome: Pope John Paul I,"
and 'The Wiz'—Most Expensive Musical Ever." One of the most important differences, I learned from the article, between the actual film
version of *The Wiz* and my fantasy version was that the real film looked
abstract, two-dimensional, and surprisingly (unaccountably, at times)
spare—for all the $28 million spent on the film, there was a capricious,
offhand curvaceousness, an odd imbalance to Tony Walton's set designs
that took some getting used to: bulbous where it might just have been
sleek (for example, his bulging, yellow and black-and-white checker-
board fantasy taxis—why hadn't he simply used real New York taxis?);
spare where I would have made it dense (his Oz skyline inexplicably consisted of five towers equidistant from each other, and there wasn't a person in sight—why hadn't he made it more like the Emerald City of the
MGM movie, a bunch of sparkling green glass tubes of various widths
and heights, or more like New York City itself, corridor after steamy corridor of great, tall buildings and apartment houses on top of each other
with roof gardens and terraces with awnings and streets glutted with ve-
hicles and pedestrians?); harmlessly childlike where I would have made

it more grownup and menacing (Evillene's costume, all reds, purples, and oranges, was "inspired by a dog's rubber toy" ["Golden" 60]—why hadn't it been, like Margaret Hamilton's costume in the 1939 film, feline, regal, and black?), all scattered and piecemeal, where I wanted solidity, conviction, symmetry.

Apparently, Walton had conceived of Oz as a catalog of references to famous New York City architectural landmarks (fair enough, I thought: after all, I had already begun planning my "Brand New Day" production number atop the World Trade Center). A series of photographs in *Life* showed what looked like an empty fountain and a highway ramp that led nowhere, transformed through the magic of special effects into an image of the beginning of the Yellow Brick Road (which emerged out of the dotted yellow line in the middle of the highway), now leading not nowhere but to a stately skyline of five Chrysler buildings—one large, central tower, and two slightly smaller towers on either side of it—in back of which you could see the twists, turns, ups, and downs of a rollercoaster.

Hmm. I didn't get it. If this was the beginning of the Yellow Brick Road, then those Chrysler buildings couldn't already be the Emerald City (because the Emerald City is at the *end* of the Yellow Brick Road, not the beginning), although there was a dreamlike air about the image (something about the slightly blurred quality of the lines of the buildings and bridge) that reminded me of the famous shot in the 1939 film in which Dorothy and her friends first catch sight of the Emerald City rising up in the hazy distance out of the wide, flat plain.

Then, what was the rollercoaster all about? A caption in the article read, "I'm a Tin Man from Coney Island, so how 'bout slidin' some oil to me?" so I thought, okay, that must be the Coney Island rollercoaster, called the Cyclone, where Dorothy and the Scarecrow meet the Tin Man (the Cyclone—oh, hey, clever! Cyclone! I get it! But in the movie, I learned, Dorothy gets whisked to Oz not by a tornado but by a snowstorm, so what was the reference to the cyclone doing in the movie?).

I guess I thought it would have made better sense if Dorothy had lived in, say, the rural South, had dreamed she got sent off to, say, Brooklyn or Newark, and then went in search of Manhattan. One of the many things Pauline Kael disliked about the film was exactly this quality of dislocation: "Although Oz is meant to be Manhattan, it includes locations in Queens, the Bronx, and Brooklyn, and after Dorothy accumulates her traveling companions, they have to go over a couple of bridges to get to the Emerald City (the capital of Oz), in lower Manhattan. Geographically, we're thoroughly dislocated. When Dorothy first arrives in Oz, she's in a dark-bluish playground with graffiti-covered walls. The cyclone [*sic*] seems to have tossed her around the corner. When she's in a rubble-strewn lot and we expect her to say 'Damn, it looks just like home,' she dithers, 'Where am I?'—as if she'd never seen a burned-out block in Harlem" ("Saint Dorothy" 138).

I *was* delighted by the inventive ways the movie was going to translate the identities of the characters in the stage version: the Tin Man, an amusement park/junkyard heap (as *Life* magazine explained, "the Tin Man appears beyond repair but manages to pull himself together—with odd cogs and gears . . . spinning tops [bow tie], rusted food and beer cans, scouring pads [hair] and a pie tin [hat]" ["Golden" 59]); the Lion, one of the lion statues at the New York Public Library; the Scarecrow, a trash bag slung over a TV antenna stuck in the cornfield-garden of a tenement apartment building (well, this translation didn't quite add up: why had the filmmakers not decided to transform the story *fully* into urban terms? How many cornfields could there be in New York City?). All in all, the movie characters made their Broadway counterparts look low-budget and amateurish by comparison.

The Witch's henchmen were now not flying monkeys but Hell's Angels–style monkeys on motorcycles, or rather monkeys-*as*-motorcycles (my friend James and I admitted to each other to being shocked and titillated by how scantily clad the Winged Monkeys were in the Broadway production—we remarked how they wore nothing more than g-strings, and we speculated that those may even have been made of fishnet). And the munchkins were playground kids sprung to life from graffiti walls. Now *that* was a good idea! These were gimmicks I probably couldn't have devised on my own, because although I loved New York, there were aspects of it I didn't pay attention to or know anything about.

But I was ready to learn. For example, the Poppies. In this film version, the field of poppies was a crowd of prostitutes, an idea I could never have dreamed up—although it's true, during my high school years New York had already come to mean "sex" to me. My parents' gift to me for my sixteenth birthday was a three-day weekend in New York, including tickets to two Broadway shows (*They're Playing Our Song* and *Ain't Misbehavin'*) and, the *pièce de résistance,* tickets to see Liza Minnelli in concert at Carnegie Hall. We stayed in what was then (September 1979) called the City Squire Hotel (it's now a Sheraton), right in Times Square, which was an especially sexy place for me because during these years there was a billboard advertising The Gaiety, an all-male stripper club, right there across the street from the half-price tickets ("tkts") booth, just above the Howard Johnson's on the corner of Broadway and Forty-fifth Street. The billboard pictured a handsome young man, I forget in exactly what stage of undress, but I'm sure his torso was naked, and men's chests and stomachs never failed to make me horny and hard (I did nothing but ogle and fantasize about my high school classmates' naked torsos, and sometimes even their fully naked bodies, as they stepped out of the shower after gym class). The Gaiety man may also have been showing off those extra few sweet inches of tummy just above the pubic hair that drive me wild. So there he was, every time I walked out of the City Squire into the sizzling mid-September streets.

One night in our shared hotel room, the lights were out, Mom and Dad were in their bed, I was in mine, underneath the sheets and blankets, and I wanted to masturbate. I *had* to do it, and in my determination I figured, somehow, that I could do it without causing a disturbance or unduly calling Mom and Dad's attention to me.

I started rubbing. Rubbing, rubbing. (This was before I discovered I could do it by hand—jerking off by frottage was a lot more conspicuous than a hand job would have been.) Rubbing, rubbing. Rubbing rubbing rubbing rubbingrubbingrubbingrruubbbiiinnngggg————!!!!!!!!!

Mom's voice, only a few feet away: "Hey, what's going on over there? It sounds like you're on a rollercoaster."

Aside from the depiction of Oz as New York City, the other stunning difference, of course, between the film version of *The Wiz* and all previous versions of the story was that here Dorothy would be a twenty-four-year-old kindergarten teacher, not a little girl, and she would be played by Diana Ross. While I had to go through a period of adjusting to the particular ways in which Oz was designed in the film, I instinctively and immediately understood the logic of making Dorothy an adult. For one thing, I had learned years earlier to accept and even to cherish Barbra Streisand's unorthodox portrayal of Dolly Levi, and in a way, there was little difference between a twenty-something woman (Barbra) playing a middle-aged widow (Dolly) and a thirty-something woman (Diana) playing a twenty-something schoolteacher (Dorothy). Plus, the risk of spending tens of millions of dollars on a Hollywood musical seemed to warrant an equivalent risk in characterization and casting. But most important, the idea of an adult Dorothy made sense to me given that the story now took place in New York City. To me, New York was an escape from the evils of my adolescence in Reading, and when I learned that Dorothy would now be an adult, for the first time in my life it occurred to me that adulthood, too, could be a kind of escape from childhood, that just being grown up meant that you had gotten out of the trap of being young, powerless, and provincial. In the movie version of *The Wiz,* then, and particularly in Diana Ross's performance as Dorothy, those two things would finally merge in my consciousness: New York City and adulthood.

The opening few scenes in the film establish Dorothy's ambiguous predicament. It's holiday time, and family and friends are arriving for dinner. When Dorothy's cousin arrives with her newborn baby, all eyes are upon them. At dinner, Aunt Em sings a song about how much love exists within the family, and she addresses the song initially to her daughter with the new baby. She then walks into a bedroom, interrupts a young man and woman who have been kissing (it's not exactly clear who these young people are or what relation they bear to Aunt Em), and ushers them with a knowing smile into the dining room. When the couple make their belated appearance at dinner, the entire family gives them a hearty round of applause, as if everyone in the family knows and fully approves of what they'd been doing in the bedroom (if you had been caught doing something like that right before dinner in my house, you would have gotten in trouble).

During all of this, Dorothy is busy, like Cinderella, tending to people's hats and coats and putting the finishing touches on the meal. When Dorothy doesn't show any interest in a handsome young man who has come to the party, Em explains to him apologetically, "don't worry, Gale, she's just a little shy."[1] And during Em's song at the dinner table, Dorothy looks confused and embarrassed when Em sings to her that one day she, Dorothy, will be "out in the world . . . on your own." Promptly she rushes into the kitchen to look after the dessert cake and to be alone for a few moments. She sings a song written expressly for the film, "Can I Go on Not Knowing?": "Something tells me this is more than I can deal with." What can't Dorothy deal with? It seems to have something to do with the fact that nearly all the affection and attention in her family goes to the children who exhibit strong heterosexual tendencies (the young woman with the baby, the guy and the girl necking in the bedroom).

After the party is over, Em encourages Dorothy to take a job teaching high school, arguing that exposure to high school students would be good for Dorothy—"such an important time in their development," Em says. (In other words, Dorothy needs to be around people who are going through puberty?) But Dorothy insists that she is content teaching kindergarten. Em assures her, "I know gettin' out in that world ain't easy, even for Uncle Henry and me. But we'll always be here for you, Dorothy. And whatever your fears are, well, they'll be defeated just by facing up to 'em." (This wasn't all that different from the advice the Reverend Mother gave to Maria in *The Sound of Music*: "Maria, our abbey is not to be used as an escape. . . . You have a great capacity to love. What you must find out is how God wants you to spend your love. . . . Maria, these walls were not built to keep out problems. You have to face them. You have to live the life you were born to live.") Dorothy's problem has something to do with love: the love she feels for her family, the love they feel for her; but it's also a love that goes beyond family, a love she's afraid of. "Now you take that new job and find a place for you and Toto. It's time for you to make a home of your own," Em says firmly.

"A home of your own"—no wonder Dorothy was frightened. Aunt Em and Uncle Henry loved Dorothy, that was clear, but they were also always pushing her away. Although as an adolescent I wasn't at peace with my home surroundings, and although the older I got the more enamored of New York I became, the thought of actually being out on my own was beyond frightening—it was a thought almost inaccessible. I just couldn't picture it: where exactly would I live? How would I eat? What would I do? Who would I know? I didn't know how to answer any of these questions apart from my immediate family and the life I knew with them. I was caught between wanting, *needing* to get out and not knowing where to go or how to get there. Diana Ross's Dorothy seemed to be caught in a similar bind.

The solution that the film offers Dorothy is an interior one: she must understand that "home" is inside of her. As Glinda the Good Witch of the South (played by Lena Horne) explains toward the end of the film, "Home is a place we all must find, child. It's not just a place we eat or sleep. Home is knowing—knowing your mind, knowing your heart, knowing your courage. If we know ourselves, we're always home, anywhere." When the wizard (played by Richard Pryor), now discovered to be a fraud, asks Dorothy if there is anything she can do for him now that she's learned the secret of home, she answers him, "I don't know what's inside you. You'll have to find that out for yourself. But I do know one thing. You'll never find it in the safety of this room. I tried that all my life. It doesn't work. *There's a whole world out there!* And you'll have to begin by letting people see who you really are."

But in the end we never quite find out who Dorothy really is, nor do we know what path she now intends to follow or where it will lead her. Will she take that job teaching high school? Will she take a liking to Gale, the handsome young man Aunt Em is trying to fix her up with? Will she find the words to name her fears? And will she have the imagination to overcome them?

I saw *The Wiz*, finally, with my friend John (with whom I used to look at *Playboy* magazine, only it was pretty clear to me that we were both focusing mainly on the guys in the pictures. There was one spread that we spent a lot of time looking at which involved a farm scenario, and there was this really cute guy with his legs spread, and with a hard-on, leaning against a bail of hay inside a barn, waiting for a cowgirl or a milkmaid or someone like that to come in to have sex with him). The act of seeing the film became almost as sacred as the film itself. I had already done so much thinking about the film before I saw it that, when the time finally came to see it, I didn't just watch the movie—I watched myself watching it. I remember, as I sat with John waiting for the lights to go down, and then all throughout the film, being acutely conscious of the fact that I knew exactly what kind of socks I was wearing (white tube socks, each with two bands of purple around the calf).

My favorite scene in the film was and still is the one where Dorothy, the Scarecrow, the Tin Man, the Lion, and the Winkies sing "A Brand New Day" upon Evillene's death (Dorothy melts her by activating the sprinkler system). Though the number didn't end up looking anything like the one I had planned atop the World Trade Center, it nevertheless had the uplift and the sheer spectacle that always appealed to me in big, expensive Hollywood musicals. Tony Walton's sweatshop set eventually took its place in my heart alongside the von Trapp foyer, the Harmonia Gardens Restaurant, and the SS *Poseidon* saloon: it was a vast, gable-roofed warehouse divided into three airy sections by rows of slender pillars and two long, low work tables (perfect for singing and dancing on top of). The place felt more like a church than a factory: at one end of the wide, central aisle sat Evillene's throne, a huge and grotesque toilet seat mounted on a pedestal, which looked, on a much larger scale, like the baptismal font in my hometown church. And along three of the four walls loomed handsomely arched stained glass windows, filled with Gothic, cobwebbed leading and topped with exhaust fans in place of rose windows.

The number contains two movements. In the first, Dorothy leads the former slaves in a disco-dancing rendition of "A Brand New Day" ("We always knew that we'd be free somehow—*free at last!*" the Tin Man ad-libs). With their Muppet-like, heavily padded bodysuits—androgynous hodgepodges of dopey face masks, skirts, pantaloons, and aprons—the Winkies sing and dance and jump up and down for joy, but they never look anything more than earthbound, and that's what I loved about this part of the number. The down-to-earth disco beat and the dancers' thumping tread made me feel that their freedom was still very much of *this* world. Freedmen, they looked and moved pretty much the same as when they were enslaved. Everything *looked* the same—the only difference was that whereas before they were slaves, now they were free. Freedom had a clear, visible relation to what came before it, and that, somehow, was a deep comfort to me when I was fifteen.

The second movement of the number, however, felt different. At a certain point, the disco beat pauses, the actors freeze, and they begin to unzip their thick, rubbery costumes from head to toe, revealing their lithesome bodies underneath, clad only in scant yellow undergarments. What follows is a series of closeups (anomalies in a scene made up mostly of long shots—one of several things Pauline Kael objected to about the film's handling of the musical numbers: "The big production numbers are free-form traffic jams. They're shot the way a fagged-out TV crew arriving at the scene of a riot in the streets might grab whatever it could from behind the police barriers. Was Lumet trying to get the whole block in every shot?" [142]): a young woman's face drinking in daylight as if for the first time in her life; a young man, his shaved head beading with sweat, eagerly pulling himself out of his suffocating overalls; a young woman looking in awe at her own freshly ungloved hand; another woman shrugging off her costume, her long hair falling in innumerable tight braids around her bare shoulders; a man's well-developed pectoral muscles flexing as he inches off his shirt. Suddenly one by one, their garments burst into flames and disappear. The Winkies resume their dance, infused now with classical balletic moves, leaping higher, doing somersaults, looking lighter and more airborne than ever before.

For some reason I didn't like this part of the number as much as the first. It seemed redundant to me that the Winkies, fully dressed, should sing and dance about how happy they were to be free, only to then peel off their clothing and go through the whole number again. Could it be that the sight of half-naked brown and black bodies, male and female, offered up as objects of unequivocal beauty, made me uncomfortable? Would I have felt differently if these had been white bodies? Had I not yet learned to appreciate the beauty of the unencumbered, athletic human body? (Well, I *was* having all kinds of fantasies about naked guys, including athletes, around the same time that I became mentally and emotionally involved with *The Wiz* . . .) Was it that musicals and nudity—musicals and sexual liberation—just didn't go together in my waking imagination?

Or was my quarrel with the second part of the "Brand New Day" number *not* that it was "too black, too sexual," but that it wasn't black *enough* —not sexy *enough*? For one of the advantages, I felt, of the Winkies' bulging costumes, as opposed to their unadorned dancer's bodies, was that the costumes filled the screen and gave the first part of the number a much-needed look of density. This, after all, was the look I had in mind when I imagined the Brooklyn Bridge traffic jam scene for my personal film version of *The Wiz*—the look of thick-textured, gritty reality as I felt it on my skin every moment I spent in humid, midtown, lunch-hour Manhattan. I guess Pauline Kael lived in New York all year round, so traffic jams had lost their charm for her ("the big production numbers are free-form traffic jams"). But she was right about Lumet's mishandling of the musical numbers: he stands back, surrounding his actors with empty, unused space. The camera rarely interacts with them when they sing and dance, and what good is singing and dancing if you can't *feel* it when you're doing it, if you can't feel it when you're witnessing it? "Can't you feel a brand-new day?" Not really. And that was the problem with the second movement of the liberation number. The slaves' bodies had been gorgeously revealed, gloriously set free, but just at that moment the camera's distance from them and the overwhelming size of the surrounding sweatshop set made them look shrunken, scrawny, a forest of undifferentiated arms and legs. Why had Lumet recoiled from the Winkies just when they had become most sensual, most free?

The number raised some other unsettling questions: Why didn't the Scarecrow (played by Michael Jackson) peel off *his* cumbersome costume (you could hardly see nineteen-year-old Michael through all the face makeup, the peanut-butter-cup nose, the wig, the baggy shirt and pants, the floppy shoes) to reveal the agile, sweet-tempered young man underneath? For that matter, why didn't the Tin Man (Nipsey Russell) and the Lion (Ted Ross) do the same? And what about Dorothy? We get no idea of what she thinks or how she feels about the seductive bodies all around her. Do they turn her on? Which ones does she desire—to have? To be? How many layers of clothing and inhibition and memory would *she* have to peel away before she arrived at some irreducible core of her sensual self?

A little more than a year after I saw *The Wiz*, my parents, my Grandmother Horrigan, and I went to New York to see a brand new musical (so new, the original cast album hadn't even been released yet, and they hadn't yet produced a souvenir booklet) about a nineteenth-century London barber who murders his customers, has them chopped up into little pieces and bakes them in pies and eats them (something like that), and it was called *Sweeney Todd: The Demon Barber of Fleet Street*. Stephen Sondheim wrote the music and lyrics, and I dimly recognized his name, though I had never to my knowledge heard his music, and I'd never seen any of his other shows. It was being called "a musical thriller," not the usual "a new musical" or "a musical comedy," and that seemed intriguing. I think my mom first became interested in *Sweeney Todd* because she'd heard or read an article saying that someone from Reading was in the chorus. Then one of the Reading papers ran a story on the soon-to-open show that focused in equal parts on the man from Reading and on the set, a gargantuan nineteenth-century factory (reminiscent of the sweatshop set in *The Wiz*) filling the entire stage of the Uris (now Gershwin) Theater and even spilling into the first seven or ten rows of seats. (The seats had to be removed to accommodate the massively elaborate set. I loved learning anecdotes like that: how nature had to be wrestled with in order for art to proceed, or how people became so crazed by art that they turned violent, like the original audiences for Stravinsky's *The Rite of Spring*—somewhere along the way I'd learned that the opening-night audience was so incensed by the music that they *ripped out the seats!*). Eventually, I would discover that everything that could be said of the set (it wasn't so much a filling of space on stage as it was the creation of stage space itself) could also be said analogously about Sondheim's ambitious, capacious, dissonant, mind-altering score.

That Saturday afternoon in New York, it was raining. We headed all the way downtown to the World Trade Center to see the view from the observation deck and then to have lunch at the Windows on the World restaurant. The observation deck and the restaurant were just fine, terrific even, but all I could think about (apart from anticipating *Sweeney Todd*) was seeing the plaza where the great Emerald City sequence in *The Wiz* was filmed. We walked across the plaza when we arrived, but I don't remember the experience all that well. I do remember, though, wondering why the plaza looked so different in real life than it did in the movie (figs. 19, 20). I assumed—wrongly, it turned out—that anything used for location shooting in *The Wiz,* as a number of New York City sites had been, would be instantly recognizable. The first unmistakable difference was the missing Z from the "OZ" sculpture in the middle of the big fountain on the plaza. In the film, you saw a huge bronze globe with, here and there, sections carved out of it and other pieces of it bulging forth as if it were a living organism (the O), and a zigzag structure (the Z) superimposed upon it. But now there was just the globular O. Then in the film there seemed to be neon rings around the fountain, but no such rings were now in sight. If these things were added to the fountain for the making of the film, why hadn't any of them been retained—especially the Z? It was a lesson, if I hadn't already learned it, in how magical Hollywood filmmaking really can be, but also, in how disappointing life usually is in comparison to the movies.

Our table at Windows on the World was also disappointing because I couldn't get close enough to the glass to look down squarely on the plaza and enjoy the same—*almost* the same—bird's-eye view of it as the camera sees in the film (we were separated several feet from the window by a golden railing, apparently for safety reasons). From our table I could just barely make out one corner of the plaza, but not enough to fully conjure up the missing pieces in my mind. Or rather, I could imagine the rest of the plaza, the parts I was prevented from seeing because

Figure 19. The Emerald City (filmed on location at the World Trade Center, New York
City) in *The Wiz*. (Reprinted by permission of the Museum of Modern Art)

of the angle of my vision, but now that I had gotten this close to the
real thing, mental drawings of the space were a poor substitute. I was
closer than ever to the real thing, but, ironically, the real thing was further away from the "truth"—the *screen* truth—than before I'd gone to
the World Trade Center.

But I can't say that I was ultimately let down by my visit to the World
Trade Center and to the site of the filming of *The Wiz*. As usual with *The
Wiz,* and with all the movies that became my love objects during these
years, I rallied my strength and adapted to each new stage in the un-
veiling of its mystery. From my fond fantasies of what *The Wiz* could be
if only it dared, to the intractable reality of the actual film (I figured
the film's success was also seriously damaged by its "G" rating—no important or respectable films, it seemed, were rated "G" anymore), to the
even cruder reality of the stuff from which it was made, again and again
I realigned my expectations and standards in the face of what the world
gave back to me, and to tell the truth, I think I derived as much pleasure—maybe *more* pleasure—from that mental exercise than I would

Figure 20. The World Trade Center.

have if I had just been left alone with my untouched fantasy or if my every wish had been fulfilled.

IV

A couple of summers ago my then boyfriend Joe and I decided to celebrate our three-month anniversary at the Windows on the World. It was a Saturday and we made a reservation for 11:00 P.M. that night (the earliest we could get). I needed a jacket and tie, so we spent the afternoon searching to buy me a new set of clothes. After looking in several stores but not finding anything that suited my taste, we decided I might as well splurge at Barneys. With the help of Joe and a very sweet, obviously gay clerk named Richard, I bought a crisp, light-weight woolen black jacket by Paul Smith; a pair of creamy bone-white Calvin Klein pants; a finely ribbed Georgio Armani dress shirt with thin blue, gray, black, and white stripes spaced close together, creating an overall light blue-grayish effect; and a tie by Ermenegildo Zegna featuring a collage of large black, gray, and blue vertical rectangles, as well as blue squares with little golden classical portals drawn inside, the rectangles and squares alike outlined in thin strips of golden white. It all worked together beautifully.

Windows on the World had recently been remodeled, and its new architect had finally removed the brass rails that made me feel so cut off from the views outside when I first visited there in 1979 (but I still couldn't see any more of the plaza down below). The tables were now arranged, like seats in a theater, on platforms that rose higher the farther away you got from the windows, so that no matter where you were sitting you had a more-or-less unobstructed view. Our table was located in the center of the restaurant, along the central aisle running the length of the room, overlooking a sunken area of tables against the windows.

At the end of the night, still high from the wine and food and coffee, and from the joint we'd smoked before heading downtown, we asked for our check, and our waiter said, "There's no check; your dinner has been paid for by Mr. Lee, a member of the restaurant." Shocked and curious to know who this mysterious Good Witch "Mr. Lee" was, but hesitant to ask too many questions for fear of discovering that a mistake had been made, we said, "Please tell Mr. Lee we said thank you very much," and we said good night. After intense speculation, we decided the best hypothesis was that Mr. Lee was a wealthy older gay man who saw us together, thought we looked handsome (which we did!), figured we were in love and that tonight was a special occasion, and so wanted to give us a gift.

Around 1:30 in the morning, the last ones to leave the restaurant, Joe and I had the elevator to ourselves, and we kissed each other down all 107 flights. It was a magical night. And this time it *was* magic like you see in the movies. For a moment, I—we—felt at home in the world.

OUTTAKES IV

Gigi (1958)

I liked the old, overstuffed apartment where Gigi (played by Leslie Caron) lived with her grandmother, "Mamita" (Hermione Gingold). The walls were red and most of the furniture was red too. Mamita was always disappearing into the kitchen through a doorway in the back wall, serving tea and saying how happy she was to see Gaston (Louis Jourdan), a friend of the family and, later, Gigi's suitor, whenever he would come to visit. The apartment was a wonderfully unpredictable mixture of informality and tradition. Gigi's bedroom was just off to the left as you walked in the front door, which seemed a little precarious but exciting at the same time; bedrooms as I'd known them were always sequestered safely away from the front door, somewhere else in the house where visitors couldn't see them. Adding to the sense that Gigi and her bedroom were "on the verge" of something, her bedroom door was more like a *closet* door than a regular door to a room, with horizontal slats (like the closet doors in my bedroom), as if you might be able to see through it into the bedroom. And there was a charmingly regal little flight of steps, not more than two or three, leading up to her bedroom door, as if it were on a pedestal (which seemed to contradict the informality of her bedroom door and its placement so near to the front door of the apartment). These steps made her look even more stunning than she already was when, late in the film, she descended them, a "lady" for the first time, no longer a girl, wearing a white dress with a high white neck, to go out with Gaston for the evening.

But even more than Mamita's warm, inviting apartment, I loved the long, irregular staircase that led up to it. It had two landings and seemed to curve slightly as it rose. The railing was thin, not heavy, almost unsteady looking, but that enhanced the charm of the staircase. Like Mamita's apartment, like Gigi herself, it was somewhat fragile and aged (for much of the film, Gigi, despite her youth, is too smart to fall in love as everyone else around her seems to be doing), yet springy with youthful optimism, wise yet head-over-heels in love. There *was* a head-over-heels quality to the staircase, perhaps because that's how Gaston feels when, at the end of the film, having realized that Gigi is not just "that funny, awkward little girl I knew," but, in fact, the woman he loves, he races like an impetuous boy of sixteen (though he looks to be a man of thirty at least) up the long staircase, burning with the revelation that he loves Gigi and that he is ready to marry her, not keep her as his mistress as he had intended before, and he bounds up the stairs, skipping two and three steps at a time, to tell Gigi and Mamita the joyous news.

Grease (1978)

The first time I saw *Grease,* I was horrified by the cynical ending
in which Sandy, played by Olivia Newton-John, turns herself from a
normal, pretty, polite girl into a black-leather-clad, cigarette-smoking,
spiked-heeled vamp to win back Danny, played by John Travolta, who
thought it was too uncool to go out with a square girl like Sandy. Of
course I assumed that ultimately Danny would realize that good girls
were better than bad girls and, anyway, it didn't matter if Sandy was a
little square on the outside because he loved her for who she really was
on the inside (i.e., a good, decent girl who doesn't drink, swear, or tease
her hair). At the end-of-the-school-year carnival, Danny, who has been
experimenting with a change of image himself (he's wearing a respectable letter sweater), catches sight of Sandy, all done over in her "bad
girl" look. They sing and dance together ("You're the one that I want,
oo oo oo, honey"), chase each other through a fun house, then get into
a car that, magically, flies off into the clouds, and the movie ends.

I couldn't believe that was the ending! I thought for sure, Danny
would be so upset to see Sandy using her sex appeal in such a grotesque
way to get his attention that he would say, "Okay, enough, let's call a
truce. You can go back to being the way you were, and I'll ignore all the
peer pressure and I'll be good to you and you alone from now on." But
unfortunately it seemed that being disobedient and sexually promiscu-
ous won out over following the rules and abstinence before marriage.

On the other hand, the way John Travolta peeled off his letter sweater
and swiveled his hips when he saw that he didn't need to dress like a
good boy for Sandy any longer *was* an unbelievable turn on.

Somehow, I felt differently after seeing *Grease* a second time a couple
of weeks later. For one thing, "You're the One That I Want" was such
an infectious number that it seemed a perfect way for the movie to
end—upbeat, melodic, fun to sing and dance along with, and the more
I watched John and Olivia in that last scene, both dressed in skin-tight
black clothing (god, those tight black pants on John Travolta!), their
look began to seem much better than the nerdy 1950s fashions that
everyone else in the movie was wearing and which all the characters wore
on the TV sitcom *Happy Days.* The ending of *Grease* seemed, in a way,
to point towards the future, although I'm not sure I thought it was the
future of the 1960s exactly (which is what the future would have been in
terms of the time period represented in the movie), and not necessarily
the 1970s either (which would have made sense given that the movie
was made in the 1970s and succeeded in turning the gaze of the 1950s
ever toward itself). The "future" that Grease looked forward to was not

a temporal future, but an attitudinal future, an emotional future. And a sexual future. Between my first and second viewings of *Grease,* I had learned, without realizing it, not to care if Sandy remained a "good girl." I even came to like the off-balanced feeling the movie gave me in the end; I *liked* the idea of taking a bad turn and never coming back from it — of just driving off into the sunset and never looking back, of being bad and staying bad. That felt exciting and daring in the same way that John Travolta's gyrating torso made me want to have sex with him so badly that I started dreaming up scenarios in which we were having an affair that got leaked to the press, and then everywhere we went we were hounded by reporters and gossip columnists and we never seemed to get a moment's privacy. Even when he would pick me up in his private helicopter and fly me out to his secret mansion in California or Washington state (sometimes you just need to escape the big city), somehow the press always found out about it and wrote stories speculating about our relationship and insinuating that we might be gay.

5

Coming Out, with Al Pacino

I

After seeing *Dog Day Afternoon* (1975) for the first time when it premiered on television in 1979, I began to fantasize at length and in detail about making love with Al Pacino, who played Sonny Wortzik, a Catholic, bisexual, big-hearted, small-time Brooklyn bank robber.

By this time I was fifteen years old, a sophomore at Holy Name High School, was feeling intermittent anxiety that I might be gay, and had fooled around sexually the previous summer with my friend James, much to our subsequent shame, while we did volunteer work in the office of a local cerebral palsy services agency. The idea that James and I were using these poor disabled people, and the nurses and social workers who ministered to them and who needed our assistance, to find occasions for pulling each other's pants down and doing things with each other's cocks when no one was looking or when the office was empty except for ourselves, was too much for my already always-guilty conscience to bear. James and I never talked about what had happened between us, and of course I never told anyone else, not even my parents, who repeatedly assured me and my siblings that no matter what it was we could tell them anything, we should never feel as if we had anything to hide from them, there was *nothing* we could do or say that could ever make them stop loving us — they might get angry, they might feel disappointed, but they would love us no matter what. Somehow I knew that this was a lot more complicated than they made it sound.

When the summer and our volunteer work ended, I thought, I'll never look at anyone with cerebral palsy, or at James, again. But James would remain my estranged high school classmate for the next three years, even though we quickly drifted into different circles of friends, took dif-

180

ferent classes (mine were all "advanced placement," his remedial), and generally managed, politely, to ignore each other completely. The last I heard, James had entered an ROTC program.

I kept many more secrets from the world when I was growing up than just my occasional sex encounters with James. No one knew it, but since about the time I was ten, my interior life was dominated by the fantasy that I was an important, hugely talented, Hollywood actor. I was always *me* in my dreams; just as Barbra Streisand didn't change her name or her nose when she became a star, I basically didn't change anything about myself—my name, my age, my short height, the sound (embarrassingly effeminate) of my voice, my blue eyes, my red hair, my freckles. I wanted to make sure, also like Barbra Streisand, that when I became famous, everyone would know it was still me. I wanted to rub their faces in it (fig. 21).

At some point in my preadolescence, I realized that I could escape into a world inside my head where I had power and freedom, while on the outside I simply bounced a basketball in front of our house. There was a hoop over the garage doors and a basketball key painted on the driveway, so while I imagined I was Barbra Streisand leading the well-dressed citizens of Yonkers to the train station, singing "All aboard!" like a whistle blowing or a siren calling, as everyone boarded the train, rushing past her like beautiful, strong horses jumping fences in a race, or while I fantasized about what my next film project would be or about the lukewarm reviews I was getting on my most recent film, for the rest of the world I was perfecting my basketball shot. (I loved getting "lukewarm" reviews for my performances and films. It made more sense than the praise my parents always heaped upon me for whatever it was I had done—played the piano, built a model airplane or house, painted a picture; their praise never seemed 100 percent sincere to me, whereas mixed praise at least meant that the critic had thought long and hard about what you had done and that you were being taken seriously and not being dismissed with kindness.)

Now and then I would let members of my family join me on the court for games of "Around the World" or "HORSE" (a shorter variation was "PIG") or "21" (which seemed endless), but mostly I craved solitude, and I got privately furious whenever anybody would come outside to watch me shoot, or to talk to me, or to ask if they could play along. I didn't even like it when my mother would watch me, as she often did, from the dining room window—she could see my lips moving, I was sure, when I talked to myself. And in the fall and spring she would turn off the air conditioning and open up the windows, so that the noises I

Figure 21. Thirteen years old, spring 1977.

made, the things I was saying and singing, could be heard through the window screen or through the screen door of the kitchen, where she worked much of the long day preparing dinner, doing wash, ironing, making and receiving telephone calls, marking her calendar.

Sometimes when I would be singing a song, gamboling about on the driveway, the orchestra building to a climactic, sizzling drum roll, aiming to shoot the basketball from the middle of the court, the camera zooming in for a close-up, I would turn to shoot, and there at the window stood my mother, looking at me. Our eyes met. A blood-rush of embarrassment ran cold through my entire body. I had been observed. How long had she been standing there? (I resumed my basketball playing as if nothing had happened.) What would I say if later she asked me, casually, as she sometimes did, I thought I heard you singing when you were outside playing—what were you singing? (She lingered there in the window in silence for another moment.) What did she think of me now? What was the expression on her face?

When I turned to look for her again, she was gone.

My imagination went everywhere in those days—from Reading to New York to Hollywood to London, on location in the Soviet Union. I had made eleven films by the time I was nineteen, and since I had only made my first film in 1977 when I was thirteen, that meant eleven films in seven years. But in real life, by the 1970s at least, Hollywood movies couldn't be made that fast, so I had to do some manipulation of the facts to handle my overwhelming career ambitions. For example, my first film, I decided, was really made in 1976 but wasn't *released* until 1977. That made eleven films in eight years—still not plausible; basically I was aiming for one film per year. In two of the films I played supporting roles, so I figured that I could make two films in one year if I had a minor part in at least one of those films. And if I needed to, I could allow myself to jump ahead a year or two and pretend that the film I was currently involved in would be made and released in, say, 1983, when in fact at the time I was living in the year 1981. And sometimes, in order to gain a year or two, I would abandon a film project (much to producers', critics', my agent's, and the public's dismay) either because I realized that the film didn't have any substance to it (at one point, I had begun filming a big-budget musical starring me and Andrea McArdle, then the star of Broadway's *Annie,* but I just couldn't come up with any kind of plot that would include the both of us, so I quit the picture) or because the film I had started to make turned out to be too derivative of some actual film I had just seen (for a long time, I worked on an epic musical that was a bizarre coming together of *Hello, Dolly!, Mame,* and Walt Disney World's

Main Street, which I visited in 1973 and fell instantly, madly in love with—but the film was plagued by script problems, so I eventually had to give this one up, too). Once I realized that I could make these mental leaps—in moderation, of course—I immediately felt more at ease. I was always worried about being as honest with myself as I possibly could be.

In my film debut, I played an obedient, musically inclined but unathletic boy who dies from being underappreciated by his parents, played by Louise Fletcher and Edward Fox. I won best actor for this astonishing performance. In my second film, I played a nice young boy whose father, played by Gregory Peck, murders him after losing a presidential election. For this I won best supporting actor, thereby convincing anyone who might have doubted it that the brilliant success of my first film was not just a fluke. (Cybill Shepherd played my older sister in the film, a performance critics are still calling the best of her career, though, incredibly, she didn't even get an Oscar *nomination* for it.) In my next film, I played a younger-than-average college freshman (he was allowed to skip a few grades in high school—lucky him) who has an affair with one of his professors, played by Meryl Streep, and in one controversial scene, he has sex with both her and her Siberian husky. I was nominated again for best actor for my performance in this film, but I lost it to Dustin Hoffman because, you know, they can't keep giving it to the same person every year.

Seeing Al Pacino's performance in *Dog Day Afternoon*, however, permanently altered my fantasy life by making me realize that, at least in my head, I could play a gay person, and that being gay wasn't, as I had felt, shameful, frightening, not to be spoken of or even thought about. Being gay, as Al Pacino played it, suddenly seemed attractive, nerve-racking, authoritative, irresistible—above all, *possible.*

II

Dog Day Afternoon begins unexpectedly with a lengthy montage of scenes of a hot summer afternoon in New York City. We see, among other things, first one, then three Circle Line sight-seeing boats at the midtown docks; a dog rooting through garbage; a kid jumping, *splash!*, into a swimming pool; fat construction workers digging and standing in a ditch; someone watering his small patch of front lawn in Queens; someone else hosing down a city sidewalk; a highway tollbooth with a sign saying "PASSENGER CARS 50¢"; an airplane ascending overhead across the humid, gray-blue sky; people playing tennis; the outdoor café, a dense patch of umbrella tables, at Rockefeller Center; old people, one under an umbrella, chatting on the boardwalk at Coney Island; someone sunning himself by a reflecting pool at the base of a skyscraper; a man lying on his back on the sidewalk in the sun; a woman (who we'll later discover is Sonny Wortzik's female wife, Angie—he also has a male "wife" named Leon) walking with her two kids, and a straight couple crossing the street toward them as the girl squeezes her boyfriend's ass; a lime-green Volkswagen Karmann Ghia in the middle of a highway traffic jam; sanitation workers tossing empty garbage cans onto the sidewalk; speedboats zipping along a crowded shore; several young women with a baby carriage, chatting on sidewalk benches; a Dannon yogurt truck lumbering down a Brooklyn street in front of a bank; the massive New Calvary Cemetery in Queens; an electronic Kent cigarette sign that reads "2:57 P.M."; and a street cleaning truck slowly passing in front of the same Brooklyn bank and, now, a parked car in which Sonny and his accomplices talk over last-minute details.

Unlike other 1970s films whose visions of pregentrified New York City tend to appeal to a disapproving yet still prurient *sub*urban sensibility, including Al Pacino's *Serpico* (1973), about corruption in the police department, as well as *Network* (1976), about corruption in the television industry, *Dog Day Afternoon* (like *Serpico, Network,* and *The Wiz,* directed by Sidney Lumet) shows an urban scene that is both dirty and livable, ugly and pleasurable. The camera is positioned *among* the people and things it films; in several shots, a vehicle passing by is made to appear so physically close to the camera that it momentarily disorients the viewer's perspective. A third of the images include water, restorative and abundant—the sequence almost looks like an "I Love New York" tourist advertisement. The people in these images are dogged; they go about their business, take advantage of the sun and water, and survive the heat. Most of them are not isolated but located within family and friendship networks, and the two who are alone (one sunning himself by a reflecting pool, the other sunning himself on the sidewalk) seem blissfully so. Crowds are an inevitable, but not necessarily an unpleasant or dehumanizing, part of the urban scene; indeed, in the midst of crowds, human touch abounds—the young man's butt, the lime-colored car, the time of day in lights, "PASSENGER CARS 50¢." These workaday images of water, pleasure, and the *Volk,* all of them exuberantly out of doors, confer a baptismal blessing over the entire film, setting a charitable tone of forgiveness and preparing us to feel ourselves part of the events and characters (criminal, bisexual, transvestite, transsexual, violent) that we are about to witness.

Sung during the opening sequence as a voice-over (not, however, obliterating the cacophony of city sounds, but rather coexisting with them), Elton John's "Amoreena" echoes, but also complicates, the meaning of these prologue images. The song features an exultant piano, organ, and guitar, spluttering drums, overall a lush, orchestral sound; and Elton John's epicene, pubescent-sounding voice hyperexpressively adds coloratura to the melody. Lifted for the film off of Elton's 1970 album *Tumbleweed Connection,* a song cycle about old soldiers, the Old South, and the bittersweet pleasures of life on the frontier, "Amoreena" recalls a mythical female beloved whose absence is both mourned and relished; the singer describes lusty, golden days spent with his now-distant "lady," eating apples, running through cornfields, dreaming of "crystal streams," "rolling through the hay like a puppy child." The effect is to invest the film's images of mediocrity, work, middlebrow lifestyles, deteriorating bodies, and urban sprawl with a keen, pastoral wholesomeness that produces, finally, not irony or detachment or alienation (each a hallmark effect of classic 1970s cinema), but a roving, Whitmanesque sense of innocence, affirmation, sentimentality, and hope.

Ensconced inside the bank he has tried unsuccessfully to rob in order to pay for his boyfriend Leon's sex-change operation, Sonny has taken hostages and is negotiating with police captain Eugene Moretti (played by Charles Durning) and FBI agent Sheldon (James Broderick) for safe passage out of the country with his partner-in-crime, Sal (John Cazale). As day turns into night, a crowd of people gathers to witness the showdown between Sonny and the authorities. The film, based on a true story, is structured around thirteen "coming out" scenes in each of which Sonny comes out of the bank in order to negotiate with the police and, on one occasion, to talk with his mother (fig. 22). In the most famous of these scenes, Sonny stirs up the crowd of onlookers by telling the police to put their guns down and invoking the name of the New York state prison, Attica, where, in September of 1971, a prisoners' insurrection was put down by the National Guard, leaving thirty-nine prisoners and nine prison guards dead:

> SONNY: [*referring to a cop approaching him with a gun*] Hey, what's he doing?
> MORRETTI: [*to the cop*] Will you get back?
> SONNY: What are they movin' in there for? Get on back there man! He wants to kill me so bad he can taste it! Attica! [*the crowd cheers*] Attica! Attica! Attica! Attica! Put your guns down! Tell 'em to put their guns down! They'll kill us all! Put the fucking guns down! Put 'em down! Put 'em down! Attica! Attica! [*to the crowd*] You got it, man! You got it, man! You got it, man![1]

When I first saw *Dog Day Afternoon,* however, I knew nothing of the political and historical context for this and other scenes where Sonny

Figure 22. Sonny Wortzik (Al Pacino) in *Dog Day Afternoon*. (Reprinted by permission of the Museum of Modern Art)

wrangles with the police. What I saw and heard, instead, was a confrontation between a sympathetic, disobedient young man (a child, practically) and a series of parental figures who often seem to bear Sonny no ill will but who, along with Sonny, are trapped in circumstances that make authentic communication impossible. In my mind, the bank became a metaphor for Sonny's interior life — his private, fragile, emotional world; Sonny's crime (robbing a bank) a metaphor for Sonny's deviant, gay identity (although it isn't until at least midway through the film that we actually learn that Sonny is gay); and everyone's efforts to lure him out of the bank a metaphor for the misguided efforts on the part of his loved ones to understand him and to reestablish their connection to him. By robbing the bank and holing himself up inside it, Sonny has acted, as if for the first time in his life, on his own impulses, done what he thinks is best for him and nobody else. If he comes out of the bank now, he will come out a new person. So the question becomes, on whose terms and to what end will he come out? Will he come out to satisfy the needs of the very people whose authority he is trying to slough off, or will he come out in order to affirm himself? What is the best, safest, and most meaningful way for him to come out?

In one "coming out" scene, the police have just tried to break into the bank through the back door. Inside, Sonny fires a shot in return, prompting Moretti to summon him outside to talk:

MORETTI: C'mon out, Sonny. Sonny, come on out. Come on out here now. Come on out, Sonny. Sonny? Come on out here Sonny. [*Sonny comes out; Moretti shouts angrily at him*] What the fuck is the matter with you?

[. . .]

SONNY: [*also shouting angrily*] Get somebody to talk to me. I'm not talking to you anymore.

MORETTI: Let me talk to you. Let me talk to you. Aw, now wait, hold it a second.

SONNY: Yeah, you tell me one thing, then you do another. What're they doin' back there?

MORETTI: I don't know what the fuck they were doin' back there.

SONNY: Yeah, you don't know—you're full of shit. You don't know.

MORETTI: I got a force back there, a tactical force—

SONNY: A tactical force, yeah, yeah—

MORETTI: —they like to shoot, they like to jump on ropes, they like to climb in through windows.

SONNY: They like that, right? Without your orders, right? Without your orders.

MORETTI: No!—Yes! Without my orders, yes!

SONNY: How do I know you're not gonna come through the roof?

MORETTI: 'Cause I'm telling you that we're not.

SONNY: Yeah, you're tellin' me a lot of things but you're not doin' 'em.

MORETTI: Oh goddamn, when I told you—

SONNY: What were they doin' back there, that's what I want to know!

MORETTI: I don't know what they were doin'.

SONNY: You can't answer me. You can't answer me.

MORETTI: What?

SONNY: You can't answer me.

MORETTI: Yes, I can answer you.

SONNY: Tell me what they were doin'.

MORETTI: We don't have our communication set up there. No communications.

SONNY: Look, I got a guy in there—I got a guy in there's gonna kill somebody, that's your responsibility, understand? Not mine, that's yours.

MORETTI: [*no longer shouting*] Now wait a minute, hold a second, listen. We got everything you wanted.

SONNY: [*starting to calm down*] Oh yeah?

MORETTI: Yeah, we can't get a helicopter in here, but we got a bus coming. We got a jet coming into Kennedy. All right? Okay? All right? Now we got a—we got a hold of your wife—your wife is coming—we've reached her, and she's coming here, all right? Okay?

SONNY: [*as Moretti approaches him*] Where you goin'?

MORETTI: I'm right here, I'm right here, all right? I thought we were gonna talk.

SONNY: I thought so too but we're not talkin'. We're tryin' to get through the back door, that's what we're doin'.

MORETTI: I'm talking now. We reached your wife, she'll be here in about a half hour. Okay? Okay?

SONNY: [*referring to nearby cops*] What are they doin'? They're still pointin'! They love to point!

MORETTI: [*to the cops*] Holster that weapon! Holster it! Holster that weapon! You too! [*to Sonny*] All right, come on. What else do you want me to do? Huh? I don't know how you can do any better, huh? We got everything you wanted, everything. I'll do everything I can to stop anything I can, all right? Anything else?

Sonny then asks for food, something to drink (Cokes, no beer, Moretti insists), and aspirin, all of which Moretti gives him. Like an estranged father and son, Sonny and Moretti start by shouting and hurling accusations at each other. But then Moretti confesses his mistake ("our communication isn't set up yet"), tries to give Sonny what he needs (Sonny's wife, the bus and jet for passage out of the country, the food, the aspirin), even tries to offer *himself* to Sonny ("I'm right here, I'm right here. . . . I thought we were gonna talk"). But Sonny knows that Moretti's kindness is at least partially a ploy—his words sound soothing, but his intention, as Sonny points out in an earlier exchange, is to "bury" him.

And in a later scene, Sonny's mother (played by Judith Malina) encourages him to come out with her ("What would be the matter if you came out with me?" she asks; "Because I'm not coming out with you, Mom, please," Sonny answers, as if the answer should have been obvious). She claims that "the FBI understands everything. They understand that it is not you that is doing this, it's the *pressure*—it's from your—from your home life . . ." And she assures him, "I talked to the man from the FBI and he says—he says if you come out now everything's gonna be alright. . . . Listen, I'm trying to get you out of this! I told them how you were in the war in Vietnam, I told them you always had good jobs, I told them you were with Goldwater in '64 and the convention . . ." But she can't resist criticizing him: "Everything in your life is sweetness and roses, and you—you wouldn't need Leon if Angie was treating you right, you know that. I don't understand—I don't understand why you want to sleep with her anyway—you got two kids on welfare now—what do you want to sleep with her [for]? [*shouting*] You got a wife and two kids on welfare!" In a final attempt to get him to come out on her terms, she urges him to run:

SONNY: Run? Where am I gonna run, Ma? I can't run.
SONNY'S MOTHER: Well, don't—maybe—maybe—
SONNY: There's no maybes. No maybes, Ma. Please, you gotta go home
   now. Where's Pop? Did he come—he didn't come down here, did he?
SONNY'S MOTHER: Oh, is he pissed off at you! He says—he says he doesn't
   have a son. He says you're dead. You know what he says—
SONNY: He's right, Ma.
SONNY'S MOTHER: No!—no—no—
SONNY: Look, Ma, I'm a fuckup and I'm an outcast and that's it. You come
   near me, you're gonna get it. You're gonna get fucked over and fucked
   out. Now I gotta go, Ma, please. [*shouts to the cops*] Get her home, okay?
   Just take her home!
SONNY'S MOTHER: [*as she is led away*] How beautiful—how beautiful you
   were when you were a baby . . .

Sonny's mother's love for him, laced as it is with anger and bewilderment over his sexuality, makes her an unwise counselor. If he came out
according to her plan, he would only fall into the hands of men, like
Sheldon, who want to kill him (Sonny tells him, "I hope the guy that
kills me does it 'cause he hates my guts, not because it's his job") or who,
like his father, already pronounce him dead.

When Sonny displays himself outside the bank on his *own* terms, however, the crowd adores him, chanting "More! More! More!" They tease
him about his sexuality (when he frisks Sheldon before admitting him
inside the bank so that he, Sheldon, can make sure the hostages are un-
harmed, someone calls out, "Pussycat!"), but their whistles and applause
suggest, at least, that they don't *hate* him because of his sexuality. And,
perhaps most important of all, they *don't* greet his sexuality with polite,
stone-cold silence. That was a revelation to me when I first saw *Dog Day
Afternoon*. When Sonny comes out to pay the pizza delivery boy, he has
enough extra cash (fistfulls of it from the bank—never mind that it's
counterfeit) to throw into the crowd, making them beg for more. The
pizza boy shouts, "I'm a fucking star!" once he has delivered the food
and enjoyed his minute of fame in front of the TV cameras, but clearly
it's Sonny who has star quality.

"When I'm being fucked, I like to get kissed alot," Sonny tosses off
when Moretti assures him that he won't have to serve more than a year
in prison if he surrenders now. Sonny knows it's a lie. But now that he's
out and in command of the sidewalk, he can say *everything!*

Late in the film, Sonny speaks with his male lover, Leon (played by Chris
Sarandon). At Sonny's request, Sergeant Moretti escorts Leon from the
psychiatric hospital, where he has been recovering from his recent sui-

cide attempt, to the scene of the crime in order to persuade Sonny to give himself up to the police. At first, Leon refuses to speak to Sonny. But then he relents, speaking by telephone from a barbershop across the street as Sergeant Moretti and others secretly tap into the phone line. Sonny's and Leon's long conversation ranges over several different topics—Leon's unstable psychiatric condition, his fears of being implicated in the robbery, Sonny's unpredictably violent temper, Sonny's near-to-nervous breakdown over the unexpected turn of events, and both Sonny's and Leon's melancholy uncertainty about what the future holds in store for them. Here for the first time in my life I was seeing two gay men (or more accurately—though these nuances didn't impress me at the time—one bisexual man and one gay man who wishes to become a straight woman) speaking intimately, honestly, and at length with one another on screen:

SONNY: Hello. Hello? Hello, Leon?

LEON: Hello. Hello, Sonny.

SONNY: What happened? How ya'—how ya' doing?

LEON: Well I'm out of the hospital.

SONNY: Yeah, I know. You know I thought you'd never get out.

LEON: I never thought I'd get out this way, I'll tell you.

SONNY: Yeah. So, how you doin'?

LEON: Uh—I'm a little shaky.

SONNY: Oh yeah? Yeah, well, Moretti told me, you know, that you were all drugged up, so, uh, I figured that's why you didn't talk to me, you know, 'cause I was wondering why you didn't talk to me.

LEON: Yeah. It's really terrible, you know. I mean you walk in and right away they say you're crazy and then they start sticking things in your arm. I mean how do they expect you to get uncrazy if you're asleep all the time? I'm—I'm—uh—just starting to come out of it now.

SONNY: So.

LEON: Well, so, uh, how are you?

SONNY: How? I'm fine. It's something, huh?

LEON: Yeah. Yeah.

SONNY: [*starts to cry*] I don't know, Leon, you know I'm dyin' here. I'm dyin'.

LEON: Don't you ever listen to yourself when you say that? You're dyin'. Did you ever listen to yourself?

SONNY: What are you talkin' about?

LEON: What do you mean, what am I talkin' about? You are dyin'. You know that you say that to me every day of your life?

SONNY: Oh—

LEON: "I'm dyin'." Well, you're not dyin'. You're killin' the people around you's what you're doin'.

SONNY: Oh come on, Leon, don't give me that shit. I don't need that deep shit now.

LEON: Well I don't think you realize what it means, Sonny. You know, do you realize the things you do?

SONNY: Yeah? I know what I do.

LEON: You stick a gun to somebody's head.

SONNY: Yeah, well I don't know what I'm doin' sometimes with that.

LEON: Yeah, well obviously you don't. "Go to sleep, Leon, so it won't hurt when I pull the trigger." What do you think I've been doin' in the hospital? I mean I take a handful of pills to get away from you, right?

SONNY: Yeah?

LEON: So, now I'm talkin' to you on the phone again, right? I got no job, I don't have friends, I can't live. I have to live with people. This death business. I'm sorry.

SONNY: I don't know, Leon, you know, I don't know what I'm gettin' here with that shit. You know, what am I supposed to say to that shit? You know, this is goin' on and you're givin' me that shit.

LEON: I'm sorry.

SONNY: You know what's happenin' with me. You know that. You know the pressures I've been havin', right? I mean I got all these pressures and you know about it. You're in that hospital there with all them tubes comin' out. You want that fuckin' operation. You're givin' me that shit, right? Everybody's givin' me shit. Everybody needs money, you know what I mean? So, you needed money, I got you money. That's it.

LEON: Yeah, well I didn't ask you to go and rob a bank!

SONNY: I know you didn't ask me! I know you didn't ask me! Look. I'm not puttin' this on anybody. You know? Nothin' on nobody. I did this on my own, you see? All on my own I did it. But I want you to know something. I want you to know that I'm gonna—I'm gettin' out of here. I'm gettin' a plane out of here, and I just wanted you to know it, that's all. And I wanted you to come down, [*his voice trembles*] and, uh, I wanted to say just good-bye to you, or, if you wanted to you can come with me. I mean you're free to do what you want. That's what I want—that's just what I wanted to say to you. That's all.

LEON: Uh, I'm free to do what I want, huh?

SONNY: Right.

LEON: Yeah, well, uh, I've been tryin' to get away from you for six months and I'm gonna go away with you on a plane trip, huh? Well, where? Where are you goin'?

SONNY: I don't know where yet. Well, we said Algeria, I don't know. So, I'll go to Algeria, I don't know.

LEON: Why are you goin' to Algeria?

SONNY: I don't know why. They got a Howard Johnson's there, so I'm goin', you know what I mean?

LEON: Howard Johnson's. You're warped, do you know that? You're really warped.

SONNY: I'm warped, I know I'm warped.

LEON: God, Algeria. It's—uh—they walk around—they got masks on—they got things on their heads—they're a bunch of crazy people there.

SONNY: So, what am I supposed to do?

LEON: Well, I don't know. You could have picked a better place.

SONNY: Like what? Sweden? Denmark?

LEON: Yeah. Yeah. Like that, yeah.

SONNY: You know what? Sal wanted to go to Wyoming.

LEON: Oh, Jesus.

SONNY: I had to tell him it's not a country. He don't know where Wyoming is. See, I'm with a guy who don't know where Wyoming is, you think you got problems?

LEON: Whew! So, Sal is with you, huh? Oh, boy. You'd be better off givin' up.

SONNY: Well I'm not gonna give up, because what have I done this so far? You know what I mean? I've gone so far with this. Why should I give up now? I can't give up.

LEON: Well, would you do me a favor, then?

SONNY: Yeah, what?

LEON: Well these guys that have me down here, you know, they think I'm—uh—they think I'm part of it—you know, they think I'm part of the plot to rob the bank—

SONNY: Oh that's crazy, Leon. That's crazy. They're just—they're bullshittin' you—they're givin' you a snow job.

LEON: Well, no, they told me I was an accessory.

SONNY: No. That's just a con job on you, Leon, don't listen to them.

LEON: Well I have to listen to it.

SONNY: No!

LEON: Well I can't survive in prison, Sonny.

SONNY: Oh, Leon, you're not going to prison, nobody's gonna—

LEON: Well how do you know?

SONNY: Because I know, you're not going to prison. Believe me.

LEON: Well please—

SONNY: Please what? What? What do you want me to do?

LEON: Just tell them—

SONNY: Tell them *what*? That you didn't do it? Now where am I gonna—where—are they on the phone now? Are they on the phone now?

LEON: Yeah.

SONNY: That's terrific. You talk to me with them on the phone, that's really smart.

LEON: Well I don't have a choice.

SONNY: What do you mean you didn't have a choice?

LEON: Well they're standin' all around me. There's seven thousand fuckin' cops all around me.

SONNY: Who's on the phone now?

LEON: Look, don't lay it on me.

SONNY: I'm not layin' it on you, but you knew that was goin' on. What are
    you talkin' about, layin' it on you—you knew what was happening, right?
LEON: Yeah. Yeah.
SONNY: Who's on the—I wanna—who's on the phone now? Moretti—
    Moretti—is that you on the phone? Hello! Will somebody talk to me? Is
    somebody gonna talk to me, or what? They on the phone now?
LEON: They won't talk to you.
SONNY: All right, he didn't do it. Okay? He had nothin' to do with it. All
    right? Now will you get the fuck off the phone? Are they off the phone?
LEON: Yeah.
[*Unbeknownst to Sonny, Moretti and the others remain on the line.*]
SONNY: All right, Leon, that was terrific. That really convinced 'em. That's
    what they wanted to know, right? Did I do it for you or what?
LEON: Yeah, thank you.
SONNY: Okay. So now what? What are you gonna do?
LEON: Well I thought, uh, I thought that I would go back to the hospital,
    you know. They're really nice there, I mean they really seem like they're
    tryin' to help me.
SONNY: So then that's good, then, right? You found something.
LEON: Yeah, well, I don't know if I have or not.
SONNY: So are you gonna still have the operation?
LEON: Yeah. Yeah.
SONNY: So then, what do I s'posed—what am I supposed to say to you?
LEON: Thanks a lot. And, uh, bon voyage.
SONNY: Yeah, right. See you sometime.
LEON: Yeah. I'll see you in my dreams, huh?
SONNY: Right. I'll write a song. Oh, I don't know, you know? Life's so
    funny.
LEON: You said a mouthful, sweetheart. Well, good-bye, huh?
SONNY: Bye.

Leon was the type of person—cowardly, self-centered, effeminate, de-
ceitful, a woman trapped in a man's body—whom I had always been
taught to hate. But Sonny doesn't hate Leon. His voice is plaintive, almost kittenish, when he asks Leon, two times over, why Leon didn't
talk to him at first. I was amazed that, in spite of all of Sonny's masculine bravado (displayed everywhere else in the film), he could still need
somebody like Leon. Sonny even forgives Leon when he discovers that
they are being listened to by the police and that Leon knew it all along.
His anger is not finally damning of Leon but is only one expression of
a much larger, more complex emotional entanglement. In fact, Sonny
loves Leon so much that he is even willing to accept Leon's desire to become a woman; that was the kind of self-sacrificial love that I had been

taught in all my years of Catholic schooling to value above every other kind of love on this earth.

Sonny and Leon's conversation is intimate like no conversation I had ever had with any of the men in my life. My father hated it when I would "hang" on the telephone, which I did more and more the older I got, plus my friends were mostly *girl*friends, so that just confirmed his sense (or so I imagined) that phone conversations were somehow intrinsically effeminizing. His motto was, "state your business and get off." But except for the favor Leon asks of Sonny (that Sonny assure the cops that Leon had nothing to do with the bank robbery), they speak purely for the sake of being with each other. And their conversation doesn't risk ending just because it takes a turn or because its "business" is taken care of; when a moment of silence falls, Sonny isn't embarrassed by the consequent potential for intimacy, but says, rather, just "so." And Leon, too, embraces that intimacy: "Well, so, uh, how are you?" What I heard exchanged between the men in this scene, besides words, were patience, silences, and sighs.

Perhaps most affirming of all, Sonny and Leon share their deepest, most existential concerns with one another: Sonny: "Oh, I don't know, you know? Life's so funny." Leon: "You said a mouthful, sweetheart." Or again, Leon: "I'll see you in my dreams, huh?" And Sonny: "Right. I'll write a song."

And I loved the way Leon called Sonny "sweetheart."

In *Hollywood from Vietnam to Reagan,* Robin Wood argues that "keeping Sonny and Leon apart," in separate buildings, interacting only on the telephone, "spares the spectator the potential embarrassment of imagining anything they might do in bed together. It is also consistent with the film's general desexualization of Sonny" (235). But whatever the intention of the filmmakers, the film's dilation on the inner and interpersonal lives of gay men rather than on their specifically sexual attraction to each other nevertheless had the power to push me, an isolated, unworldly gay teenager, toward accepting the idea of a male homosexual relationship in a brand new way. What I *didn't* need at that time was the image of two gay men as sexual beings (although I did find Al Pacino staggeringly attractive); instead, I needed to know that being gay meant something besides sexuality. I already understood, reluctantly, that being gay had chosen me: ever since eighth grade, I knew how turned on I was by other boys' bodies. I would periodically think, I'm gay, and then I'd shudder at the thought and try to put it out of my mind (the thought would always come back). But I was starved for an understanding of all the ways that I would have to choose to be gay in order to survive and to grow. I must have dimly sensed that Sonny's physical separation from Leon meant *not* a desexualization of Sonny but, rather, the allegorized, indeed politicized, truth about gay people as I experienced it daily: they were inherently "cut off" from each other, forbidden movement, forbidden to look at each other, imprisoned, "dying here" as Sonny tells Leon on the verge of tears.

In *The Celluloid Closet*, Vito Russo, like Robin Wood distrustful of the portrayal of gay men in *Dog Day Afternoon*, argues—too hastily I think—that when "Sonny's straight accomplice Sal complains that the television news reports are calling him a homosexual, Sonny says, 'Ahh, Sal, what do you care? It's only a freak show to them.' And that was all the movie was to middle-America, a freaky, only–in–New York story that made a fair two-hour yarn but failed to touch their lives" (231). My experience of the film, and I don't doubt plenty of other people's, belies Russo's claim. This doesn't mean that *Dog Day Afternoon* represents gay people well or fairly, but it does mean that an audience's response to a film is to some degree incalculable, and so any gay-affirmative intervention in the filmmaking process needs to take into account the full complexity of the scene of response. Perhaps if critics and filmmakers acknowledge how unpredictable an audience's deepest response may be, then the quality and complexity of gay representation will change.

III

In case he should be killed while trying to escape the police, Sonny writes his last will and testament near the end of the film; by this time I had fallen in love with him. The lights and the air conditioning inside the bank have been cut off, it is nighttime, and Sonny feels exhausted and alone. He has already said good-bye to Leon. His undershirt is soaked with sweat. The deep lines in his otherwise youthful face bespeak suffering, corruption, even some inarticulate familiarity with evil. His will begins, "To my darling wife Leon, whom I love more than any man has loved another man in all eternity"; I had never heard a man speak such tender feelings for another man before. "In all eternity": that was the kind of thing Rodgers and Hammerstein wrote love songs about ("You're his girl and he's your feller") but it was always about a man and a woman. That night as I lay awake in my bed, unable to fall asleep, I kept picturing Al Pacino, in his white dress shirt, unbuttoned all the way down, his white undershirt damp with sweat, his face and hair glistening with sweat, telling me how much he loved me. Deep feelings and tender words of love and affection and kindness and gentleness poured out of him like sweat: Patrick, I love you, I love you so much, I love you as a man has never loved another man, I love you as a man loves another man, I love you for all eternity. . . and I began to realize what my next film project would be.

The film I imagined was called *Brothers,* and it starred Al Pacino and me—I graciously took second billing. I started by imagining the sex scenes that *Dog Day Afternoon* never shows, scenes with Al and me in bed, making love. I worked out a scenario in which a verbal argument would turn into a physical fight—pushing, punches, throwing things, trashing the apartment (I would have to figure out exactly whose apartment it was, and what we were doing there together in the first place, and what we were fighting about, but that could come later). At some point the fight would suddenly calm down, and turn into a love scene.

I was younger and weaker than Al, of course, and had always gone out of my way to avoid fights with other boys, but I could be slightly tougher on film than I was in real life. So Al Pacino and I would be fighting and he would be throwing knickknacks at me and I would be throwing pillows and other bed linens back at him, and he would chase me around the room, trying to grab me in order to throw me down (both of us would be in our underwear, because it was getting close to bedtime when the argument began, and it was summertime, so it was hot, and this was a run-down apartment building in New York, so Sonny doesn't have any air conditioning), and for a while I would manage to escape him, but not without doing terrible damage to the apartment: blinds would become twisted, curtains pulled down from the windows, pictures would fall down off the walls, the glass smashing as they hit the floor. The whole room, it seemed, would shake, as if there were an earthquake, as if in a disaster film! Finally, he would catch me roughly and tightly squeeze me in his strong arms and pin me onto the bed, face down, the way wrestlers hold each other to the mat, their bodies tense and beading with sweat, their faces anguished, their muscles and veins tightening visibly beneath their skin. And he would force me to submit, as I fought, but failed, to get out from underneath him. "Let me go! Let me go!" I would shout, but somehow this was not really what either of us wanted. (In *Men's Dreams, Men's Healing* [1990], the Jungian psychotherapist Robert H. Hopcke quotes one of his patients as follows: "The dream starts a split second before a film-review program I am watching cuts to a clip of a film it has reviewed. In Italian, I see and hear Al Pacino, who is a boxer named Maccagnorola, denigrating another boxer, who is named [humorously] Grancche. There is a crowd in a kitchen which leaves, ready to sit down at the table to eat an Italian meal in the dining room. Al Pacino and his wife are getting things ready, bringing plates of food out. I am waiting to hear him begin using words like 'barbaric' and 'animal' with regard to the other boxer, but he doesn't. Instead he fusses, making sure everyone is seated and all is ready" [139].)

So Al would bury his face in my neck, but rather than lift it again, he would linger there, for he had begun to kiss the back of my neck, his disheveled hair covering his face and the back of my neck. He would slowly, slowly relax his muscles and loosen his grip on me (his arms had locked themselves around me) and begin slowly, gently to shift his legs in order to feel his skin rubbing against mine and reach down with one arm and begin to caress the inside of my thigh. I too had begun to relax, and lay there, now on my back, lifeless beneath him, and looked up into his face as if to ask, confused, worried, afraid, in disbelief, but also expectant, full of desire, "What is happening to us?" (Again, Hopcke's patient: "Now I am in the movie, sitting on the kitchen counter, as if my eyes are the camera [you can't see me in the film, but I see everything] and I'm a little kid, eight or nine years old. I ask Dad [Al Pacino] for a piece of bread. He comes very close to me, his chest pressed up against the counter between my legs, so I can feel and smell his body very close. He dips a small piece of bread in olive oil with long thin tongs and gives it to me in the mouth. I barely chew this before I ask for another, which he gives to me in the same manner. I keep asking, expecting him to refuse, hurriedly chewing each morsel so he can't—but even with my mouth full, he continues to feed me. He is extraordinarily tender and generous. I feel very loved." [139]) (Fig. 23.)

Now Al Pacino was flat on top of me, and was kissing me, and calling me sweetheart, darling, and telling me that he was sorry, that he didn't want to hurt me, asking me did he hurt me, kissing the hurts here and there to make them go away, kissing my face and telling me that he loved me and had wanted this moment for a long, long time and that he loved me and would love me for all eternity. . . .

Eventually I worked out a plot to go along with the sex scenes. The film, I decided, is about a boy, around sixteen years old, named David. (Actually, I now forget exactly what my character's name was. I think I usually named my characters "Peter," but that would be odd if true, because "Peter" was the name of the boy who in tenth grade made my life miserable by throwing little wads of chewing gum in my hair during social studies class. He also punched me in front of the boys' bathroom one afternoon before lunch. I said and did nothing. For a long time, the name "Peter" meant the unbearable pain in my groin and the feeling of gum in my hair, and the anger that everyone else in the class could see what was being done to me but didn't try to stop it and the agony of knowing that after class I would rush with tears in my eyes to the boys'

Figure 23. My brother John and me, ca. 1975.

bathroom to pull out my hair stuck with gum and Peter would follow me and just stand there and watch me and the whole ritual would be repeated the next day and the next. So I'm not sure whether now I felt that I could defuse the name "Peter" of its power over me by adopting it as my own in the film or whether, probably more likely, it was the *one* name I knew that I could never, ever own. I think my name in the film must have ended up being one that I happened to have no particular relation to at the time, like "David.")

Either he has run away from home or he is suddenly orphaned—at any rate, the film begins with David leaving the suburbs and going to New York City to live with his cousin Sonny (played by Al Pacino). At first, David doesn't like Sonny all that much and doesn't like living with him. David is used to suburban comforts (like the home I grew up in) and has a tough time adjusting to urban noise, pollution, squalor, neighbors dropping in at all hours of the night, drinking, drugs, sex, and so on and so on. Sonny doesn't like David much either because he doesn't like having to be a parent, he's used to living his life sloppily the way he wants, and David is very finicky and spoiled (the way my siblings always complained that I was spoiled because I was the "baby" of the family and as a result, they thought, got everything I wanted). David and Sonny have a few nasty fights, but little by little they fall into a homosexual relationship with each other. I'm not sure, but I think it's clear to David from the start that Sonny is gay, although the film makes little, if anything, of Sonny's gayness until the scenes where he and David start making love with each other. I must have learned this narrative device from *Dog Day Afternoon,* as it isn't until late in the film that we learn that the antihero with whom we are compelled to identify, Sonny, is also a gay man. For certain, David has never had any homosexual experiences until now, and he spends a good deal of the film worrying that he might be gay and not wanting to admit the way he feels about Sonny. Sonny, on the other hand, is sure that he loves David and has no doubts about entering into a love relationship with him. One night, they try sleeping separately at David's request, but before you know it David is at Sonny's bedside wanting to come in again, and he does and they're back where they started, unable to resist their love for each other.

So things go on like this for a while until an aunt and uncle in the family, played by Estelle Parsons and Karl Malden, decide that they want to adopt David. Reluctantly, and much to Sonny's chagrin, David goes back to the suburbs to live with his aunt and uncle for a "trial run." This part of the film is blurry in my memory because it was ill-conceived from the start, but I know that there were scenes meant to show how awful life with David's aunt and uncle would be if they adopted him, despite the fact (which is supposed to make David happy, but doesn't) that they have nine children and hence, nine live-in playmates for David. In one scene, David is playing pool with a few of his cousins, but it is totally boring. In another scene, David's aunt scolds him for no apparent reason at the dinner table, and here he is supposed to be her guest, and she scolds him! (This family was modeled largely on my father's twin brother's family of nine kids, whom I hated visiting—they did have a nice in-the-ground swimming pool in their backyard, though, and instead of a regular kitchen table and chairs they had a really neat built-in table with one continuous vinyl sofa running all around it like a big booth in a restaurant, but that was about it. Their house was like a circus with millions of people always running around; finding privacy and peace and quiet in *my* house with my *five* siblings was hard enough, but finding it in their house I knew would be virtually impossible.) Desperate, David secretly arranges for Sonny to come and steal him back, which Sonny does.

The remainder of the film, inspired in part by *Kramer vs. Kramer,* which had come out the same year I saw *Dog Day Afternoon* on TV, involves a complicated court battle for custody of David between Sonny and the aunt and uncle. In the end, Sonny wins custody, although here again I'm not sure how, and anyway I also imagined a peak dramatic moment (which completely contradicts the idea of Sonny *winning* the case) where David would have to *choose* whom he would prefer to spend the rest of his life with, and shockingly he chooses Sonny over his aunt and uncle.

The very last scene in the film shows a bittersweet embrace between David and Sonny in some tiny room that, I imagined, could be found in courthouses for keeping witnesses or for sending defendants while they await the verdict or maybe where they send the jury to *decide* the verdict or maybe where the *judge* (played in my film by Sir Lawrence Olivier) goes to decide the verdict. I didn't quite know if there was even going to *be* a jury making the decision or just the judge. In fact, I imagined very little about the courtroom scenes, not because I didn't suspect they would be crucial to the working out of the plot, but because I usually hated courtroom dramas, I always got bored watching them, and I never understood exactly what was going on in them anyway. The important thing was the reunion scene between Sonny and David after Sonny wins the case, or the scene where David makes his choice and ends up in Sonny's arms.

About a year after these initial fantasies came to me, I made one other scene for *Brothers* that actually contradicts the plot in a serious way; the scene never quite found a secure place within the film, but I nevertheless felt compelled to make it with care. In this scene, it is Al Pacino/Sonny, not I/David, who is shown to be extremely uneasy about his homosexuality. Sonny is restless one night and decides to sneak out and go to a gay bar. Obviously I was confused: if Sonny were openly and comfortably gay, as I had otherwise imagined him to be, why would he be "sneaking" out to gay bars? I think my only conception of gay bars and the people who went to them came from seeing brief clips from the movie *Cruising* on the nightly news when, upon its release in 1980, members of the gay community protested it for suggesting that there was some inherent connection between, on the one hand, gay identity and, on the other, sadomasochism and murder. Newscasters would show gay activists picketing outside a movie theater where *Cruising* was playing, cut to the line of people waiting to buy tickets, cut to a five-second segment of one of the apparently objectionable scenes in the film—usually a scene in the leather bar where the hero, Steve Burns (played by Al Pacino), goes to track down a serial killer. All you saw in the clip were ill-arranged masses of oddly dressed or shirtless men dancing in the dark and grabbing onto each other and huddled together in groups of three or more doing it was hard to tell exactly what.

So I decided that in *Brothers*, Sonny would go off to one of these mysterious places, just to see if he really is or if he really wants to be gay, or is it just that he loves David and that this is not otherwise the life for him? To make a long story short, he goes in, has a beer, someone starts feeling him up, he goes along with it for a little while, but then two other guys join in, he gets nervous, blows up, throws his drink in their faces, and storms out of the bar. We see him charging down the alley behind the bar, enraged but also shaking with fear. In his bewilderment, he kicks over a garbage can and its contents spill out into the filthy twilight—and the scene fades.

I wanted *Brothers* to have a depressing, somewhat sleazy look and feel to it. I imagined Sonny's New York apartment building to be a grim, walkup affair with a creaking staircase and sinister-looking tenants. I thought it would be good to have me/David accidentally enter the wrong apartment in my quest to find Sonny's door at the beginning of the film. I would be walking down a dark, ugly, narrow brown hallway and pass by an open door. Inside would be a group of people, very rough and unattractive-looking with their undershirts and beer bottles and fat bellies, men and women, assembled underneath a swinging lamp or maybe just a light bulb, around a table, playing poker (this image seems to have been inspired by the poker-playing scenes in *A Streetcar Named Desire*, which I may have seen on TV around this time). I would walk in and they would tell me scornfully that I got the wrong apartment.

I would say innocently, "where does Sonny live? I'm his cousin, David."

"Oh, Sonny?" they would all chant in chorus, and cackle as if they knew something I didn't. "He lives upstairs in 6H—" (I just picked any number) "—last door on the left. *All* the way at the end of the hall, you can't miss it—heh, heh, heh!" One of the fat men would chuckle and nudge his partner and point his thumb at me and chew on his cigar, as I humbly turned around and continued on my way, mounting the seemingly interminable stairs with a suitcase in each hand (not unlike Maria when she journeys out of the convent to meet the von Trapp family).

During the opening credits, though my memory of this is weak, we would see a succession of desolate New York City street and rooftop scenes—garage doors; trash cans; dark and empty alleyways (at the time, I didn't know that New York City doesn't really *have* many alleyways, at least not the kind you can freely enter and walk through like we had in Reading); streets with lots of parked cars but otherwise deserted, except for maybe a stray cat, a stray *black* cat; empty front stoops; chimneys smoking, or maybe chimneys not smoking—just acres and acres of crooked chimneys and TV antennas and water towers like sculpture on

since Judy Garland and James Mason had done it, they always thought, so handsomely in 1954.

I, on the other hand, thought Barbra looked gorgeous, she sounded better than ever, and I loved the way the camera panned around her while she sang "Evergreen," almost as if she were an object of sacred veneration. And yet, I too was a little disappointed with what I saw. To begin with, I wished Kristofferson were just out of the picture altogether. And I didn't like all of the "realistic" touches—Streisand's impromptu laughter before the line "and their dance is unrehearsed" and the way she "worriedly" touches her throat near the end of the song as if to suggest that she must *work* to achieve her perfect tone quality! The fact that she sang live here on camera, rather than lip-synching as in her earlier film musicals, didn't please me at all. Her magnetism was always real to me no matter through what special effects it was achieved. In fact, I suspect that the more artificially constructed the effects of her performance, the more they intoxicated me, because they proved (as the promotional slogan for her 1983 film, *Yentl,* would have it) that "nothing's impossible!" I wanted Hollywood musicals to be honest about what they were (a fantasy), but it seemed to me that by having the story take place in the contemporary, vulgate world of pop music, this version of *A Star Is Born* was covering up for the fact that it was still a Hollywood musical, so that if the characters should ever break out into song, as in this scene, there would always be an alibi: of course they're singing, not because that's what their wildest fantasies and deepest urges tell them they must do (as mine would if my life were a musical) but because after all they're pop singers and that's what pop singers do in real life—they sing. I still wanted Barbra to make another big-budget show biz musical like *Hello, Dolly!* where any stroll down Fourteenth Street turned like a miracle into a production number with hundreds of extras singing and dancing and tons of scenery and a full-scale orchestra filling the blue sky. Obviously those happy days were gone forever.

I was also disappointed in Barbra's choice of Jon Peters as a boyfriend (a slimy hairdresser?!) in the same way that I always hated the guys my sisters used to date. Plus I was having a hard time adjusting to Barbra's new frizzy hairdo, which Jon apparently talked her into getting.

However, disappointment and moral outrage were precisely the feelings I wanted people to have about *me* in my film *Brothers* and in the late night Dick Cavett interview with me and Al Pacino (actually, I never really worried about anybody's reaction to Al Pacino either in the film or in the interview—in fact, I could barely think of anything for Al to do or say during the interview). I wanted people to think, Patrick's not the boy I used to know. And it wasn't long after seeing the Barbara Walters interview that I began to think that the whole *purpose* of that interview, in a way, was to disappoint people, to disappoint Barbra Streisand's fans, to show the world what a brand-new, liberated, grown-up person Barbra could become if she wanted to—if she had to—after all this was 1976. I came around to thinking that Jon Peters wasn't all *that* bad (in fact, he was kind of cute!), and Barbra would wear her hair any way she liked (fig. 24). I felt that my Dick Cavett interview should send a similar message to the world: that I was grown up now, that I could and would do what I wanted, and that included playing a homosexual character and even suggesting if not saying outright that maybe Al Pacino and I were also having an affair in real life on the side. (At midnight mass one Christmas Eve during the mid-eighties, I got into a fit of uncontrollable laughter with my sister Karen over something one of our former high school English teachers, Mrs. Bromfield, was doing in the pew in front of us, I don't remember what. After mass she turned to me and said, "Patrick, I heard you laughing all throughout mass. I'm surprised at you. Not only do you look different [I was sporting a new perm], but you act different, too. You should be ashamed. I don't know what's happened to you!" This, of course, only increased our laughter.)

Whenever I thought about my interview with Dick Cavett, I always insisted that Al Pacino and I should be wearing black tuxedos for the occasion. Somehow the tuxedos heightened for me the shattering discrepancy between my public image (nice, clean cut, obedient, from a good Catholic family) and what I was doing privately (having sex with men on screen, talking openly about it on TV), between my ostensible identity as an "artist" and the homosexual content of my art. But the tuxedos also domesticated and legitimated, in my mind, the frightful power of my sexuality, of my character's homosexuality. I had also seen a picture of Barbra, Jon Peters, and Kris Kristofferson on a talk show with Geraldo Rivera from around the time of the release of *A Star Is Born*, and both Kris and Barbra were wearing tuxedos.

> *Dick Cavett:* Hi. It's good to have you here again.
> *Patrick Horrigan:* Thanks, Dick. It's good to be back on late night TV.
> *Dick:* How long has it been?
> *Patrick:* Oh, God. Let's see. I haven't been here since—I think you had me on just after the '77 oscars?
> *Dick:* You've had probably the most successful acting career of anyone under twenty-one in Hollywood history. You won best actor in 1977, best supporting actor in 1978, and now there's talk of another best actor nomination for *Brothers*—both you and Al Pacino, best actor nominations.

Figure 24. Esther Hoffman Howard (Barbra Streisand) in the 1976 version of
A Star Is Born.

Patrick: Well, I don't know, I mean sometimes it amazes me to think about that—you know, being fourteen and playing in these really serious films about death and trauma and suicide [*laughs*]. But—I—you know, I hate the word "superstar"—I hate that word. [*pause*] I think I missed a lot of the normal things kids grow up with. School has not been a regular part of my life, what with growing up half the time in Pennsylvania, half in Hollywood. I mean I've missed whole years. I have had wonderful private tutors whom I just adore, really, and they've been very good to me. You know, they've been like surrogate parents. Especially my piano teacher, she's—well, I don't know where to begin. But I didn't have a regular childhood, and, you know, I would sort of think, shouldn't I be going to a basketball game or something normal like that, rather than, you know, getting up at five o'clock in the morning to be on the set and ready to shoot by seven or going to parties at producers' houses where everyone else is drinking martinis and I'm having 7-Up. It's funny.

Dick: I'm wondering how you would compare your career with that of other child stars—I'm thinking of Brooke Shields, Ricky Schroder, Jodie Foster, Tatum O'Neal. Do you see any similarities between your career and theirs?

Patrick: Well, yes and no. I mean, I've been very lucky, and I know that. One thing about Hollywood is, for young people, you have to go through an exploitation period when you're starting out—you're either a sexpot or you're "the brat" or "the kid" or you're "precocious"—and the thing about Brooke Shields is, all anybody could talk about when she did *Pretty Baby* was, "Is she wearing a body stocking?!" Whereas I, on the other hand, feel as though I've been treated like a full human being right from the start, and my first film was a major role, and, okay, I was playing a ten-year-old, but it's a real part and he is a real person, you know? But I don't want to make it sound like I'm knocking Brooke's work, I mean she and I have talked about this, and I know that I'm not saying anything out of school—I mean, she's said the same things about her work to me, so . . .

Dick: So your new film is due to open—when?

Patrick: December something. I guess Christmas day, now. I'm not sure. It keeps getting pushed back. First it was a September opening. Then Thanksgiving. Let's hope sometime before 1990!

Dick: Because—

Patrick: Because of all the changes that are being made to it—every hour on the hour, it seems. This film has been through so many incarnations. I've never worked on a film like this before.

Dick: Can you tell us what it's about?

Patrick: [*laughs*] I suppose so. Well, I play this—boy, who runs away from home and goes to live with his cousin, who is Al Pacino, I mean who is played by Al Pacino [*laughs*], and, basically, they fall in love with each other.

Dick: They fall in *love* with each other?

Patrick: Yeah.

Dick: How do you feel about playing what I take you to mean is a homosexual character?

Patrick: I feel fine, really. And I don't believe all that stuff about how it damages your career and you'll never work again or you'll be forever typecast as a homosexual. I think if the work is good then the work is good and that's all that matters and you'll keep on working, knock on wood. I guess I feel like I'm at a point in my career where I want to take chances. I don't want to make movies about just ordinary people like you always see in the movies. I wanted the chance to play someone who, in many ways, is different from me—someone who is not sympathetic. Also, I mean, who could turn down an offer to work with Al Pacino?! But you know this is not a film [*makes quotation mark signs with his fingers*] "about homosexuality," it's really about just two people, one of whom happens to be another man, and they fall in love and they discover that they need each other and that's really all it is. The other big reason for doing this picture was that we had almost complete freedom in creating our characters.

Dick: I understand that this film has had, at different times since its inception, sixteen scripts. *Sixteen?!*

Patrick: [*laughs*] Yeah. I think, *more!*

Dick: Why?

Patrick: Well, the original idea for this film was Joan Didion's, oddly enough. She had written a script with her husband, John Gregory Dunne, around the same time that they were collaborating on the script for the Streisand version of *A Star Is Born,* and then it got tossed around Warner Brothers for about three years until finally Irvin Kershner was signed to direct. There had been some talk of William Friedkin directing it, but that never got beyond the bright idea stage. Now at that time Kershner was still thought of as a kind of semidocumentary director, but he had also directed Barbra Streisand in 1972 in *Up the Sandbox,* which is about a woman who is trying to decide whether she should have an abortion, so I guess Warner Brothers thought, okay, here is someone who can direct a "problem" picture. They probably thought *Brothers* was going to be another TV movie of the week about teen pregnancy or something ridiculous like that. I don't know. But anyway, um, all of a sudden it was like there was no script. We were doing scenes and we started improvising a lot, and we began to just write our own dialogue or not even write it, just, you know, it would just come out as we were doing the scene, and then we found that our characters were changing in unpredictable ways—but good ways. I mean the whole courtroom sequence was really up in the air during the whole shooting and Al and I had different ideas, in fact, about how it should go, and we even made two completely different versions of the ending.

Dick: I heard Lawrence Olivier wasn't very happy about that.

Patrick: Yeah. Well, I don't know—I do love Larry. [*laughs*] But—so anyway, it had become clear to us that this was a totally different project from the one we started out with. It was very important to me, and really for both me and Al, that this was a film where *we* were as much responsible for the finished product as anyone else, and Irvin understood that—I don't think another director would have gone along with that— not like Irvin. He doesn't have an ego, you know? He's a total . . . artist. I can't think of another word for it.

Dick: You're not only one of the most respected actors in Hollywood, you're also one of the busiest. Not to jump too far ahead of ourselves, but what's next for you?

Patrick: Well I'm really excited because this summer I'm going to have fun. I have a small part in a film called *Cancer,* which is going to be a big all-star thing, it has a big budget [*laughs*]—it's very big and very Hollywood and I love it!—I mean, there's nothing like working with Marlon Brando and Lucille Ball in the same picture! And I play a young—very young— doctor who knows something about a cure for cancer, which has just been discovered—the *cure* has just been discovered—and—well I better not say anything more about it, but I get chased around a lot! I have a stunt double in this movie, can you believe it? It's a thriller, you know? And then after—oh, and Jane Fonda's in it as well, did I say that already? —anyway—and then after that I'm not sure. There are a few projects that I'm sort of developing on my own, which I don't think I would know how to even begin to explain at this point. Oh yeah, and I have a small but really juicy part in *The Stand*—based on the Stephen King novel— but that's at least a year down the road. But I get to play an absolute villain, and the kid I play is supposed to be fat, so I'm going to have to put on something like, I don't know, fifty pounds! I don't even want to think about it. But, you know, if Shelley Winters could do it for *The Poseidon Adventure,* I can do it for this, that's my philosophy. The price of character acting! [*laughs*] For some reason I'm much more comfortable right now with small parts that allow me to do more character acting, and preferably unsavory types—for some reason, please don't ask me why!

Dick: Why! Why! [*laughs*]

Patrick: See, I want to stay away from parts that just allow me to "be myself." I guess I'm looking for a different kind of challenge. Of course, it's a myth that when you play a character who is very like yourself, you're really just being yourself—I don't think that there's really ever any such thing, for an actor, as just being yourself, you know?

Dick: Let me ask you a more difficult question.

Patrick: Please.

Dick: You and Pacino may very well both be nominated for best actor for this film. How would you deal with that? I mean, you'd want to kill each other, right?!

Patrick: [*lengthy pause*] You know, it's great to be recognized by your peers and I'm grateful and flattered and honored and all of those things— all of those good things—but I do have to say that it just doesn't matter. I mean I would be happy to win and I would be thrilled if Al won and I know that I'm not—I know that he feels the same way—I mean, I don't want to speak for Al, but, uh . . . I think a lot of people would like to hear things like, oh, you know, there's this rivalry between them, or they really didn't get along when they made this picture and the behind-the-scenes this and that, but, you know, I'm sorry if people are disappointed when I say that nothing could be farther from the truth. I mean, people like to gossip. And we've had so much of it for this film that at this point, they can say anything they want—they've practically said everything already, I think! I just know what this film is really all about and the Oscars and all the press and the lies—the hype—they're not what this film is about for me.

Dick: There's been trouble at Warner Brothers because the film is perceived as being—and I'm quoting the studio head of Warner Brothers—the film is "pornographic, with little artistic—"

Patrick: "—with little artistic merit," yes, I know, I read the article in *Rolling Stone.*

Dick: Oh, hey, by the way, that pinup—I mean, the picture of you on the cover of *Rolling Stone*—whew! Hide that one from Grandma and the kids!

Patrick: [*laughs*] Yeah, you know, at first I said to my agent, are you kidding? Pose in the nude?! But then I said, oh what the hell, and I just did it. It was fun, what can I say? But you know, I see it more as an art photograph than a pinup.

Dick: It's a beauty. But I interrupted you.

Patrick: What were we talking about? Oh yeah—well, anyway, the film is *not* pornographic. The studio heads have not seen this picture, and they're sabotaging it—well, they're *trying* to sabotage it before it even has a chance.

Dick: Why?

Patrick: [*sigh of frustration*] I don't know. For a while it was supposed to have an X rating, which, I mean, it's ridiculous! Can you imagine?! It would kill the movie—but that's not even the point. I mean, this is not a pornographic film! What can you say? People are going to be afraid of what they don't know or what's unfamiliar, but this is not a pornographic film.

Dick: Now I've been told, and I have not seen the entire film—we're going to be showing a clip a little bit later on—

Patrick: [*laughs*] Which one are you going to show?!

Dick: [*laughs along*] Don't worry! One of the less steamy scenes. But I'm told that when the two of you have sex in this film that it was. . . more than acting. There's a moment where you have an orgasm. Now what about that?

Patrick: [*laughs*] What *about* it?

Dick: What—I mean—well, let me ask you this. Is it real?

Patrick: Is it real. Is *what* real?

Dick: The orgasm. Your orgasm in the film. Is it real?

Patrick: [*pause*] Well—[*annoyed*] I'm an actor—this is a film—I mean, "is it real?" I don't understand what—why can't anyone talk about this film as a piece of art, which after all, I mean, that's what it boils down to. I'm an artist, artists create illusions, that's what they're paid to do, and I think the question is, how well can they do it, not what is real. Reality, unreality—I honestly don't understand the question, you know? I mean, it's not a question that interests me, let's put it that way. I mean, what does my personal life or what I was feeling when I did the scene—what does any of that have to do with the finished product—with the artifact, with the *art,* with the art that gets made and sent out there to give pleasure—for—for entertainment purposes alone? Why do people want to know this kind of thing?

Dick: [*turns to face the camera*] And we'll be back in just a few minutes.

IV

Recently I turned down my first movie offer. After years of looking down my nose at gay men who work out, thinking they are so worried about how other gay men see them that they sell their souls to the fickle winds of fashion and pump up their bodies, no matter how painful and boring the task may be, I joined the gym a couple of years ago with my then boyfriend Brian as a loving way of making myself better and stronger for him—for us. So I arrived at the gym one day a couple months ago only to discover a film crew busy at work. I wanted to walk on the treadmill, but the film crew were filming in the area where the treadmills were located, and it looked like I might end up being in the film depending on which treadmill I chose. I felt angry that they were invading my gym space. I always hate it when someone on the street, someone I don't know, takes my picture or films me inadvertently with their video camera. I guess I'm one of those people who believe that when someone takes your picture, they've captured your soul, and I want to be the one to decide who gets my soul and who doesn't. (As many people did at the time, I probably would have reacted with horror in the mid-nineteenth century to the newfangled and godless daguerreotype.) I started walking on my treadmill but was extremely uncomfortable because the floodlights were all around me and I wasn't sure if they were planning to film me and the people in my vicinity walking on the treadmills or if the lights were there for some other shot that didn't involve me. I watched the filmmakers at work and felt how arrogant, how uninteresting they were—and they were ruining my workout! Unable to relax, I got off my treadmill and moved to another one in a less conspicuous area (I was also annoyed that the bright lights were making me hotter than I would normally be just working out on the treadmill).

But then I thought, how strange that I should be so uncomfortable in front of the camera, given that all my life I've wanted to be a movie star. Maybe I just don't want my film debut to be a supporting role, I thought; maybe, I thought, I want my debut to be a big splash like Barbra Streisand's debut in *Funny Girl.* I imagined what I might say if they should ask me to be in their film, and I pretended it would be something like, "What, are you kidding? I'm a star! I'm not going to condescend to be in your little movie! I can wait until a bigger, better part comes along."

A little later, while I was working out on one of the weight-lifting machines, I watched as the filmmakers photographed a young, cute, though kind of bland-looking guy, with a tatoo around his left bicep, doing biceps curls. I was jealous. Why hadn't they asked *me* if they could film *me* lifting weights? Obviously, they didn't think I was muscular enough or cute enough or WASPy enough or maybe it was because I didn't have any cool tatoos. And look at how that guy with the tatoo is enjoying the attention—he was doing his biceps curls for the camera with a big smile on his face! I thought how all these gym bunnies probably were just dying to get into this film, how they lived for nothing so much as their little fifteen minutes of fame. I wished the filmmakers would just go away and leave me alone.

Then, as I was doing my shoulder exercises, one of the filmmakers started watching me. I didn't like the feeling of being looked at like that—being assessed, sized up, made a meal of by this man I didn't know. He motioned to another of the filmmakers to come watch me and together they conferred in a whisper about me. I tried to ignore them by averting my gaze. At the end of my set, I stood up and turned my back to them so as not to make eye contact with them. One of the filmmakers approached me and said, "Hi, we're making a promotional film for the gym. You have a great little look and we'd like to film you working out. I don't know if you'd like to be a part of that."

As he said this I smiled, then said "No thanks."

"Okay," he said, and politely went away.

Rapidly I finished my workout, went downstairs to shower (and wondered if they would be doing any filming in the locker room—imagine!—naked men in the showers as part of a promotional film for the gym!—it'll never happen), and went home.

Riding the subway uptown, I wondered if I'd done the right thing. Maybe I should have said yes—after all, what harm could it have done? And I could have been in an actual movie! Who knows how many people would see me in this movie?! Maybe Brian would see me in the movie— that would be great! For Brian had broken up with me after we'd been dating for about five months, and I liked the idea that he would see me in the movie and realize that I had moved on from my relationship with him to bigger and better things—that I was doing things that he never even dreamed of. It might make him regret breaking up with me, make him see what a really wonderful person I really am, make him feel bad about himself and what he'd done to me (remember that Barbra Streisand kept her real name so, when she became a star, everyone would know it was still the Barbra they had tormented years ago in Brooklyn).

But then I thought that if these are my only reasons for wanting to be in the movie, then it's a good thing I said no; it seemed that being in the movie appealed to me mainly for vindictive reasons, and that wasn't justification enough for doing it.

Then I thought I was right to say no because if I had been in their movie, I wouldn't have been in control. It occurred to me that a big part of my wanting to be a movie star when I was a kid was being in control of the filmmaking. Even when I made a flop or got bad reviews, I orchestrated the whole thing—even when the press hounded me and I felt all I wanted to do was to be left alone with John Travolta or whomever it was that I was dating at the time, the point was, all of it was my own doing. Whereas in this case, I would have been at the mercy of someone else, of someone else's artistic vision.

Then I thought, it's kind of cool to have said no to a part in a movie. I always loved the idea that being a star meant you could go around saying, oh yes, I turned that part down, and then everybody would wonder what the movie would have been like if you *had* been in it, and they would think how different it would have been, how it might have been much better than the movie that finally got made, or how, on the other hand, it might have been awful but maybe at the same time wonderfully experimental (for example, if Carol Channing really *had* played Dolly Levi in the film version of *Hello, Dolly!*, or if Julie Andrews had played Eliza Doolittle in the film version of *My Fair Lady*, or if, as was originally intended, Shirley Temple had played Dorothy in *The Wizard of Oz*, or Buddy Ebsen the Tin Man), and how, in a way, ultimately painful and sad it all was, because, finally, no one would ever really know.

OUTTAKES V

The Long Day Closes (1992)

Movies don't have quite the same affect upon me that they did when I was a kid. I don't go to them looking for the same things, and the more I've seen and the more I've read and the more I know about the world around me, the less satisfying movies have become—or at least, the less they compel me to fantasize about them, to imagine myself inside of them, to want to improve them. Relationships, writing, and teaching, I suppose, have absorbed the creative energy I used to put into thinking about movies. And, I suspect, I mistake relationships and work—but especially relationships—in some of the same ways that I mistook movies when I was growing up. For example, just as a mere newspaper ad for a movie I loved could send my mind spinning with memories and fantasies of the movie, I'm liable to fall in love nowadays, and have been for years, with the merest idea of someone (the way he wears his cap, the thing he said about modernism, the place he grew up, the way he touched my arm when he said good-bye) rather than with "who he really is" (whatever that is).

But I still go to the movies a lot, and there are plenty of movies that I like, some that I even "love," like Terence Davies' autobiographical *The Long Day Closes*. After seeing it I thought, this is one of the best movies I have ever seen. It dramatizes the ways in which popular culture permeates the minds and hearts of a Catholic working-class family in Liverpool in the mid-1950s. At the center of the film is Bud, a solitary eleven-year-old boy, teased in school for being "queer," whose interior life is dominated by the movies he sees. Davies combines images and scenes of everyday life in postwar England (Bud asking his mother for money to go to the movies; Bud and his mother, brothers, and sister attending a local carnival; Bud getting shooed upstairs so his older brother can be alone with his girlfriend; Bud and his classmates having their hair checked for lice [Bud has it]) with sound clips from Hollywood movies—"The Carousel Waltz" from *Carousel;* a love scene between Judy Garland and Tom Drake from *Meet Me in St. Louis* in which Judy sings "Over the Banister Leaning." The contradiction between the ordinary facts of exterior reality and the extraordinary, boundless waves of inner desire evoked by popular culture is both sad and sweet: sad, because the glamour and fulsomeness of pop culture succeed in emphasizing the poverty, by contrast, of Bud's everyday life (in school, Bud daydreams about a ship sailing heroically in a stormy sea, while the teacher gives a passionless lecture on erosion); sweet, because, just as often, popular

215

culture becomes the occasion for communication and bonding among the members of Bud's family (at a holiday party, Bud and his sister, framed by a doorway as if it were a proscenium arch, take pleasure in performing "A Couple of Swells" from *Easter Parade,* singing and dancing as if they were Fred Astaire and Judy Garland, to the delight of their entire audience, their family and friends).

I love *The Long Day Closes* for exploring so patiently the inner life of a boy like Bud. Filled with melancholy images of Bud thinking, looking, and staring, overlaid with the sounds of sweeping, romantic, movie music, *The Long Day Closes* evokes the restless drama that goes on inside of "queer" boys, and it invests them with the power and beauty of classic Hollywood cinema. This is what Hollywood musicals used to accomplish: they mined everyday life for all the music and passion and spectacle it kept locked up inside of it, only they never featured boys like Bud. They came close—think of young Patrick in *Mame*—but they could never bring themselves to admit that the people most intent on seeing life this way are gay people, or at least people marked as "gay," whether or not they are in fact gay (in one telling scene, Bud stares out his bedroom window across the street at a god-like, shirtless workman, who returns Bud's gaze with a smile and winks at him; embarrassed, puzzled, Bud looks away).

My favorite sequence in the film is also its most abstractly beautiful: Bud stands at the top of the short flight of stairs leading to the cellar in front of his house, as the camera slowly approaches him. He reaches out to swing on an iron crossbar spanning the stairwell (the kind of play kids devise with limited means at their disposal—the kind of physical, rhythmic play that allows a child to become introspective without feeling unoccupied); the film cuts to an overhead shot of Bud swinging back and forth on the bar suspended over the narrow, rectangular stairwell, which horizontally bisects the screen. As the camera moves steadily left, the image of the stairwell fades into an overhead shot of the light beam (horizontally bisecting the screen in place of the stairwell) emanating from a movie projector in a crowded, darkened movie theater; we see Bud in the audience, then a man a few rows in front of him lighting a cigarette, the puff of smoke mingling with the flickering light of the film projector. The beam of light fades into an overhead shot of church pews filled with people, as bells ring out summoning the congregation to rise, and again to kneel, the priest now raising the Host in his upstretched arms (his chant, "holy, holy, holy Lord, God of power and might, heaven and earth are filled with your glory," mingling with a sound clip of dialogue from an old Hollywood movie). The overhead shot of the priest fades into an overhead shot of a teacher standing at the head of rows of schoolboys seated in their desks (which take the place of rows of church-goers in their pews from the previous shot); he dismisses them one row at a time, as they rise and file out in perfect order, saying "good night, sir," the sound of their voices, again, mingling with a sound clip of movie dialogue. The scene then fades back to an overhead shot of a horizontal row of several identical cellar stairwells, including, finally, the one Bud had been playing in, but this time he is not there. . .

All during this sequence, we hear Debbie Reynolds singing "Tammy." "Tammy's in love," she warbles sweetly, but her love floats free of the one she loves ("Wish I knew if he knew what I'm dreamin' of"). Her love is, literally, in the air ("I hear the cottonwoods whisperin' above . . . the old hooty owl hooty-hoo's to the dove"). Maybe, after all, that's what being "in love" has always meant—a lens, merely, through which one perceives and receives the world, an attitude, a point of view, an angle of vision, not a "real" and "true" response to some*one*. It's the way you live in the world when you think your own life is a movie, or wish it were so, with you the hero or heroine. By setting this sequence of images to Debbie Reynolds's "Tammy," Davies declares his love for the poor world that cushions Bud and holds him in place, even as Bud tries to escape that world (he swings, as if hoping at any moment to fly away, but gravity weighs him down—that is, until the end of the sequence, when he is gone—free?).

Being in love with love, or in love with "everything" like Patrick's Auntie Mame, doesn't make a person happy. "Tammy," after all, is a sad song, ending on a wish that is neither fulfilled nor crushed, but left, like Bud, just hanging—permeating everything but having nowhere special to go, nothing in particular to do (". . . rainy days and Mondays always get me down"). The singer sings about Tammy—is Tammy the one sing-ing? If so, why does she sing about her love as if it belonged to someone else—to a third person (to "Tammy")?

With no solid subject from which to think, feel, and express oneself, and with no stable object upon which to project all one's thoughts, feel-ings, and desires, no wonder happiness and sadness are indistinguishable here, no wonder words fail in comparison to the eloquence of images, no wonder all of *The Long Day Closes,* all of what I've longed for in the movies, is summed up in these few perfect, impossible, valedictory mo-ments.

Notes
Works Cited

Notes

Chapter 1. The Happiest Family in All the World!

1. This and the following three quotations are taken from the first page of Ernest Lehman's script of *The Sound of Music,* the first two pages of which are reproduced in Julia Antopol Hirsch's *The Sound of Music: The Making of America's Favorite Movie* (Chicago: Contemporary Books, 1993), p. 35; ellipses in original.

2. This and subsequent dialogue is quoted from the film's screenplay by Ernest Lehman. Since none of the screenplays for the films I discuss in *Widescreen Dreams* are in print, all film dialogue in the book has been transcribed from videotape.

3. For a discussion of the cultural significance of "vocal crisis," see Wayne Koestenbaum's *The Queen's Throat: Opera, Homosexuality, and the Mystery of Desire.*

4. The clinical term for this is "trichotillomania," or "compulsive hair pulling," affecting between two and eight million people, 90 percent of whom are female; see "Trichotillomania: Compulsive Hair Pulling" by Nancy Goldberg. For a psychoanalytic account of the disorder, see Louise J. Kaplan's *Female Perversions: The Temptations of Emma Bovary,* 397–404.

5. In his essay "Musicality, Essentialism, and the Closet," Philip Brett eloquently describes the connection between the pains of gay childhood and the compensations of piano playing: "Music is a perfect field for the display of emotion. It is particularly accommodating to those who have difficulty in expressing feeling in day-to-day life, because the emotion is unspecified and unattached. The piano, let us say for example, will thus become an important means for the attempt at expression, disclosure, or communication on the part of those children who have difficulties of various kinds with one or both parents. To gay children, who often experience a shutdown of all feeling as the result of sensing their parents' and society's disapproval of a basic part of their sentient life, music appears as a veritable lifeline" (17).

Outtakes I

1. Quotations from the teleplay by Tere Rios.

2. Quotations from the premiere episode of *The Partridge Family* taken from the teleplay by Bernard Slade.

Chapter 2. Love Barbra

1. Dialogue from *Funny Girl* quoted from the screenplay by Isobel Lennart.

2. The production designer, John De Cuir, had earlier designed the sets for *The King and I* (1956) and *Cleopatra* (1963), and there are traces of Eastern exoticism and Roman decadance in his sets for *Hello, Dolly!* De Cuir won an Oscar for each of these three films.

3. Quoted from the screenplay by Ernest Lehman.

4. Vito Russo died of AIDS on November 7, 1990.

5. D. A. Miller offered me this interpretation of the Streisand fan's relation to the star.

Outtakes II

1. Quoted from the screenplay by Paul Zindel.

Chapter 3. The Wreck of the Family

1. These words follow the opening credits in *The Poseidon Adventure* (1972), produced by Irwin Allen for Twentieth Century-Fox; all subsequent quotations are taken from the screenplay by Stirling Silliphant and Wendell Mayes.

2. The late-nineties rash of disaster films, including *Twister, Speed* and *Speed 2, Volcano, Daylight, Dante's Peak,* and *Titanic,* though they indulge our appetite for witnessing other people's lives come undone, differs from the seventies disaster films in several respects. The nineties heroes tend to have extraordinary expertise or access to extraordinary technology for coping with disaster, whereas the seventies heroes have to rise to the occasion. The nineties disaster is personified, making it more like a self-consciously willful monster than a meaningless natural occurence beyond human ken. The nineties films feature less blood and less individuated human suffering; they are more reluctant than seventies films to let good people die. The nineties films take a more narrowly focused look at the interpersonal dramas of the main characters, to the point where, as in the case of *Titanic,* the central, heterosexual love plot (the story of a cross-class shipboard romance) eclipses all the other characters along with their narrative possibilities. The seventies films, by contrast—and *The Poseidon Adventure* is a prime example of this—tend to view all of the characters in the same way: from a distance, as "little people," remarkable for the kinds of heroism and know-how that ordinary people are famous for showing in times of distress.

3. One could argue that, beyond the film's invitation to sympathize with all of its characters, men and women, young and old, fat and thin, adventuresome and timid, the very mise en scene of *The Poseidon Adventure* (upside-down space) evokes in the viewer a kind of gay subjectivity for which conventional positionality has been completely "inverted." See Lee Edelman's "Seeing Things: Representation, the Scene of Surveillance, and the Spectacle of Gay Male Sex" for a discussion of the psychoanalytic links, ever since Freud, between male homosexuality, spatial disorientation, and the blurring of subjectivity with objectivity.

4. In *Between Men: English Literature and Male Homosocial Desire*, Eve Kosofsky
Sedgwick suggests what might have occurred to middle-class parents such as
mine when they thought of Gothic novels like *The Picture of Dorian Gray*: "A story,
Gothic in its own right, from Beverley Nichols' twentieth-century autobiography, *Father Figure*, will illustrate the particular comic, educative, and terrorizing
potential that the Gothic novel and the 'unspeakable' had realized by the first
decades of this century. Nichols' middle-class parents had a higher-class male
friend who rouged, acted effeminate, and would to a knowing observer have
seemed from the first glance to be telegraphing his homosexuality. The elder
Nicholses, reactionary but unworldly, saw none of this. They were simply delighted that their friend took such a keen interest in their young son. One night,
though, Beverley's father came into the boy's room drunk and found him with
a copy of *Dorian Gray*—a present from the friend. The father nearly choked. He
hurled the book at his son. He spat on it over and over, frothing at the mouth.
Finally he began ripping the book to shreds—with his teeth" (95).

Outtakes III

1. Quotations taken from the screenplay by Paul Gallico.
2. Quotations taken from the teleplay by Stewart Stern.

Chapter 4. Like Home

1. This and other quotations are taken from the screenplay by Joel Schumacher.

Chapter 5. Coming Out, with Al Pacino

1. This and other quotations taken from the Academy Award–winning screenplay by Frank Pierson.

Works Cited

Barthel, Joan. "Biggest Money-Making Movie of All Time—How Come?" *New York Times Magazine* 20 Nov. 1966: 45 ff.

Baudelaire, Charles. "The Painter of Modern Life." 1863. *The Painter of Modern Life and Other Essays.* Trans. and ed. Jonathan Mayne. London: Phaidon Press, 1964. 1–41.

Bettmann, Otto L. *The Good Old Days—They Were Terrible!* New York: Random House, 1974.

Bishop, Elizabeth. "One Art." *The Complete Poems: 1927–1979.* New York: Farrar, Straus and Giroux, 1983. 178.

Brett, Philip. "Musicality, Essentialism, and the Closet." *Queering the Pitch: The New Gay and Lesbian Musicology* Eds. Philip Brett, Elizabeth Wood, and Gary C. Thomas. New York: Routledge, 1994. 9–26.

Brodsky, Jack. Liner notes. *Funny Girl.* Perf. Barbra Streisand. LP. Columbia, 1968.

Burton, Virginia Lee. *The Little House.* Boston: Houghton Mifflin, 1943.

Canby, Vincent. "On Screen, Barbra Streisand Displays a Detached Cool." Rev. of *Hello, Dolly!*, dir. Gene Kelly. *New York Times* 18 Dec. 1969, late city ed.: 62.

Coleman, Ray. *The Carpenters: The Untold Story.* New York: HarperCollins, 1994.

Considine, Shaun. *Barbra Streisand: The Woman, the Myth, the Music.* New York: Delacorte Press, 1985.

Edelman, Lee. "Seeing Things: Representation, the Scene of Surveillance, and the Spectacle of Gay Male Sex." *Homographesis: Essays in Gay Literary and Cultural Theory.* New York: Routledge, 1994. 173–91.

Edwards, Anne. *Streisand: A Biography.* Boston: Little, Brown, 1997.

Friedan, Betty. *The Feminine Mystique.* New York: Bantam-Doubleday-Dell, 1963.

Frith, Simon. "Extra Ordinary." Rev. of *Let's Talk About Love*, perf. Celine Dion, and *Higher Ground*, perf. Barbra Streisand. *Village Voice* 16 Dec. 1997: 87.

Gallico, Paul, screenwriter. *The Snow Goose.* Dir. Patrick Garland. NBC. 15 Nov. 1971.

Goldberg, Nancy. "Trichotillomania: Compulsive Hair Pulling." *Ms.* Jan./Feb. 1992: 74–75.

"The Golden Road to a Grand New Oz." *Life* Oct. 1978: 56–60.

Gottfried, Martin. *Broadway Musicals.* New York: Harry N. Abrams, 1979.

Green, Joey. *The Partridge Family Album: The Official Get Happy Guide to America's Grooviest Television Family*. New York: HarperCollins, 1994.

Hirsch, Julia Antopol. *The Sound of Music: The Making of America's Favorite Movie*. Chicago: Contemporary Books, 1993.

Hopcke, Robert H. *Men's Dreams, Men's Healing*. Boston: Shambhala, 1990.

Jackson, Kenneth T. *Crabgrass Frontier: The Suburbanization of the United States*. New York: Oxford University Press, 1985.

Kael, Pauline. "Keep Going." Rev. of *Hello, Dolly!*, set designer John De Cuir. *New Yorker* 3 Jan. 1970: 56–58.

Kael, Pauline. "Saint Dorothy." Rev. of *The Wiz*, dir. Sidney Lumet. *New Yorker* 30 Oct. 1978: 138 ff.

Kaplan, Louise J. *Female Perversions: The Temptations of Emma Bovary*. New York: Doubleday, 1991.

Koestenbaum, Wayne. *The Queen's Throat: Opera, Homosexuality, and the Mystery of Desire*. New York: Poseidon Press, 1993.

Langley, Noel, Florence Ryerson, and Edgar Allan Woolf, screenwriters. *The Wizard of Oz Movie Script*. 1939. Monterey Park, Calif.: O.S.P. Publishing, 1994.

Lehman, Ernest, screenwriter. *Hello, Dolly!* Dir. Gene Kelly. Twentieth Century-Fox, 1969.

Lehman, Ernest, screenwriter. *The Sound of Music*. Dir. Robert Wise. Twentieth Century-Fox, 1965.

Lennart, Isobel, screenwriter. *Funny Girl*. Dir. William Wyler. Columbia/Rastar, 1968.

Lucek, Gary. "Out on Vinyl: Readings Between the Grooves in Gay Male Pop Music." Unpublished paper. Outside/Inside: Third Annual Conference of the Lesbian and Gay Studies Center at Yale University, 27–29 Oct. 1989.

Lumet, Sidney. Introduction. *The Wiz Book [The Wonderful Wizard of Oz]*. By L. Frank Baum. New York: Berkley Publishing, 1978. vii–xii.

Pierson, Frank, screenwriter. *Dog Day Afternoon*. Dir. Sidney Lumet. Warner Brothers, 1975.

Pullia, Nick. "Spada: Biographer Shares Rare Glimpses Into All the Decades of 'Her Life.'" *BARBRA bilia* 6–7 (1995): 34 ff.

Riese, Randall. *Her Name is Barbra: An Intimate Portrait of the Real Barbra Streisand*. New York: Birch Lane Press, 1993.

Rios, Tere, screenwriter. "When Generations Gap." *The Flying Nun*. Dir. Leon Benson. ABC. 20 Mar. 1970.

Ruhlmann, William. *Barbra Streisand*. Stamford, Conn.: Longmeadow Press, 1995.

Rushdie, Salman. *BFI Film Classics: The Wizard of Oz*. London: British Film Institute, 1992.

Russo, Vito. *The Celluloid Closet: Homosexuality in the Movies*. New York: Harper & Row, 1981.

Russo, Vito. "Rebellion Over the Rainbow." *OutWeek* 26 June 1989: 42 ff.

Sarris, Andrew. Rev. of *Funny Girl*, dir. William Wyler. *Village Voice* 10 Oct. 1968: 53–55.

Schumacher, Joel, screenwriter. *The Wiz*. Dir. Sidney Lumet. Universal, 1978.

Sedgwick, Eve Kosofsky. *Between Men: English Literature and Male Homosocial Desire.* New York: Columbia University Press, 1985.

Sedgwick, Eve Kosofsky. *Epistemology of the Closet.* Berkeley: University of California Press, 1990.

Sedgwick, Eve Kosofsky. "Paranoid Reading and Reparative Reading; or, You're So Paranoid, You Probably Think This Introduction Is about You." *Novel Gazing: Queer Readings in Fiction.* Ed. Eve Kosofsky Sedgwick. Durham, N.C.: Duke University Press, 1997. 1–37.

Sedgwick, Eve Kosofsky. "A Talk with Eve Kosofsky Sedgwick." Interview with Sarah Chinn, Mario DiGangi, and Patrick Horrigan. *PRE/TEXT* 13.3–4 (1992) 79–95.

Sennett, Tedd. *Hollywood Musicals.* New York: Harry N. Abrams, 1981.

Silliphant, Stirling and Wendell Mayes, screenwriters. *The Poseidon Adventure.* Dir. Ronald Neame. Twentieth Century-Fox, 1972.

Slade, Bernard, screenwriter. "What? And Get Out of Show Business?" *The Partridge Family.* Dir. Jerry Paris. ABC. 25 Sept. 1970.

The Sound of Music. Booklet (author unknown). LP. RCA Victor, 1965.

Spada, James. *Barbra: The First Decade. The Films and Career of Barbra Streisand.* Secaucus, N.J.: Citadel Press, 1974.

Spada, James. *Streisand: Her Life.* New York: Crown Publishers, 1995.

Stern, Stewart, screenwriter. *Sybil,* by Flora Rheta Schreiber. Dir. Daniel Petrie. NBC. 14–15 Nov. 1976.

Stetler, Lawrence. *By the El: Third Avenue and Its El at Mid-Century.* Flushing: H&M Productions, 1995.

Streisand, Barbra. Liner notes. *Back to Broadway.* Columbia, 1993.

Streisand, Barbra. Dorothy Arzner Award acceptance speech. *Barbra: The Concert.* N.p.: J.E.G. Productions, 1994.

Streisand, Barbra. Interview with Rosie O'Donnell. *The Rosie O'Donnell Show.* ABC. 21 Nov. 1997.

Streisand, Barbra. Liner notes. *One Voice.* Columbia, 1987.

Streisand, Barbra. "Widescreen." Liner notes. *Lazy Afternoon.* Columbia, 1975.

Weinraub, Bernard. "Movie Musicals: Remembering." *New York Times* 13 June 1996, late ed.: C15–16.

Wilde, Oscar. *The Picture of Dorian Gray.* 1891. Ed. Donald L. Lawler. New York: W.W. Norton, 1988.

Wood, Robin. *Hollywood From Vietnam to Reagan.* New York: Columbia University Press, 1986.

Woolf, Virginia. "The Humane Art." *The Death of the Moth and Other Essays.* San Diego: Harcourt Brace, 1942. 58–63.

Woolf, Virginia. *Mrs. Dalloway.* San Diego: Harcourt Brace Jovanovich, 1925.

Zindel, Paul, screenwriter. *Mame.* Dir. Gene Saks. Warner Bros., 1974.